PROMISED LAND

Also by Michele Guinness

Child of the Covenant
Is God Good for Women?
A Little Kosher Seasoning

Promised Land

Michele Guinness

Hodder & Stoughton
LONDON SYDNEY AUCKLAND

British Library Cataloguing in Publication Data
A record for this book is available from the British Library

ISBN 0 340 70987 1

Typeset by Avon Dataset Ltd, Bidford-on-Avon, Warks

Printed and bound in Great Britain by
Clays Ltd, St Ives plc

Hodder and Stoughton Ltd
A division of Hodder Headline PLC
338 Euston Road
London NW1 3BH

For all my family in 'Grimlington',
a rich source of laughter, tears and inspiration!

Oh please don't cry my darling son
for the things I can't afford
because your dad's on strike lad
for his job and some day yours.
He's too young to retire love,
he's only thirty three,
so that's why there's only a sandwich for your tea.
There's this man called McGregor,
who is some seventy plus,
who's telling men your daddy's age,
'That's it lads, you've worked enough.
We're going to shut your pits down,
slim down the workforce too,
and if you don't agree with it,
there's always the dole for you.'
Well Daddy needs a job, love,
to keep the wolves at bay,
he wouldn't be very happy
sitting here all day.
I know it's hard, my darling,
after all, you're only two,
but Daddy and the other men must win this fight,
    that's true.
So dry your eyes, my angel,
cos when this fight is won,
there'll not be just a job for Dad,
but for you, my darling son.

Nicky Layton

Prologue

More than ten years have passed since I wrote *Promised Land*. I cried myself to sleep the night before we left, then woke suddenly in the middle of the night.

'I've had this awful nightmare,' I said to Peter. 'I dreamed we were leaving Grimlington.'

'We are,' he said.

And in that awful moment I knew the terrible weight in the pit of my stomach would never go away.

Bereavement eases in time. It never simply vanishes. It's accommodated somehow. The memories, the joy and the pain all become a part of us and make us who and what we are.

I am not the same today – but then neither is Grimlington. If the miners' strike is fast becoming history, so am I.

The people of Grimlington exerted their influence over me at a very formative time in my existence when my horizons were in danger of being severely narrowed by a comfortable, blinkered Jewish childhood, a privileged academic education, a traditional middle-class, evangelical introduction to Christianity, and widespread expectation that I would play the dutiful, purple-becrimplened clergy wife on those rare occasions when I managed to raise my head from endless bucketfuls of babies' nappies. The prospect of a writing career was as realistic for me as a job down the pit.

Raised in a mining town, I never really knew how the other half lived, how much history bound them inextricably together. I'm so grateful for all they taught me, so glad my children grew up to see which values really matter. When Joel reached his teens and decided to stay with his friends, rather than come with us to Grimlington for what has now become a traditional New Year's Day gathering, they said to him, 'You can be with your friends whenever you like, Joel. We're your family.' He came with us.

Grimlington folk taught me there was only one thing to do when adversity strikes – the old Jewish trick – laugh. The richness, the poignancy, the bitter-sweetness of their story has never waned. Perhaps it's more relevant today than ever, at a time in our history when we are becoming particularly aware of the social disintegration and alienation all around us, and lament the passing of those grand old British communities, where everyone was their brother's keeper and knew their brother's most intimate business, where children with special needs were supported by an extended family network, where the elderly died in their own beds, full of years and honour, surrounded by their loved ones.

It could equally have been a story about shipbuilders, or dockers – any community which revolved around the work which once made Britain a great industrial nation, giving the workers a sense of pride and achievement. None were as interdependent as the miners.

In the ten years after 1984, as the miners foresaw, the government announced massive pit closures: 140 pits shut down, 250,000 men were made redundant. And to this day, no one knows why. That's the real scandal. An apparently arbitrary and suspiciously inept decision was taken somewhere in the remote and impenetrable offices of Whitehall to end yet another major national economic resource. It was gift-wrapped, parcelled and presented in the shoddy packaging of non-financial viability – a lame, and manifestly silly excuse. Why had millions of pounds been spent barely a few years earlier modernising pits which were to close anyway? All the feasibility studies showed that mining was still potentially profit-making. The one pit the miners bought out themselves is a success story today, a real thorn in the previous government's side.

In reality it was a decision to destroy a whole way of

2

life, by people who knew nothing about it, and cared less. In the Bafta award winning film, *Brassed Off*, the conductor of the fictional 'Grimly' (yes, Grimly) Brass Band, standing in the Albert Hall, says to a packed house. 'If we were seals or dolphins you would have organised a massive, national campaign on our behalf, but we were only a few human beings, fighting for our pride and dignity – for our community.'

Brassed off? When the axe finally fell, the Grimlington community was bowed and bloodied, but not defeated. Members of the Parish Church joined with thousands of others, some in wheelchairs, some on crutches, most on foot, marching proudly through Yorkshire behind their bands, heads held high, banners flying. They wanted to say that they were the working men who once made Britain great. And now, thank them for the sacrifice of all those years below ground? No, they were being thrown on top of the slag heaps they had helped to create, an offering to the Thatcherite god of free enterprise.

One MP spoke half-heartedly about pressing on, about making the best of a bad job. The fire in his belly had long been extinguished. It was left to the Bishop of Wakefield, Nigel McCullough, to rouse the masses to a standing ovation with his impassioned appeal to everyone present, including the church, to commit themselves to the caring values which were the hallmark of their communities.

Grimlington survived. As Port Wakefield. No one was very sure how that happened, how a tunnel under the sea, linking our small island with foreign parts, could provide employment so far north. They smelt a rat. The plans proudly displayed in the town hall revealed a town ringed right round with monstrous container depots. Any remaining speck of greenbelt mysteriously untouched by mining would be swallowed into an industrial wilderness. There was a public consultation, loud protestations, and louder reassurances.

'This will provide employment. We'll build you new swimming baths too.'

The containers arrived, and one or two jobs, though many came from outside, but there is still no sign of the pool.

'We could turn our town into a tourist attraction,' said one town councillor at the monthly council meeting.

The rest goggled at him, open-mouthed. Facilities were thin on the ground, the scenery lacking. The only hills were slag heaps.

'Aye, we could buy a gond-ola and float it on lake.'

'Lake' was a twenty by twenty foot pond.

'Aye,' said another councillor nodding, carried away by his colleague's enthusiasm, 'we could buy two, and mate 'em.'

Tourists haven't been seen to flood into Grimlington. In fact, the long, main road through the town, where Alicia used to live, has been subject to stringent traffic-calming measures, with pavements forming a strange selection of indents and islands, crowned with the occasional plant or waste bin, presumably to stop cars driving through so fast.

The only real historic building, the Norman Parish Church, has been lovingly and carefully reordered inside – at great cost and personal sacrifice – to cope with the new influx. It is fairly full most Sundays. But the church has the same share of problems as any other. They still manage some rollicking good parties. We celebrated a Passover for around two hundred just a few months ago, squeezing people into every available nook, cranny, round every pillar, into every chapel. On a groaning buffet table, laden with goodies, was the wonderful coconut, celery, tangerine and marshmallow salad we used to eat over ten years ago. The love they heaped on us was as robust as it ever was. And I went to bed with my ribcage aching – both from the hugs and the laughter, just as I used to do. So what's new?

More newcomers, some professional, from beyond the Grimlington boundary, overseas visitors, the little children who played with our now strapping teenagers, back from college, hordes of new babies. The change is slow, but change there is – an almost imperceptible, slight restraint in the air, a certain holding back which wasn't there before. The next generation may never have the sense of community, commitment and belonging their parents knew and loved, may never understand what it was they fought and starved for. That's why, in a country where the south, as well as the north, now knows the pain of redundancy and unemployment, of insensitive, uncaring employment practices, of exploitation and injustice, the story of those days must be retold, the voice of the people of Grimlington must go on shouting in the wilderness, a reminder in the fight for a just, caring society, that the Church dare not keep silent. We may lose the fight from time to time, but one day, we'll win the battle.

Michele Guinness

Preface

'I think you should call your book "a turnip-head's guide to a northern church," Linda said, 'before the North becomes a distant memory! I mean the theory's all right, if you like reading the heavy stuff, but you should write a story about ordinary people for ordinary people like me.'

The name 'Grimlington' is not intended to be derogatory. By some strange quirk of fate towns in the North do seem to acquire names like Grimsby, Grotton and Foulby, whether they reflect the truth of the matter or not!

Many readers will know where 'Grimlington' is, but that is largely irrelevant. It is 'Everytown', at least every small, industrial northern town, where life has become increasingly uncertain in recent years. Grimlington people are ordinary, yet they have a resilience and humour which makes them as special as the many others in our nation who now have to fight to make a future for their children.

I have also used a pseudonym for the town to cover my tracks and protect the church from public gaze. It is an ordinary parish church, with its usual share of ups and downs. Other churches have far more dramatic, exciting stories to tell. As we struggle to come to terms with the needs and culture of the working man, we still have more questions than answers.

No book is a work of journalism. Had Edward, Anna, or Alicia written it, it would be a different story. My roots go deep into the northern soil. I know nothing else. But for Edward and Anna the transplant has not been

7

without cost and heartache. Life in Grimlington has meant a kind of death for them.

These are my impressions, events seen through my eyes alone. There have been many times in the past when, as a Jew, I have felt culturally alienated from the Church. I felt an outsider, little guessing how many others, Anglo-Saxon and Gentile as they were, felt the same. Unlike the Catholic, Pentecostal or Salvation Army churches, the Church of England, rightly or wrongly, has a certain image and tends to represent a certain kind of churchmanship, at home in a rural or professional environment, but not among the working classes. I realise that my terminology and the division it creates might give offence, but the reality is that Britain is divided into what almost amounts to two tribes, each with its own language, standards and culture. To deny it is to play the proverbial ostrich. The Church must adapt to the local environment. But more than that, it must work for understanding and acceptance. Both cultures have their strengths and weaknesses and much to give to each other, if we would but realise it.

I dare to hope that my Jewishness has invested me with a certain objectivity, which a clergyman's wife might not normally possess. I suppose I shall always feel a little like the outsider looking in, though Grimlington has done more than any church to conquer that feeling. Throughout history the Jew has been forced to wander in search of a land and like a chameleon has learnt to adapt to his environment. While preserving his own identity, he often becomes the greatest defender of the place of his adoption.

Chapter 1

Grimlington's special charm is not exactly obvious. Those who pass through are hardly aware they have been and do not come back for the scenery. But those born here believe there is no finer place on God's earth. Nowhere else can a man toil his life away underground, then for ever rest his weary bones so peacefully in his old, familiar haunt beneath the soil. A certain charm there is in the gentle whirring sound from the pit wheel which wafts its way across the farmers' fields; in its hooter announcing the end of the shift; in the sight of the distant Yorkshire hills beyond the boundaries of the town, now dwarfed by the growing mountains of slag, black against the horizon; in the terraced cottages, back-to-back with their smoking chimneys, beckoning men to a good fire and good food. For these sights and sounds have the charm of home.

Good food and fires are almost a distant memory today. The High Street is quiet for a Tuesday, market day, the day the Post Office pays out the Benefits. Women, normally glad to stop and chat, warmed by the temporary illusion of wealth, walk quickly, lest if they stop to stare in a shop window the precious coins will somehow vanish from their purses. The greengrocer, a jovial man, loads his wares in crates upon the pavement, succulent oranges, shiny red apples, large bananas firm and tempting.

'Come on ladies, pears are a give-away this week. Leave the price to me.'

The women stop, gaze wistfully for a moment, then drag themselves away.

9

The butcher's shop is almost empty. There is no demand for meat. Sausage is the only treat since the strike began. Sausage on Saturday, sausage on Sunday.

'If I as much as look at another sausage...' says Mrs Whitaker. The butcher nods in sympathy. He could happily strangle any of the poor sausages which hang from the hook in his window, were they not already dead.

But it is midday and what would a man not give for the sight of a sausage, sizzling in the pan. The thought stirs his gastric juices into action. He must stop hallucinating. He must not go home. That way there will be more food for the kids. Company will drive away the hunger pangs. So the men congregate at the bottom of the street in the Market Square at the Spittle rail, so called because there the retired miners always stand every day, leaning against the rail, watching the world go by and coughing up the thick, black stuff which lines their lungs. Once it was known as the 'hitching rail', because, years ago, before the pits existed, the weary traveller would stop, hitch up his horse, fetch it water from the fountain and find himself a pint of ale. The fountain is now a clock, but little else has changed. For hundreds of years all the news and gossip of the world has found its way to and from that spot.

There the retired have been joined by the un-employed, restless, bored and heartsick, finding a comfort in companionship not to be found at the dole office across the road. And now the strike has added many more. They are a familiar sight, and there is reassurance in the sound of their laughter. Life goes on. They say that when the strike is over they will have to erect a bronze monument where Fred Benson has stood these eight months, like a statue, his elbows on the rail, unmoving except for his eyes. The town will not seem the same once he is back down the pit.

Wives, mothers and sisters with buggies full of children stop for a word, blocking the pavement, then trudge up the High Street.

I jostle past as I always do every Tuesday, and go into the market for eggs, almost warm from the farms. Then just a tiny diversion, not to buy, I tell myself, just to peep in the wool shop window. But oh the bargains! Bags of offcuts straight from the local mills, mohair and chunky and cottons, knubbly and crunchy in irresistible emerald, fuchsia and turquoise.

'Tempted again are we?'

I jump. Laughing, hanging half out of the jewellery boutique next door is Betty, the health visitor. It is her lunch hour and the object of this visit is Marjorie, whose brother owns the shop. Cathy, Marjorie's sister, is there too, giggling as she does, like a naughty schoolgirl caught smoking in the toilets.

'I thought I heard a noise. I might have guessed.'

'Join us.'

'There's no room.'

'There's heaps of room for a little one.'

'Does no one have any work to do?'

'Cheeky beggar, isn't she?' says Betty.

Majorie smiles.

'We're not exactly busy.'

'So we're callin' instead,' says Cathy.

'Callin'', with a flat 'a' as in pally, is a practised art in West Yorkshire. Gossip makes the day pass quickly. The women do it guiltily with the disapproval of the men. The men do it naturally and no one disapproves of them.

A woman comes quietly into the shop and waits at the door. As if it is an unspoken signal Cathy gets down. 'I'm on duty at the park at one,' she says.

'And I've three more visits before clinic,' says Betty. 'See yer, Marj.'

I am about to go too when a silver chain catches my eye, the kind I have been wanting for ages.

The woman slowly approaches the counter, and lifts her left hand, the skin worksore and toughened like animal hide. She eases the gold band off her third finger.

'Will yer tek it?' she whispers, her eyes filling with

11

tears. 'I've nowt else and the kids must eat.'

Marjorie nods and lays the ring lovingly in a tiny box on a bed of cotton wool.

'I'll not sell it,' she says, when the woman has gone. 'I couldn't. I'll keep it safe for her and she'll come for it when the strike's over.'

The silver chain has lost its appeal and I walk on up the High Street. Everything seems the same, the corner sweet shop with huge glass jars of sherbet, mints and gob-stoppers lined up in rows in the window, and the newspaper shop, door propped open, stark, bare and mucky with print. Yet it is different, too quiet, almost as if rumour has it that no food is to be had in the shops today. But the bakery bulges with curd cakes and Sally Lunns, bread cakes and scufflers.

'Mornin', love. Hundred per cent wholemeal as usual?'

The loaf is in her hand already, then in mine, warm and steaming with the smell of new bread.

'Thanks, Gladys. It's quiet in here today.'

'Ay well, what can yer expect? It were a good service though Sunday night.'

'Was it?'

'Weren't yer there?'

'Babysitting.'

'Oh ay, I forgot.'

Gladys, with her smile, warm and wholesome like the bread she sells, who said months ago she wouldn't go to church. She hadn't been for years, wouldn't know anyone. And when she came she knew them all. They bought bread from her and fancy, she never even knew they went.

It was always the same with new people. They crept in and sat at the back or behind a pillar. I tried to speak to them, because, being Jewish, I remembered my first visit to a church, how strange it seemed, how out-of-place I felt.

'Hello. I haven't seen you before.'

12

'No, I've not been since we had young 'uns christened.'

'Do you know anyone here?'

'I know 'em all, love. I've lived in Grimlington all me life. That's me cousin over there. But I don't know you. Who are you?'

It was a fair question. I often wondered who I was myself. The curate's wife? The role hung round my neck like a dead weight at times and I longed to heave it off and throw it away. The curate's Jewish wife? That was more confusing, and made me more foreign than ever.

'We like you, you know, even though you're a Jew.'

'Thanks!' I said, then smiled to myself and took it as it was offered, an honest token of acceptance. Yorkshire people speak their mind. I could not ask for more. It meant they saw beyond the caricature which role and preconceptions imposed, to me as I am, always a foreigner of sorts, yet now with so much of the town in my bloodstream. Strange that I should see so much of my own struggle reflected in theirs, struggle to resist pressure, refusal to conform, insistence to be what we are, by birth and choice. Who would ever have guessed, when I first came nearly two years ago, that our lives would so intermingle?

Dear old town. When I wash your soot from my hair and the suds turn grey, when I wipe soot daily from my windowsills and watch it appear through the floor-boards in stripes on my carpets, when I see it and can laugh, then I know you have secured a niche for yourself in my heart that nowhere else shall supplant. Rumour has it that land round here belonged to Wilberforce, fighter of slavery. Later, strange irony, its harvest made other slaves, men, women and children, who hacked it day and night, and were just as black and bowed. Land always tugging at my heart strings, once fair, then raped and plundered for its treasure, now abandoned, bruised and scarred, its attractions gone. What will become of it and the men whose destiny is buried in its soil? What will all our striking and starving achieve? Will it preserve the community we love or drive it further towards its destruction?

Chapter 2

I never dreamed of being a clergyman's wife. Not that I imagine many girls do these days. It just so happened that mine was the strange fortune, strange for a Jewish child, of attending a Church of England girls' school. And there I discovered that some girls, and even certain teachers, are very susceptible to the sight of an attractive young face emerging from a dog collar. Whatever it was that made them weak at the knees, I never succumbed to it.

I never wanted to marry a rabbi either for that matter. Although we kept most of the Jewish festivals at home and Mother's cooking was strictly kosher, yet they were far too pious for us. Besides, rabbis were not attractive. They had beards and their wives wore wigs!

And then events took over. At seventeen I read a forbidden book, the New Testament. And because of that apparently innocent exercise the course of my life was changed. Such are the fruits of curiosity! Mother's plans for me of a hard-working, if not wealthy Jewish boy were doomed from the moment I opened its pages. I became a Christian, but not a convert. How I hated the word! Christ was the logical extension of my Jewishness, not an alternative. Years later, after I had fought my battles to be a Christian and a Jew, I met Peter, not Jewish and only a schoolteacher, but a nice enough boy. Or so my mother thought, until he announced his sense of calling to the Church of England ministry.

She was not the only one to be horrified. She at least saw the funny side. I was devastated. By then we had been married four years, had our own home and up to that moment had been nonconformist! I prided myself on being versatile, especially when it came to the denominations, but there were limits. The vicar's wife could hardly try another church if she did not enjoy the one where her husband ministered. She was stuck for life with one denomination and all its foibles and with her husband's sermons. She had no choice. She fitted in. She did as people expected. She was bland, safe, without opinions and without friends for who would want their private thoughts to find their way back to the vicar?

I pushed my fears away for the two years of training, stimulating, happy years, a chance to read and think, to shake off inherited attitudes I felt were unreal. But I still did not confront my real self and its refusal to come to terms with its destiny, not until that first weekend we drove into Grimlington with a view to a possible curacy. 'For better, for worse', I had vowed only six years ago. And this, I decided, was worse, far worse.

We drove in silence up the one long road which stretched from the motorway to the centre of the town. On either side were rows of uneven, red-brick terraced housing, broken by a side street or a dingy corner shop. I looked for greenery, but there was none: no trees, no shrubs, no sign of spring, though March was almost past. The tiny gardens, separated from the pavement by two foot high walls, were muddy and bare. It occurred to me that it would take a fairly determined flower to fight its way to daylight through gravy-stained cartons, scrunched up newspaper and empty pop cans.

'Well,' Peter said, breaking into the silence, as we stopped at the traffic lights, 'could you live here?'

So many impressions were flashing through my mind in a confused mass. The impression of 'once had been': a chapel now a warehouse, a cinema now a factory, a thriving, busy town now past its height. Yet also the feeling that in the occasional splash of colour for a front door, the fancy brickwork and hotch-potch of modern-isation, bottle-bottom window panes and frilly net curtains, hope and pride survived.

16

'Oh, it's not so bad,' I said, transported in time to Felling, the little pit town in Gateshead where I had grown up. My father was the local doctor and he loved the little community in his care. Back-to-back terraces, cobbled streets and smoking chimneys were sights I had seen from the window every day. I would watch for hours. And sometimes, our Albert, a retired sailor and postman, who trained the dog, did the garden, collected us from school, sang us to sleep and kept the whole family in order, would take me home with him. Home to his Nelly, a real fire, home-made scones and endless cups of tea. I shook myself back into the present.

'There are far worse places to live,' I said.

'Ashton!' said Peter and rammed the car into gear.

His associations were not nearly as positive as mine. He was an eight-year-old once again, forced to leave behind a lakeside apartment in Geneva for Ashton-under-Lyne where his father was to be the new vicar. For the first weeks the family stayed with the church-warden. All went down with gastric flu and the only toilet was out in the backyard. Peter did not understand and it was a trauma he never forgot. The Ashton of thirty years ago symbolised for him all that was drab, grey and depressing about small northern towns.

But I never expected to live anywhere else. Two years at theological college in the suburbs of Nottingham were the nearest I had ever been to beautiful surroundings. And while in mad moments of fantasy I dreamed of hearing a divine command to head south to a house on the coast with a sea view, I knew my chances were slim. I could live in Grimlington. But whether I could live there as a clergyman's wife was another issue. That was my struggle.

We turned up a long drive and as if by magic the scene changed into one of almost rural tranquillity. We were surrounded by trees, shrubs and riots of daffodils. A path led through a rustic gate to a rather picturesque old church ahead. For a moment it seemed we had come to the very heart of rural England – until I opened the car

17

door and an acrid, sulphurous smell hit my nostrils and ruined the illusion.

'Pwah!' I said. It never occurred to me that the thick black smoke which poured into the sky from every chimney and hung over the town in a heavy brown pall would smell quite like that.

'I suppose you get used to it,' I said hopefully.

'Ashton!' was all Peter said and sniffed, wrinkling up his nose.

Meeting a prospective vicar is the closest equivalent I know to a blind date. We had been sent to two vicars already and neither seemed right. We were in danger of appearing too choosy. But our whole future happiness hung in the balance. We had a right to be sure. We walked up to the front door of a large, modern vicarage, rang and waited, as the condemned man waits to hear the footsteps of those who will take him to his execution.

The door opened and a striking-looking man appeared. We stood for a while, weighing each other up, wondering, I suppose, whether each was the answer to the other's prayer. For our part the poor man had a great deal to live up to. We had a definite blueprint: someone strong, forceful, determined, warm, caring, enthusiastic, all that and with a sense of humour too. Whether such a mortal, let alone a clergyman, existed was another matter. Given that we were also anticipating a fair measure of theological agreement and a willing partner in our plans to revolutionise the Church of England overnight, Edward Huntingdon was at some disadvantage. Nevertheless when, after half-an-hour's basic probing, he disappeared to fetch the coffee, we nodded to each other in agreement that he was faring quite well on our mental identikit. How we were faring on his remained to be seen.

Anna, Edward's wife, came in with the coffee.

'Cherchez la femme,' they had warned us at college. 'Look out for the wife, the power behind the man.' She was young, with a strong, attractive face. I noticed the firm jawline of someone who knew her mind and stuck to it. She did not appear to be someone whose life would consist of meetings, jumble sales, flower arranging and benevolent visits to the sick.

'I do little in any official sense,' she said. 'Only one committee, and that by choice. We've only been married a couple of years and I'm still getting used to everything. It takes me all my time to cope with the telephone, the doorbell, this big house and garden and a baby.'

I sighed with relief. The last thing I wanted was to provide a church with the sweat, blood and unpaid labour expected of many a minister's wife. I had supported my husband when he was a teacher, been involved in the life of the school, but no one had assumed I would do his job. I hoped it would be the same now.

'I'm warming to this place all the time,' I whispered to Peter as we went into lunch.

Alicia, the deaconess, joined us.

'Oh, this is nothing, dears,' she said, conscious that we were watching her struggle into a chair. 'Spondylitis of the hip. No pain, just a nuisance, a little stiffness.'

Alicia had had years of experience as a deaconess – twelve of them in Grimlington – and left us in no doubt that she regarded it as the third best place after heaven. Second was her native Scottish Highlands, but Grimlington was very close behind. She regaled us throughout our meal with an enthusiastic account of all its comings and goings, births, deaths and the best take-away food. Edward had only been vicar five months and obviously had much to learn.

'You remember Molly Fairclough, whose sister we buried on Tuesday? Her youngest daughter is married to the brother of the man whose daughter you're marrying on Saturday. The groom is the nephew of Jim Burton, whose wife's sister I went to see this morning. And she's promised to come to church this Sunday.'

The tale was obviously perfectly comprehensible to Alicia and little short of a minor triumph, even if it was lost on Edward, who seemed a thousand miles away and

19

stared abstractedly at a little blond, blue-eyed baby in a high chair, who was plastering food in her eyes, ears, up her nose, anywhere in an attempt to find the right opening. Just like our little Abby.

'Everyone here is related to everyone else,' Anna said, coming to the baby's rescue, 'a fact you may discover to your cost.'

She grinned knowingly at Edward. 'So never be rude about anyone. You'll probably discover you're talking to their mother-in-law, or a fifth cousin twice removed.'

'We wanted somewhere with a strong sense of community,' I said to Peter.

Alicia nodded in agreement. 'Then how,' he asked quietly, 'does an outsider fare?'

Alicia smiled.

'You're an outsider here, darling, if you come from the next town, or the other side of the motorway. Just be yourself. It's sham they've no time for. And I must go.'

She hobbled to the door, and, turning, left us with the ultimate encouragement. 'The bird life is quite exceptional round here.'

I looked out of the window. Birdsong was not a sound I had noticed.

'I mean, we have an ings nearby, reclaimed land filled with water. If you do decide to come you can borrow my binoculars whenever you like.'

No one had said anything yet about the house. College had buzzed with incredible horror stories of curates' houses, damp, cold and in disrepair. Why did they not mention the house? It did matter. Other people could choose theirs.

'Shall we go and see the house?' Anna asked at last. 'I haven't seen inside it myself yet.'

We drove through the town, a leaden weight of dread resting on my stomach.

'How big did you say the town was?' I asked.

Anna watched my face, amused.

20

'About eighteen thousand,' Edward said from the front.

'And no Boots, no Woolworths?'

Anna laughed. 'I asked the same questions a year ago. No, no Boots or Woolworths. There were once, but they had to close. Hard to imagine, isn't it? Apparently the turnover was bad, and the service was worse. The pace of life is slow round here. No Sainsbury's either and for a southerner like me that's hard to bear. But don't despair, the town got its first purpose-built supermarket two years ago. It's a Co-op, adequate, if not exciting, as long as you're not an exotic cook.'

We drove on towards the outskirts of the town and into a large area of council housing. No high rise blocks, but only, I suspected, because the planners had run out of money before they remembered Grimlington's existence. There were some advantages in not being strictly inner city.

At the furthermost edge of the town, in total isolation, stood a modern detached house, separated on all sides from every other house by a thousand square yards of grassland. There was no tree to soften its starkness or shelter it from the wind. There it stood, the only private house, the only house without a chimney, looking for all the world like the folly of a man with too much money, who wanted to impress but had made a big mistake.

The car came to a halt and my heart sank. The curate's house, of course, what else? Built to look as if its inhabitants were somewhat superior to the rest of the neighbourhood, either that or carriers of the plague. Edward was obviously struck by its oddity too.

'It was built seven years ago,' he said. 'The idea was to establish a kind of church presence up here where we have so little contact.'

'Then why not rent a council house?' I asked. Living like the lord of the manor could hardly be called identifying with the people and I was not sure I fancied being a presence.

21

'I think the church members hoped the curate would soon attract a small congregation, then a church would be built on the spare ground.'

'How many curates have lived here?'

'Two.'

'And no congregation?'

Edward surveyed the grassland and shook his head. 'What church members there are want to move down into town. There's nothing here, no shops, no heart to the community.'

The exterior was all that was imposing about the house. Inside it smelt musty and looked pokey, painted as it was in a lurid, midnight blue.

'I'd no idea it was so shabby,' Anna said, looking round apologetically. 'Don't you think a coat of paint will work wonders?'

I tried to summon some rapidly dwindling enthusiasm, but such as there was evaporated when I realised the full extent of its catastrophic design. Some diocesan architect had excelled himself this time. Every room was completely overlooked from outside. The kitchen, apart from having three doors which collided when opened simultaneously, had no space for extras like a fridge. The previous curate's fridge stood where he had left it, in the centre of the room, and we walked round it as if it were a museum piece. There was no dining room, just a tiny square alcove off the kitchen. And the third 'bedroom' was too small to take a bed. The only concession to this being a purpose-built clergy house was a large downstairs toilet.

'The only room big enough for a filing cabinet,' Peter commented.

For two years in our small temporary house in Nottingham I had been forced to climb over his desk, mounds of books and papers and half-written essays to get into bed. It had been a veritable feat of mountaineering. I had dreamed of a house with some space. But here all we should have were two average sized bedrooms. The children were small enough to share, but how could I invite friends to stay? Leaving so many behind was wrench enough without the added pain of being unable to offer them hospitality.

And my poor parents! I had always said to them, 'Whatever happens, wherever we go, there will always be room for you.' Where would I put them? In Nottingham I juggled with cots and squeezed them in. It would take more than invention to do the same in this house.

Edward and Anna looked out over the garage roof. 'I wonder if we could extend out?' he asked.

I clung to the idea as to the only strand of hope. And I yearned for Manchester, for our first home, an old terrace lovingly renovated to meet our every need, then left behind when the call came. From now on we were doomed to other people's taste and other people's follies. My stomach turned over. I wanted to say, 'Thank you very much for showing us round but Grimlington isn't for us,' before running as fast as I could back to Nottingham. But something kept my mouth closed and fastened me to the spot. Had I become so inflexible? It was a roof over our heads. And life is more than houses. Though what that 'more' was I could not remember, not until later that evening, when we were introduced to some of the congregation.

Chapter 3

They came shyly into the room, as frightened of us as we were of them. Edward introduced Marjorie first as one of the churchwardens. She was a warm, motherly woman, round and dimpled, with a shock of white hair which framed a face which must have once been the toast of the town. I felt at ease with her at once, and so did Edward, judging from the merciless way he teased her. But there was respect in his voice too.

'Keeping vicar in order is her hardest job, isn't it Marj?' said a voice behind them.

'And this is Lucy,' Edward said, drawing forward a shy-looking woman with bobbed hair, who nodded at us nervously. She perched on the end of the settee.

'I were just sayin',' she said, in the uneasy silence which followed, 'Council have been after us again about state of our back garden. It's like a wilderness and I can't get Dad to do it. It's getting past 'im.'

'Offer it back to the Council as a cemetery,' Peter suggested, 'and then they'd have to do it.'

She looked at him, shocked, realised he was joking, then laughed uproariously. The ice was broken.

'Oooh, do excuse me,' she said, as a loud gurgling sound filled the room. 'It's Oscar,' she patted her stomach, 'my peptic ulcer. He's always lettin' me down.'

The doorbell went again. Moments later Alicia brought a small, neat woman into the room. A quiet, dignified man stood slightly behind her. She looked round to see who was there, smiled at Marjorie and Lucy with satisfaction, then introduced herself.

'I'm Vera, and we represent the older generation, don't we Arnold?'

Marjorie laughed. 'Hey, Lucy, that makes us spring chickens. I suppose we should feel flattered.'

Anna brought in the tea and suddenly everyone was talking at once. I gave up trying to follow any line of conversation and enjoyed watching them. Peter's eyes were moving backwards and forwards too, like a spectator at a tennis match. Eventually Edward managed to persuade them to tell us one at a time how they had come to be involved in the church. From the deferring looks Marjorie understood that she was to begin. She explained how the church had gone through a time of great upheaval since she had started going. That was years ago, when her children were small. She had an asthma attack one night and nearly died.

'I was in hospital struggling for breath when I felt someone take hold of me hand and will me to live. I thought it were Charlie, me husband. Only he loves me like that. But when I said to him later, "I was glad they let yer stay with me," he said, "They didn't. They thought yer'd had it!" Well this may sound funny to you, and don't ask me how, but I was sure it were Jesus who had stood at me bedside that night.'

There was silence for a time, except for the ticking of the carriage clock, then Marjorie laughed.

'And here I am. Mind you the church was posh in them days. I felt a bit out-of-place. It was so...'

'Traditional?' Vera suggested.

'Full of people like us,' Vera added smiling. 'Well, we didn't know any different then, did we, Arnold? We went because we always had. Arnold's father was in trade and it was expected of us. Then one day a team of young people came. They stayed in our homes. And we suddenly realised we'd little real faith at all.'

I watched Arnold, wondering how he felt about this revelation. He was chuckling to himself in recollection.

'We told all our friends,' he said quietly, 'even customers who came into the shop. They think you're in your dotage when you become religious in later life.'

'Although they were churchgoers themselves,' Vera added. 'And they've found all the changes very hard indeed. It's been difficult for us. We're often in the middle.'

'I get my share of complaints too,' Marjorie said, shaking her head.

'Mother to the town, aren't you, Marj?' Edward said.

'I don't know about that.'

'And you, Lucy,' Edward said, suddenly turning to her. She jumped. 'It's your turn.'

'Me? I've nothing to tell.'

'Go on with you,' Marjorie said.

'Well, my speaking to yer now's a miracle. Yer can hear me stammer?'

I had barely noticed it.

'That's nothing. After me twin died I couldn't string two words together. I'd no confidence at all. I suppose I'd say God gave me a voice. Now, well, that one,' she said, pointing at Alicia, 'has me birdwatching, going to opera and all sorts.'

Alicia chortled to herself.

'Alicia has a lot of people doing things they never dreamed they'd do,' Edward agreed, catching Alicia's eye. 'I think it's called the gentle art of persuasion. When I ask people what made them start coming to church the most common reply is, "It was the only way to stop Alicia visiting."'

All this time Arnold had been studying us, watching and waiting with his eyes, like an owl.

'And you,' he said suddenly, 'what brings you to a place like Grimlington?'

Peter shared his chequered history and I shared mine. To be anything less than totally honest would have been an affront to their openness. They had already given so much of themselves.

'So you see,' he said, 'I don't want to come in as the traditional curate, good at almost everything, pretending I can do it all, because I can't. Edward says you need someone with special gifts in youth work and mission. I've neither. All I know is that somewhere there is a church with a Peter-and-Michele-shaped hole. And when we find it we'll know.'

'Well all I can say is that our curates seem to like us,' said Vera, as she collected her things together. 'They stay at least four years.' I was not sure whether that was a threat or a warning.

'Lucy,' I said, before she had a chance to disappear, 'tell me what you do.'

'I pack for Asda. You know them packs of apples wrapped in cling film? Well I put them together.'

'Do you enjoy it?'

She thought for a moment. 'It's a job. And that's something these days. I'd rather work with people though. Wrappin' apples gets a bit monotonous. But then,' she said, a twinkle in her eye, 'some days, for variety they give us avocados or kiwis. The excitement! We'd never seen them before.'

She got up, went to the door, then came back and put her arms round me. 'Whatever yer decide, tonight's been special,' she said.

As the front door closed Peter and I looked at each other knowingly and smiled. Here were people who did not try to hide their true selves or their feelings and made no attempt to impress. We had found what we were looking for.

'I feel as if I've come home,' I said.

But it was an illusion. There in the vicarage with Edward and Anna we were safe, cocooned. The reality of the situation hit me again with all its force the following afternoon when Peter went to measure up the house. I took the children to play amidst the broken glass, litter, dog mess and dereliction on some swings on the spare ground opposite. From every house coils of black floated up into the air. The smell of sulphur was stronger here than anywhere else. Would I never be able to open my front door and breathe in fresh air again? I suddenly felt numb and desolate. I had not even the

27

energy to push the children. I wanted to cry, but the tears would not come. I sat on one of the swings and rocked backwards and forwards. A child spoke to me and seemed puzzled when all I did was shake my head. I looked at the brick monument in the distance. Today it did not even look imposing, just pathetic, stuck out there on its own, as if it did not know how it got there or where it really belonged. Everything seemed so hopeless. Who would ever pop in for a cup of tea? The whole neighbourhood would know where they were going. How would we ever be accepted or get to know anyone, living such a strange, separate existence? I had always loved having neighbours and hated the isolation of the clergy. My worst fears were coming true. I would have no friends. It was all very well telling myself that if this was where we were meant to be I would have to cope. But what if we agreed to come and my feelings did not obligingly fall into line? I had to use my common sense. I would be no good to Peter as a lonely, quivering heap.

'Say no,' said a voice inside. 'That's all you have to do. Walk over there and tell him to put his tape measure away. He's wasting his time. You're not coming.'

I tucked Abby under one arm and with Joel trailing after me, lamenting leaving the swings behind, I marched up to the house, ready to offload all my misery on my poor longsuffering husband. He was sitting in a corner on the floor. One look at his face told me that he was contending with enough of his own. We looked at each other for a while in a helpless silence.

'Well,' he said, turning to stare out of the window, 'I do seem to ask a lot of you.'

I went over and sat next to him.

'Whatever happens, wherever we go, at least we have each other, and the kids.'

The thought cheered us a little, or at least helped us get ourselves together enough to follow Edward's street map to the other side of the town, where we had been invited for tea. We walked for what seemed an age, then turned into a new estate of tiny, box-like, neo-Georgian semis. 'Superior housing of distinction', we were informed by a large sign, but it was really very little different to the estate we had just left.

We were lousy company. Conversation was an effort and despite the warmth of their welcome, Rick and Julie and Mick and Karen were obviously unsure about how to handle our gloom. They agreed about the house, but were as helpless as we were about a solution. Julie disappeared quickly into the kitchen to make the tea.

'And all this smoke,' I grumbled rudely. I was too fed up to be polite.

'Why does everyone burn coal round here? Haven't they heard of the Clean Air Act?'

Mick surveyed me with the sort of quizzical expression that says, 'What have they sent us this time?' Then he seemed to remember we were foreigners after all.

'They burn it because it's free if yer work for Coal Board, like I do.'

'Then why don't they give them anthracite?'

'They do,' said Mick, with more grace than I knew I deserved, 'but not nearly so much. And none of us can afford to be finicky. It's the only real perk to working down pit. There's not much else to commend it, but at least yer don't have to worry about keeping warm.'

'You're a miner?' Peter asked.

'No, an engineer. There are as many of us, and electricians and joiners, as there are colliers.'

'Do you enjoy it?'

Mick grinned, a warm, infectious grin, with an almost schoolboy appeal, and looked round at Karen, who had been sitting quietly at his side, smiling at us sympathetically.

'It's a job,' he said and I remembered I had heard that before. 'There's talk, yer see, rumours, about pits closing. A man's glad these days he's work at all. But what I'd really like to do,' he paused with a faraway look in his eyes, 'is 'ave a recording studio.'

Karen smiled at him, her face a mixture of motherly

29

indulgence and despair. 'Oh Mick,' she said gently, and sighed. 'Him and his audio equipment!'

'No, no,' he insisted. 'I could use it for the church. A man can dream, can't 'e?'

'And he's another one,' Julie said, cocking her head at Rick as she sailed in from the kitchen with a large plate of buns. She was heavily pregnant and it seemed to suit her joviality. 'He'd like to be making music all day.'

Rick, who seemed quite an earnest young man, told us enthusiastically about a music group he had started in the church. My spirits began to lift slightly. Mick, aware of the fact, weighed us up, then decided to take a chance.

'If you think Grimlington's bad,' he said, 'you should see Ossleforth, other side of motorway. If this country were a human body, Ossleforth would have the haemorrhoids.'

'Oh Mick,' Karen said, tugging hard at his pullover sleeve, but his face broke into an enormous grin and Rick and Julie shook with laughter. We laughed too, and it brought a sudden surge of relief.

Rick's music group were certainly not in evidence at the evening service. It was a laboured, traditional affair, using the old prayer book. A choir of five took what looked like a last stand and tried to rouse a sleepy, unresponsive congregation to worship. I wondered whether it was really as dreary as it seemed or whether it was just my Jewish nature with its love of life and colour playing tricks on me again, when a young couple in front of us who had been shuffling uncomfortably for a while, suddenly got up and walked out. The droning of the psalm had evidently finished them off. I had a deep desire to run after them and apologise for the church. Either that or escape from the boredom as well. 'At least,' I thought with relief as we sang the final hymn, 'on future occasions I'll be babysitting.'

I headed for the door. It had been a long weekend. Arnold was there before me.

'Grimlington's not such a bad place,' he said. 'We once had one of the most important railway stations in Europe. The Queen slept here.'

I tried to look impressed, then noticed the twinkle in his eye.

'In a railway carriage, in the sidings,' he chuckled.

'Which queen was that, Elizabeth or Victoria?'

'Touché.' He laughed, then said seriously, 'If you don't come back, don't forget us, will you, because we won't forget you.'

A lump came to my throat. I turned and went quickly out of the door.

Chapter 4

We moved on the two most depressing days of the year. The sky was a heavy, leaden grey and the rain poured incessantly, not easing for a moment. The removal lorry with the ramp had broken down and was replaced by one with a tail-gate lift. We watched our furniture, bedding and precious belongings being battered and soaked.

'Never mind,' we said to each other, 'it can't possibly rain like this tomorrow when we offload in Grimlington.' But it did.

I hate moving. It is like turning over the final page of a good book. The experiences, relationships and emotions of that particular story are gone, never to be recaptured in quite the same way again. They disappear into the past, the silent secret of the bare walls and floorboards that make up the empty shell of the house that is left behind. As the last cup is wrapped in newspaper and placed in the crate, the remains of the sugar bowl thrown into the dustbin, a piece of toy, found under the carpet, shoved into a pocket, many scenes and sounds float back eerily, then vanish, gone for ever. It is hard to close the door for the last time and say goodbye to part of oneself.

I wondered how many goodbyes there would be in the future. They would be real separations, final, a kind of death. Clergy rarely haunt an old pitch. Perhaps it would be less painful not to love at all, than love and lose all the time.

I sat in the car, watching our belongings in the lorry ahead, feeling like a caveman's wife, being dragged by the hair where she never wanted to go.

'What sort of a vicar's wife will you make?' taunted an inner voice. 'You can't even say the Lord's Prayer without looking at the book. You're Jewish. You know nothing about the Church of England. What have you got to give the people in Grimlington?'

Then words came back to me, spoken by a friend when I had admitted my conflict.

'There's buried treasure in that town. Dig for it like a miner.' And the feeling, deeper, quieter than my fear, that told me Grimlington would not be a dead end, but a place of open doors. With a struggle we had said yes to house and all and then discovered it would only be a temporary home. The PCC had decided it was inadequate. They would sell it and buy us another. Our gratitude was enormous. We detected glints of that treasure already.

In the rain Grimlington looked greyer than I remembered and as miserable as I felt. By the time we turned into the estate and pulled up at our front door I was fighting the tears.

'Let's go home,' I said.

'Where's that?' Peter asked.

'I don't care. Anywhere you like.'

I would have happily crept into any hole as long as it was warm and dry.

Peter struggled for a while, trying to fit the key into the strange lock, then he flung the door open.

'Come and see,' he called, with excitement. I followed him half-heartedly, then stared in amazement. The lurid, claustrophobic blue was gone and instead we walked into a light, clean, airy house. The walls had been painted white, the floorboards scrubbed and the paintwork washed. I walked slowly into my new kitchen which sparkled as if it were in a detergent advert on the television. There, filling the entire double bench was the largest food hamper I had ever seen. It was packed to overflowing with tins of steak, chicken, salmon, strawberries and pineapple. There were packets of soup

33

and sauces, jars of jam and pickles. We could have survived a siege for a year. Beside the hamper was a basket of fruit and with a bouquet of flowers was a card which said, 'With love from your new family.'

I could not speak. Peter took the card from me.

'Goodness,' he said. 'This lot will have cost some of them a week's housekeeping.'

The removal men, as bedraggled as our belongings, began to offload them, cramming them into every available space, smearing black stuff everywhere as they did so. As I was directing the traffic, I noticed a young woman wobbling up to our door on a bike, a fruit flan precariously balanced on one hand. It was an acrobatic feat requiring some precision.

'Hello,' she said shyly, taking note of the chaos, 'I'm Mary. And this is Louise.'

She beckoned to a teenage girl who had biked up behind her and was waiting at the gate.

'Your daughter?' I asked carefully. I reckoned Mary was probably about my age. She was also very petite, smaller than the girl at the gate. She nodded.

'But you don't look old enough.'

Her face showed a mixture of pride and pleasure.

'I've two older than her at home. Anyway, we're not stopping. We've been told not to bother you, so I've just come to give you this.' She shoved the flan into my hand. 'If you need anything, I'm just at the bottom of the street,' she called, jumped on her bike and was gone.

The flan tasted wonderful later in the evening, when a counter had been taken out and the washing machine installed, and we sat down to eat, exhausted and ravenous.

Slowly some of the crates were emptied and others stored in the garage, temporary carpets and curtains were found, we put up pictures and ornaments and began to feel more at home. One or two church members popped in to see if we needed anything and were all right. Then they disappeared fast. There was no

34

chance to find out anything about them or the community. Then one morning the doorbell rang loudly and insistently.

'Someone with determination,' I said to Peter. There on our doorstep was a small, smartly-dressed woman with greying hair and an attractive, lively face.

'Hello, love, I'm Betty,' she said. 'We met at the service when you were here on a visit. I don't know if you remember.'

I remembered her very well, and the large golden earrings that swung jauntily as she spoke, which she did, persistently. To out-talk me was quite an accomplishment. I remembered too that Anna had told me she was one of Grimlington's four health visitors.

'Professional or social visit?' I asked, as she came into the living room and had a good look round.

'A bit of both, let's say. Killing two birds with one stone. Haven't you made it nice?' she said appreciatively, taking in every detail of our plants and pictures.

I was only too aware that our carpets looked like handkerchiefs on the bare floorboards and the curtains stopped several inches above the window-sill.

'A bit makeshift, but since it's temporary it'll do.'

'But it was so dark and pokey before.'

'Well the difference is thanks to you lot.'

'Weren't those dark blue walls awful? It took six coats of white emulsion to cover them.'

I was staggered. Such effort for a temporary house.

'In fact,' she said, following me into the kitchen where I had gone to put the kettle on, 'you see that ceiling up there?'

I followed the direction of her finger and we stood gazing at the ceiling together for some time.

'One evening my Frank was up there and on to his fourth coat. He drove us mad with his moaning. I said to him, "If you can't do it in the right spirit don't do it at all." He stopped dead and put his brush down. I thought yer'd had yer ceiling. Suddenly he started

35

singing hymns at the top of his voice and the ceiling was done in double quick time. I'll never look at that ceiling again in the same light.'

We took our coffee and sat down. After a few thoughtful mouthfuls, which seemed to help Betty warm to her subject, she said, 'What I've really come about is ... well, sooner or later you might be needing my services.'

I knew what was coming, Anna had warned me, but I could not resist playing the innocent.

'Baby clinic?' I asked. 'Abby is ready for a measles vaccination.'

'Er, yes. What I really meant was family planning,' she said in a conspiratorial whisper. 'I help with the clinic. Now if you need anything, you know, all you have to do is give me a wink and a nod in church.'

'And you'll pass it down the pew?' I asked innocently.

'Go on with you!' she laughed and got up to go. She stopped at the front door and looked round the estate.

'You know,' she said, 'Grimlington's a great place. It's a tight-knit community. Mining people always stick together. But if yer come from elsewhere and the Council stick yer in a house up here, it can be terribly lonely. I feel for some of these girls, so young, tied in with babies and they don't know anyone.'

'It's a long walk into town with a pram,' I agreed. I had tried it. 'But there's nothing up here, no shopping centre or anything. Are there no toddler clubs?'

Betty shook her head.

'Like you say, not up here. There's one fortnightly at church and some girls come to the clinic for company, but it's an almost impossible walk with a pram and a toddler.'

'Playgroups?' I asked.

Betty shook her head again.

'Only one down in the town and it's more than most mums can afford. Then the church runs one two mornings a week.'

'For a town this size? I can't believe it.'

Betty smiled.

'There's nothing, love, only one small youth club, no cinema, no facilities at all. But we survive. We make our own entertainment. And I'm off. Oh, by the way,' she said, as she turned to go, 'your little boy, what's his name, Joel, he'll soon get to know me. We go into school to check their 'eads. In fact I'm known locally as "Nitty Norah, the big game hunter".'

I hardly felt reassured and scratched involuntarily as I went back into the house. Peter was packing his case in preparation for his pre-ordination retreat. When I deposited him in Leeds it would be the last we would see of each other until he emerged from the cathedral four days later, a fully-fledged clergyman.

'We're not allowed to see each other before the services,' he said. 'No chatting and certainly no kissing.'

'It seems daft to me. I can understand you need time for quiet and reflection, but to go to such lengths?'

'I'm in purdah, I'm afraid.' He grinned. 'Don't you remember how in the Old Testament, before special ceremonies the priests of Israel had to stay away from women?'

'I thought the Church of England was Christian not Jewish!'

'I sometimes wonder,' he said wryly.

When he went I felt an enormous void. We had been apart before, but this was different. We were on the threshold of a new existence, in a strange town, where I knew almost no one. I understood his need for quiet reflection. The paradox was that if ever we needed to be together it was now. I resented the Church. It seemed a formidable rival, demanding a total disruption of my life and giving nothing in return. Let there be no doubt, it was my husband she really wanted. I would always count for little.

I made up my mind not to enjoy the ordination ceremony. All the other ordinands had hordes of family supporting them, mothers and aunties in large hats, clucking and cooing and puffing out their feathers as if it

37

were a wedding. I could hardly expect my family to be there, but it was still a source of pain that they never were at the great occasions in our lives. Most of Peter's family were abroad, but his sister and nephew came from Geneva and how we valued that.

Despite myself I found the pomp and ceremony impressive. Peter stood head and shoulders above the rest, looking handsome and dignified in his cassock and surplice. I felt so proud of him, until I remembered that those were probably not the thoughts I should be thinking on such an occasion. I tried to marshall my powers of concentration, when Joel, sitting quietly next to me up until that moment, suddenly tipped the contents of his little brown case on to the pew. I had been too busy to check what he was bringing. Several dozen large, brightly-coloured pieces of Lego hit the polished wood with a clatter which resounded through the building.

'Shhhhhhhh!' came from all sides.

I felt like retorting, 'It's his father being ordained, you know, he has a right to be here,' but decided that our assailants were probably too set in their ways to accept that a child has a place in God's house. Unperturbed, Joel built the pieces into a gun and shot various members of the congregation throughout the service. Our attempts to teach him non-violent games had failed.

Across the cathedral I caught sight of Betty, Marjorie and Lucy smiling and waving. They nodded and winked at me in the sermon when the archdeacon warned the congregation not to expect another curate in the man's wife. I was glad to have them there. Their bright faces were a striking contrast to some of the others around them. More than that their presence enabled me to make the commitment I had been unable to make before.

As Peter publicly swore his allegiance to Church and Queen, as he vowed to pastor and teach his flock, the enormity and folly of what we were doing hit me again.

We had given up a secure teaching job with prospects, a reasonable salary, a home of our own and the friends we loved, for what? A crazy job with no prospects, unspecified commitment, unlimited hours, minimal pay and life on a council desert island. All that and the weight of carrying around a role with all the expectations that created.

Yet suddenly I realised that the urge to run away and hide in a hole had gone. I was ready to face the future and commit myself, not to some great and noble vocation, that just seemed a surfeit of piety, but to Grimlington. The town had began to touch in me emotions of which I was unaware until that moment. It seemed so much like a neglected, unwanted little foster child, spurned by the vast metropolitan borough, passed over when the goodies were handed out. It reminded me of a runny-nosed child with tear-stained cheeks, yet still too proud to be patronised. I would give whatever I could, and that seemed appallingly little. The 'call' when it finally came was bigger than all my resources to fill it.

'Help me, God, you've brought me this far, screaming and kicking all the way. I feel helpless, inadequate, but here I am, for what it's worth.'

The steward put his hand on my shoulder and encouraged me to leave before the masses so that I could see my husband before they did. I joined Peter, took his arm and together we walked out of the cathedral into the warm sunshine.

Chapter 5

Acclimatising to life in a goldfish bowl was a slow process. We had never exactly been very private people, but nor were we goldfish. Most mornings a row of noses would appear squashed against our downstairs window panes. The school holidays were long, there was nothing to do, and a clergyman was something of a peculiarity. They did not need to come that close. There was a perfectly good view into every room of our house from a radius of about a hundred yards. The bus-stop for the main bus route to Leeds was right outside and when I opened my bedroom curtains in the morning, I frequently found myself staring into the face of an upstairs passenger on his way to work. Even the bathroom window was not opaque and the front door was made of glass.

At first I took care to be decently dressed at all times, but it soon became an effort.

'Blow modesty,' I said to Peter one day, when he was reminding me for the umpteenth time not to provide added local colour. 'If you can't relax in your own home, where can you?'

So he insisted we put up netting like everyone else, but I did not feel more private, just more enclosed. We were only cutting ourselves off completely.

I waited, hoping some of the local people would call, welcome us and see if we were all right, but they never did. Sometimes, particularly if we were working in the garden, I was sure we were being watched from a distant window, but when I looked up only the curtains moved.

But the girls came in their dozens, teenagers and tiny

ones, lured by the irresistible attraction of a baby. They waited in queues at the front door, arguing over whose turn it was to take Abby out. There was great prestige in having a pram to push. Some of them were sensible and doing a child care course in their last year at school. The younger ones were not and abandoned the babies while they played on the swings. If I said no they came back a quarter of an hour later and asked again. If there was no reply at the front door they hammered at the back. In fact there was so much ringing and knocking that I had little time to do anything except answer the door.

The local lads, of all sizes, used our outside walls for football practice. They drew a goal then took it in turns to score. Every time the ball hit the wall there was a thud so violent that the house shook and bits of plaster fell off the ceiling. I endured with gritted teeth, especially if I had just put the children to bed. It was a harmless enough pursuit. And most of the boys were bigger than me!

Joel was longing to play with them, but only the girls came to the house, and for Abby, not for him.

'The girls round here are stupid,' he said in disgust. 'All they want to do is push a pram.'

'It's like playing with a doll,' I explained to him, but he was not impressed.

He suffered more than all of us. At first he was thrilled by the sight of so many children playing out in the evening and he rushed out to join in. But it was not like the square in Nottingham where all the children played together. Here he was an oddity. He talked posh. He lived in the posh house. He liked dressing up and playing imaginative games. All they did was stand around doing nothing, he said. And it took him a while to understand their language. He came in one day, shouting, 'Mum, what's a bastard?'

'Why,' I asked.

'Because one of the dads has just called me one.'

'What were you doing?'

'Getting my football from his garden.'

'Well, Joel,' I said and lifted him on to my knee, for a four-year-old is still a baby, no matter how big and sturdy, 'you may be many things, but a bastard you're not.'

He seemed satisfied and ran out to try again.

I had to admire his determination. Day after day he sat around watching the older children playing cricket and football, waiting for a chance to field, or run and fetch the ball for them. I watched him from the window, my heart aching for the little chap, sitting alone on his football, his head in his hands, waiting so patiently. And sometimes they let him have a go and he would come in, his eyes shining and his chest puffed out with pride.

At other times he curled up in a corner of the house and cried quietly for his friends in Nottingham while I felt a heel and reproached myself for what we had done to him. What right had we to make him the innocent victim of what we understood to be God's will for us?

A story from the Old Testament came forcibly to my mind, probably because it was so familiar. When I was a child it was recounted every year at the Passover. My ancestors were slaves in Egypt when Moses went to bring them out and take them to the promised land of their dreams. In typical Jewish fashion the great adventure quickly disintegrated into chaotic schemozzle and a forty-year trek round the desert. And how they moaned!

'We've no food. Our children will die. We should have stayed in Egypt.'

Eventually the Almighty could take no more.

'All right,' he said, 'die in the wilderness, but your children, whom you called innocent victims, they will see the promised land.'

No matter how much I loved my children I could not use them in an argument against God. And perhaps, I told myself, one of these days Joel will look back and be glad that he discovered that relationships are not always easy.

*

42

Peter was eased gently into work. Alicia offered to show him the ropes, and that she did, literally.

'Pull, Peter, pull. That's it, harder. Now tie a bowline can you?'

'I've done some sailing in my time, Alicia,' he said, as they hauled the screen for the overhead projector into place. It was an extraordinary feat of engineering, suspended precariously at forty-five degrees over the pulpit and attached by a motley collection of ropes and knots to pillars, beams and the organ.

'Fun, isn't it?' she said, gazing fondly at her invention. 'Jack and I made it. If there are three of us it only takes fifteen minutes to get it up.'

'But Alicia,' Peter said, the words tumbling out despite himself, 'we used the latest equipment at college, out and up in two minutes. Think of the time saved.'

'And the satisfaction missed,' she said, smiling at him benignly. 'Anyway, darling, this is Grimlington. Money is hard to come by and there certainly isn't enough for new equipment. So we make do.'

She examined some of the knots to make sure they were secure.

'Are you sure it's safe?' Peter asked.

She nodded reassuringly.

'Well, I only hope the organist enjoys my sermons,' he said. 'If he doesn't all he has to do is cut a rope and I'm silenced... for ever.'

The transition from schoolteacher to clergyman was not going to be easy for Peter. He liked order and organisation, and it was not until our first family service that we realised just how alien both were to the local temperament.

The day began badly. It drizzled. Peter grumbled as he draped his cassock and surplice round the saddle bag of his bike and covered them with polythene. He hated wearing what he called his 'medieval angel kit'. He had never enjoyed dressing up, not even as a child.

'The uniform is only there to separate us from the people and impress them with our superiority,' he said.

43

'It creates a false impression.' Yet the ministerial garb had cost almost as much as a Belville Sassoon ball gown, and since it had to be worn it would have been a shame to trail it in the mud or catch it in the spokes.

I stayed in bed, warm and dry, then drove down to church in style, by car. Outside stood an excited, noisy band of Cubs and Brownies with banners.

'Strange!' I thought. 'Peter never mentioned a procession. He must know.'

Edward was away, but he had left instructions.

'Be adequately prepared for a service well in advance,' they had told us at college, 'and prepare the church. Allow for an atmosphere of quiet meditation before worship begins.'

Whoever said that had never been to Grimlington.

The noise met me before I reached the door. The church seemed fairly full, but it was hard to tell with so much happening. The music group was tuning up and wrestling with chairs and music stands. Mick was having trouble with the PA and could do little for babies shuffling down the aisles. Children catapulted over pews and tripped over wires or the edge of the carpet. People called to each other across the church and waved to their friends. A small group of older people huddled together, probably for protection.

Peter walked in, looking very much in control and commanded a certain quiet, if not exactly silence. He announced a hymn and the organist struck up a chord. In from the back with dignity and determination marched the Cubs and Brownies. Peter looked up and for a moment his mouth and eyes opened wide with astonishment. He turned to Alicia, who sat smiling at the little gaggle now waiting patiently at the level of his knees, waving their banners expectantly.

'Sorry, dear, forgot to tell you,' she whispered. 'Just ad lib.'

'I never even knew there were Cubs and Brownies in the church,' he said with a chuckle over lunch. 'Good job my dad was a vicar. At least I remembered what to do.'

'I expect that won't be the last time you have to ad lib either,' I said to him.

'No. A congregation isn't a classroom full of kids, is it? You can't organise adults in the same way, especially here.'

I laughed. 'Someone on the way out said to me, "Yer can tell he were a teacher by way he scowls at yer over 'is spectacles."'

'A fat lot of good it did.'

'At least they're honest. One thing we can guarantee, what they say behind our backs will be said to our faces sooner or later.'

Alone in the house that evening, the children in bed, and Peter at the evening service, there was time to think. There had been changes since our exploratory visit in the spring. The new prayer book for one, but also more life and spontaneity. And I had feared cold, reserved, British Anglicanism! I had been sure I would not cope. But what I had seen this morning was much more like the synagogue. Most people seemed relaxed and warm and glad to be there.

'You know I've been thinking,' I said to Peter, when he came in.

'Fatal!' he said and sat down next to me with a mug of Ovaltine.

'The noise this morning, the chatter before the service . . .'

'It was similar tonight,' he said, 'very informal, but the congregation was much smaller and there was more opportunity for quiet without the children there. Still, it is different from our last experience, a welcome surprise!'

'I'm glad you're not tempted to shut them up. I've always thought it was a nonsense to talk about going to church to meet God. That traps him in a building and divides the sacred from the secular. The Jewish idea seems more sensible. Since God is with us all the time, going to the synagogue is an expression of community. On that basis we do go to church to meet each other, to experience corporate worship, otherwise why not stay at home to pray? The British concept of private religion has always left me cold. What's private about loving your neighbour as yourself? It seems only right and natural to say hello to one another and find out how everyone is. That's what they'd do in the High Street.'

'I only wish I could make myself heard,' Peter said wistfully.

'Then you'll have to do what the rabbis do. Either wait for some quiet or carry on despite it.'

Peter shook his head and smiled. He had been amused in the synagogue at the rabbi's struggle to keep control, never dreaming it might happen to him.

'Well, Mick's working on the PA. At least they don't seem to have picked up the cultural tradition that the church is an awesome, holy place where everyone talks in deferential, hushed whispers. I can't bear that. Middle-class propriety disguised as piety. Long may such traditions go on changing.'

'What if it's too late?' I asked him.

'Too late for what?'

'For estates like this. Say there were about two hundred people in church this morning and half that this evening...'

'Less.'

'In a town of eighteen thousand! And it's obvious that those who do come don't live up here. Hasn't the Church become such a Victorian, middle-class anachronism that it's been failing them for years? How do we persuade them it's the institution, not the message which is at fault?'

Peter shook his head sadly.

'I don't know. Perhaps our image communicates the wrong message. Only radical change can alter that. And that's a daunting prospect.'

Chapter 6

Autumn slowly crept up on us. The last few sparse leaves which the trees had managed to produce turned a sickly yellow and tumbled dejectedly to the ground, making muddy, slimy heaps upon the pavement. The grassland around the house and at the play area became a boggy swamp and the children had to wade to the swings in their wellingtons. If they fell their clothes were pasted with a greasy black substance, largely soot and water, which no amount of washing would remove. The farmer whose fields stretched out to the pit, behind the houses which faced our front door, was covering them with manure and the air was ripe with its scent.

'Victims we are of industrial and rural life,' I said to Peter, ruefully, as our nostrils were filled with this latest perfume.

But soon even those fields would be swallowed up. One day, as we took our usual walk, closing our eyes and ears to the sight and sound of the vast iron structure ahead of us, pretending we were miles from civilisation, we noticed the tell-tale, heavy tyre marks, criss-crossing the fields. The Coal Board lorry had been prospecting. The farmer's days were numbered. It was wiser not to become too attached to any hill or patch of green.

On some days the Coal Board lorry moved slowly round the town, dumping mounds of coal in pyramids all over the pavements. I watched fascinated as the women appeared, only to vanish in a black haze, coughing all the while, as they shovelled it into their coal bunkers. On a blustery day the wind whipped up a blinding dust and more fool she who hung out her sheets to dry. In they came, spotted and speckled, and worse than when she started.

But in those chilly late September days Joel made a friend. At first Claire stood around and watched his antics in a bemused sort of way. Then one day I looked out of the window and saw her chasing after him, both dressed up as firemen in kagouls and wellington boots, wearing toy hats and with a mock hose made out of an old vacuum cleaner pipe.

Every evening, after dusk, gangs of older teenagers congregated in the play area and with nothing better to do, wrapped the swings round the top bar so that the little children could not play with them the next day. I watched them from the kitchen window, becoming more and more annoyed, until one evening I could bear it no longer and tore across the road in a fury. I poured out on them all the pent-up anger I had been storing up since our move. Words like stupid, selfish and childish poured out through my clenched teeth in a torrent. Then I ran dry. I paused, hunting for inspiration and to my amazement they grinned at me sheepishly, and stopped. Conscious of them staring after me and feeling a deep, inner satisfaction, I marched back to the house, which seemed to blaze in the dark like a beacon on an island.

The next night they were back. But Peter had a much more charitable solution to the problem. He took a ladder across and unwound the swings. From then on, every afternoon, as soon as school ended there was a queue at our door. 'Would vicar come and get swings down?'

'At least you're in demand with the children,' I said to Peter one day, when we were lamenting the fact that we still knew so few of our neighbours. We had made ourselves as approachable as we could and refused to hide. I sat out in the jungle which was our garden, on a deckchair which wobbled about on the tufts of couch grass and the downhill slope. It was a bit unnerving to be the focal point of attention for such a wide radius.

Children came and I gave them squash and sometimes, on a wet day, we read a story. But their parents did not come near.

In fact I was always amazed at how little sign of life there was at all. It was such a contrast to the High Street, where people would stand and chat all day. There was no community centre on the estate. The only place where people congregated for any length of time was at Maggie's, the newsagents.

I had never met anyone who worked as hard as Maggie. She opened the shop at eight and stayed open without a lunch hour until past seven o'clock, seven days a week. In a spare moment she slipped into the back to put the washing on or put tea ready for her two children and elderly father.

'I'll put papers through yer door,' she said.

'No, I'll come in. I like to catch up on the gossip.'

'Ay, yer hear it all in 'ere.'

Everyone who came into the shop knew who I was. They began to tell me stories: what vicar said at our Tracy's wedding, what last curate were like and the lovely funeral 'e give Grandad.

'Leavin' us already, are yer?' Maggie said, the day the For Sale sign went up outside our house.

I tried to explain. We did not want the estate to feel we were abandoning them, but I could see from the cynical expression on her face that my words had little effect.

'There's a lot'll be sorry ter see yer go,' she said. 'We've not much up 'ere, but at least we 'ad us own vicar.'

'A fat lot of good he is to you,' I said.

'We knew 'e were there if we needed 'im.'

I went home feeling sad and torn. She was right. If the Church talked about love it had to show it. But how could I explain to her that I could not cope with being the Church's representative, treated as an object and not a human being. I needed friends too. I hated the deferential look I saw in their eyes as I walked into the

49

shop. 'You're not one of us,' it said, before I had a chance. The Church created a divide no one would let me cross. And yet there was the uneasy feeling too that time, patience and perseverance could break down the years of mistrust. But we were one family alone and in the wrong house.

In the event the house was to be our home for another fifteen months. One or two potential buyers looked round and quickly decided it was the wrong house too. Those months, endless at times, as the price dropped and still no customers came to our door, gave us an invaluable opportunity to discover that on our estate to go to church was almost as alien as a visit to a mosque.

One Saturday night we went to bed early. Peter always needed a lot of sleep and especially before a Sunday.

'I wish several church families would come and live up here,' I said to him, as he settled down, tucking in the bedclothes, 'a sort of mini-community, drawing others in, not a figure-head who poses a threat. That way they'd see the church wasn't just a social service, providing occasional weddings and funerals, but a way of life that has something to offer.'

Peter yawned.

'And who are you going to get to do that? Most of the church members who live up here want to move down into town.'

'Well, I don't know. I suppose no one is willing to do it.'

'Right! If they were they wouldn't have put us up here,' he said and switched off the light.

We must have been asleep barely a couple of hours when we were both jolted from our slumbers by blood-curdling screams. Peter leapt out of bed and pulled back the curtains.

'What is it?' I asked. My heart was pounding.

'It looks like a fight.'

For a few moments there was no sound at all. We held our breath in the strange, unnatural silence. Suddenly the air was split with shrill screaming, then a girl's voice wailing over and over again, 'Yer've killed me dad, yer've killed me dad.'

'It's nasty,' Peter said. 'I'm going to phone the police.'

I went to the window and peeping out from behind the curtain, saw several figures below stagger over to our car, take off their jackets and lay them on the bonnet. Then they took their shirts off too. I blinked, wondering what was coming next. Half-naked, they lurched at each other, swiping and punching and beating with their fists. They butted each other in the stomach. Keeping their balance was such a delicate art that they often missed and landed head-first in a crumpled heap on the ground. When one fell, the others gathered round and kicked his head as if it was some kind of grotesque turnip. I rubbed my eyes. This was not the television. It was real and there was something nauseating and terrible about the sight of naked human aggression.

'We've got to do something. We've got to stop them,' I said to Peter as he joined me at the window. 'They're killing each other.'

'There's nothing we can do, love,' he said, 'except wait for the police. They're so much the worse for drink, they don't know what they're doing. They'd start on us.'

All this time the wailing continued, interrupted only by the occasional hysterical scream. And so did the punching and kicking, but there was no sign of the police. Peter rang them again. They were waiting for reinforcements. Grimlington, although known on citizen band radio as 'Crazy Town', still only had a skeleton police force. I left the window, unable to watch any longer, feeling angry and helpless at the sight of such unnecessary violence. I realised with a sickening awareness that aggression is buried so deeply in the human subconscious that when drink robs a man of reason and control his whole mentality is one of ruthless, angry self-assertion.

After what seemed an eternity, in roared the police panda cars, vans, and motor bikes, lights flashing and sirens howling. The street had been in darkness and I thought that we were the only ones watching. Suddenly lights appeared at almost every window and people were framed in their open doorways. The culprits disappeared into a house opposite and the police pursued them in. One by one a string of silhouettes emerged and were pushed calmly but firmly into the police van. An ambulance arrived and several figures were lifted in. There was a chase as someone tried to make an escape, but they were brought back, handcuffed. The walkie-talkie droned on for another hour and at last, by four-thirty, the street was quiet again.

Peter came in. With an anorak over his pyjamas he had been walking up and down, chatting to people as they stood and watched.

'Apparently it's always the same family. No one seems too upset. Oh, and by the way,' he said, as we crawled shivering back into bed, 'the car only has a few scratches and a broken aerial, again! My salary should include danger money.'

Life the next day was a bit of a daze. We both staggered to the morning service, bleary-eyed. By the time we came home for lunch the curtains at the house opposite were open.

'I think it's time for a pastoral visit,' Peter said, 'before I take my dog collar off.' He took a deep breath.

I waited nervously. He came in half-an-hour later, shaking his head and laughing.

'It was an engagement party!' he said. 'The fiancé came within a fraction of killing his future father-in-law, or at least kicking his eye out. He almost had a cerebral haemorrhage, but never mind, all's forgiven. They sat me down, gave me a cup of tea and laughed in an embarrassed kind of way about the whole thing.'

It was a fortnight later that the doorbell rang and standing shyly on the doorstep was a slim, pretty girl, who backed when I opened the door.

'I'm from 'cross the road,' she said, needing to say no more. 'Am I bothering you?'

'No,' I said, 'come on in.'

But she was not too keen, and kept turning to look behind her like a frightened doe.

'I only want to know if vicar'll marry us,' she said sheepishly.

Peter appeared at the top of the stairs. 'Of course I'll marry you, Carol. But no booze before the wedding!'

She grinned. 'It's a promise.'

'Well,' Peter said, 'and that was the first local person to come to our door!'

We both laughed, but the incident affected us more deeply than either of us cared to admit. For months the slightest noise outside our bedroom window woke me with a start and made my nerves jangle. And never again could either of us bear to watch violence of any kind on the television.

Chapter 7

A person might be forgiven for coming to the conclusion that life in Grimlington came to a very slow standstill about twenty years ago. The railway station, once its pride and joy, a major junction and a grand, bustling metropolis with arches, mosaics, fine glass and marble has become a hideous, derelict heap. The restaurant has long since gone. So have the attendants in their high-necked black dresses and frilly white aprons. Now there is not so much as a coffee machine. The entrance hall leaks rain through its broken roof and window panes and the puddles absorb the litter, turning the ground into a dirty, soggy carpet. Timetables hang in tatters from the noticeboard and everything smells dank and musty. Anyone arriving at night in the eerie light of one inadequate electric light bulb might think they had come to a ghost town. The wind which howls down the deserted platforms seems to carry echoes of a distant past, when a thousand employees joked, chatted, blew their whistles and polished the brasses.

'Ay, I drove the steam trains once,' an old man once said to me wistfully as I waited for the pay train to Leeds. 'Beautiful they were and the speed of 'em! All the best trains came through 'ere. The second biggest marshallin' yard in Britain it were.'

The drivers reckoned they were somebody in those days, one cut better than a miner. You could tell a railway worker by the hat he wore, be it a silk topper, brown bowler or a trade cap. Then the railways were reorganised. A thousand jobs were lost. An old elite, an upper working-class vanished and the trains, mosaics, and marble were removed, to be displayed in the Railway Museum in York.

Going to the doctor's or the dentist's was like stepping back in time. The doctor's waiting room is a large airy cellar with painted bricks and old slatted wooden railway benches for seats. Sitting there the years vanish and I am a little girl again, creeping down the back stairs of our large, old house, peeping round the surgery door to see if the patients have gone yet and my father is alone. The medical care is just as my father would have given too. The doctor is meticulous, insisting on doing the children's vaccinations himself, knowing his patients and giving time to them, the old values of general practice, miraculously kept alive.

I was less at ease at the dentist's surgery with its dark corridors, peeling paintwork and old-fashioned, cracked linoleum, the sort I remembered on our kitchen floor in the fifties. Large posters on the cramped waiting-room wall are a gruesome reminder of the dangers of too much sugar and not enough brushing. But many young people in the town have false teeth anyway or gaping holes where teeth should have been. It was hardly a great encouragement to those who appreciate that part of their anatomy.

Every clergyman is called to make countless unusual errands of mercy. Peter's first left a lasting impression. Cathy, who lived on our estate and had been faithfully popping in to collect and forward the previous curate's post, asked Peter if he would mind taking her husband to the dentist to have fourteen teeth out. Peter was not too sure if his presence was required to hold his hand, carry him out or to say an appropriate blessing.

'You're only young,' Peter said to him nervously, as they drew up at the dentist's door. 'Can't they be filled?'

'Oh ay,' the victim replied, 'but it's not worth it. I might as well get rid of them now, then they'll cause me no more bother and no more money.'

Peter came home, feeling weak at the knees and more

determined than ever to hang on to his teeth as long as possible.

Some of the older men, like Lucy's dad, did not bother to wear their false teeth at all. I found their nods and gummy grins endearing as I walked down the High Street, but it puzzled me, until I was enlightened. No collier goes down the pit wearing false teeth. A piece of grit under the palate is excruciating. And they get used to leaving them out.

'Do they just eat baby food for the rest of their lives?' I asked naively.

'Don't be daft, their gums get so hard they can bite through an apple.'

But even so, Dad Barker, Lucy's father, could not manage the celery and apple salad I offered him inadvertently when he came to tea.

'He won't eat unusual things,' Lucy reassured me when I told her what I had done. 'He won't eat what 'e calls "foreign muck", lasagne or spaghetti bolognese. It's got to be pie and chips all the time and it doesn't exactly stretch me.'

I began to realise how little I knew about miners for one who had been raised among them.

'You'll be all right there,' my mother said, when I told her where we were going. 'Miners are the kindest, the most generous people. When food was rationed they came to the house with tins of salmon for the doctor. They'll give away their last penny.'

My father agreed. Although he was a doctor, he was the son of a poor tailor and never forgot his origins. He regarded medicine as a privilege and a responsibility. I learned from him the value of people.

'We who have been shown the greatest intolerance must show the greatest tolerance,' he said, 'otherwise the lesson of the holocaust is wasted.'

Yet he was the doctor and social distinctions were clear. He could mix with other professionals and shop keepers, and the vicar, of course. My father often chose to defy convention. Life would have been colourless without the companionship of Albert, his mate. But the mining community kept themselves very much to themselves.

I remembered the craggy, wrinkled, friendly faces, covered in tiny blue-black marks, but only now did I discover that those were the tell-tale signs of a collier, pieces of grit embedded in the skin of his face, hands and arms. There they were in Dad Barker's face, as I examined it one Sunday after lunch at Lucy's. After dinner he sat warming himself by the open fire, his toothless gums chewing on his pipe and a look of supreme contentment on his face.

'Nothing like a good coal fire, that's what I say, especially after a good, traditional Sunday dinner.'

Lucy caught my eye and shook her head.

'I see you're a man who enjoys retirement,' Peter said.

'What!' Dad Barker snorted. 'Me? I'd give anything to be back down pit.'

'They had a trip down pit last year from church, the clergy wanted to see it, and who do yer think put 'is name down to go?' Lucy laughed affectionately. 'Yer'd have thought he'd 'ad enough. Right put out 'e was when they wouldn't tek 'im.'

'I just wanted to see the old place once more,' he said wistfully. 'Yer don't forget yer know, not after fifty years. I were thirteen when I started as a trapper, opening doors for ponies, then I drove 'em. It were two more years before I went on 'note and were a proper collier. Given me chance again, I'd do same.'

'After all that time in the dark and dirt I'd have thought you'd have been glad to see the back of it,' I said.

'Ah, Michele,' he said, with a distant, far-away look in his eyes, 'how can I get yer to understand what it were like, the good times we 'ad, the way we all stuck together and helped each other out? We all lived together too, yer see, up on Crossfarm View, where your estate is now. But in them days we all knew each other. We never locked us doors. Yer could leave anythin' out. Nothing were ever nicked. We shared everything, even a toilet at bottom of street.'

'The key hung on an 'ook in t'scullery. Yer had to be a fast runner in them days,' Lucy said, smiling at the memory.

'Do you miss them, Lucy?'

She thought for a bit, took her pinny off and came and sat down with us by the fire.

'Ay,' she said, 'I suppose I do. Give a man garden walls and a gate and it's never the same.'

She took the poker and banked up the fire. 'I tell you what, though, I wish Council would give us another 'ouse. This one's too big. At least the old cottages were easy to heat. It's perishin' cold and damp. The water trickles down walls. We've been on Council list for ages. Dad retired early because of ill health. I sometimes wonder if 'is chest'll survive another winter if we stay 'ere. Come December I'll be scraping ice off inside o' winders so we can see out.'

I shivered. My back, which was away from the fire was chilled already and it was still September.

'That's other thing,' Dad Barker said suddenly, only half with us and half back in that other world below ground. 'It's changed down there. It were clean work once.'

I looked at him, puzzled.

'We carried us own blades. There was no machinery. That's what started all the dust and made our chests bad. Ay, and there were none of these strikes all the time.'

'There were a few Dad, as I remember,' I said.

'But we'd just cause in them days. Yer couldn't live on pay. Now they're just young hot-heads,' he said and puffed at his pipe. 'I tell yer this. I'd not let my sons go down.'

He smiled as if in self-congratulation.

'Now then, that surprises yer. I'd no choice, but they could choose National Service. I told 'em which to tek and they've not regretted it, have they Lucy? No, it's not the same any more.'

We got up to go, thanking Lucy for her lavish hospitality.

'Two puddings was a real treat!'

'I always make two, one for 'im and one for us,' she said, with a grin in the direction of the figure in the armchair, who, with a headful of happy memories and a tummy full of sweet mince pie, was now quietly nodding off.

'It's funny, isn't it,' I said to Peter as we walked up to the estate, 'how companionship can make a heaven out of a lousy job?'

'That's probably the only way to cope with it,' Peter said.

Suddenly it seemed a great many things were clicking into place.

'Hey, all the spitting that goes on in the High Street...'

'Pneumoconiosis, the miners' disease. Alicia says that's why there are so many inquests and post mortems in the town. If pneumoconiosis can be proved the Coal Board has to pay the family compensation.'

'It's only right if we rob a man of his health.'

'Ah yes, but life isn't as fair as that, is it?' Peter said.

Life in Grimlington had a slow, unhurried pace, which I found refreshing after the rush and bustle of city life. With its routine, traditions and strong sense of community it still revolved around the pits. People had time for each other. I discovered that any piece of information I let slip in the High Street at ten o'clock was the gossip of the town by eleven. Everyone minded everyone else's business. There was no such thing as a secret. For years every experience, good and bad, had been shared by all. And they had been through much joy and sorrow together.

Everyone still remembered the great day the pit-head showers were opened.

'I were a little girl at the time,' Linda told me, her eyes still sparkling with the memory of it. She was one of a group of young women with small children, who had, I gathered, recently started coming to the church. Her capacity to see the funny in the most ordinary situations provided me with an instant soul-mate. She could send people up mercilessly, especially if they were pompous. With her short fair hair and rather arch way of looking, I could imagine her as a little girl wearing a gingham frock with a bow at the back. She must have been just as her little Tracy was now, a real bundle of mischief.

'I ran down the street shouting, "There's a strange man eating me dad's tea." Well, I'd never seen him clean at teatime before, had I?'

From then on the men developed a taste for gossip. Every young girl lived in fear lest her name be mentioned in the showers and her father overhear it! It ensured very high moral standards in the town.

Many still remember the night the men were having a quiet drink in the Crossfarm Club, when a collier burst in in his overalls, his eyes wild and his face ashen behind the dirt and grime. No one needed to say a word. Every man rose in silence, then ran to collect boots, helmets, belts and ropes. They fought for hours, up to the waist in water, to free brothers, fathers, sons and friends. Many were bereaved that night and rumour has it that five men whose bodies were never found are still up there in the disused pit.

Grimlington had the first Mines Rescue Training Centre, and the first national mining hero, who lost his life leading a rescue team after an underground explosion in Birmingham. But despite the danger, there was a long waiting list for the job. Linda's husband, Joe, was turned down because he was the son-in-law, not the son of a miner, and the pits were closing anyway. I began to pick up a great deal of tension and fear. If jobs went so would a whole way of life.

'Where's it all going to end?' I overheard one woman calling to another, as she laid out a selection of goods on her market stall. There was no modern shopping centre in Grimlington, just this, a new market of makeshift stalls, a token, a courteous nod from the planners in the direction of the nineteen eighties.

'God, I 'ope they don't strike again,' the other woman shouted back. 'It were bad enough in 1971. This stall doesn't make enough to keep us.'

'They won't strike,' the other woman said. 'No one wants to.'

'Yes, but what future is there for our kids?'

And then they were taken up by customers.

If the town struggled with problems of employment, so did we. But our own private struggle was rather different. Peter's job was a source of frustration to both of us. I knew I would have my battles, but I thought he would take to being a clergyman at once. He hated it. His organised mind wrestled with the lack of routine and structure. I could not get used to having him under my feet all day. Neither could the children. He was there, yet he wasn't there. He came in and they leapt with joy. Then he disappeared into his study and closed the door and they howled with frustration. Some Saturday mornings the two of them stood banging at the study door, demanding he come out and play, while I wrestled with the weekend's shopping and cooking.

'My sermon preparation!' he shouted.

'Football!' Joel shouted back.

'Why don't you go to the vestry or the public library?' I joined in. 'Then we'd all have some peace.'

Slowly the realisation dawned on both of us that it was no use lamenting what once was, no more than a clock can work backwards. The steady routine, organised days, relaxed weekends were gone for ever. The new life was here to stay and I would somehow have to make the best of it. I did not mind the evenings in alone. It was the fact that I could hardly ever plan a day out for just the two of us without being disappointed. It was usually a funeral. People did not die to suit my convenience.

Peter popped down to see Mick one night, knowing from the first time he met him that here was someone he could talk to, who would understand.

'It's the lack of job satisfaction that gets me down,' Peter said to him, 'especially after teaching. I get to the end of the day worn out, with nothing to show for it.'

'Join the club,' Mick said. Then, noting Peter's surprise, 'Well, yer never thought anyone worked down a pit or in a factory for job satisfaction, did yer? Yer work to keep the family and try not to think about anything else. Yer'd go mad if yer did. Most of us are lucky to have work at all these days.'

'Yes,' Peter agreed, 'at least I haven't got that to contend with. No redundancies in the Church of England.'

'Ay, if pits go so does my job.'

'What'll you do?'

Mick shrugged, then he smiled, embarrassed. 'Sometimes I think I'd like to work for the church. It's a bit of a dream I 'ave. Karen says I spend so much time there that I do that already and I'm only an engineer in me spare time. She's always complaining she never sees me. So, it sounds as if you and me 'ave a lot in common.'

Peter came home in a pensive mood, but with a much lighter heart. 'That'll teach me to grumble,' he said. 'You know, until tonight I never realised that for most people job satisfaction is a luxury, not a right.'

Chapter 8

I often wonder what possessed me to start a Drama Group. Perhaps because I did not seem to fit in anywhere else. Although motherhood had its enjoyable moments, it had its days of excruciating drudgery too. If I had any contribution to make to the church I hoped it would have nothing whatsoever to do with babies or children.

In the event, the Drama Group turned out to be my lifeline to sanity. It provided me with that precious commodity I thought had gone for ever, friendship. Every Tuesday night I lay awake in bed with aching sides, from laughter, not exertion.

My dramatic skills were minimal. I had studied it at university, the theory, rather than the practice, in true academic fashion. I took it up again years later, when Peter was at theological college, but then I had to drop out because my pregnant bump limited my versatility, and agility. Yet instinct told me that drama had a vital place in the Church, in a visual age when television had weakened our ability to listen and concentrate. But it would have to be good, not so hick and amateur that our audience squirmed with embarrassment and missed the message.

Uncertainly, I put an announcement in the weekly newsletter. Would anyone interested in forming a Drama Group please come to a meeting on Tuesday evening in the parish hall. And I prayed no one would come. But there were six of them.

'Only one man?' I said.

The girls smiled. So did he.

'The men round here don't go in for this kind of thing,' Jan said. She was petite and fair, with large owlish glasses. Linda had already introduced me to her Canadian friend, but the faint drawl still sounded strangely out of place after weeks of hearing only Yorkshire. I wondered what had brought her to Grimlington.

'They reckon they're macho, y'know,' she said, flexing her muscles. 'It's not that they're not creative. They just don't dare let it show.'

Her voice had just a hint of, 'believe me, I know from experience'.

'Oh well, it just means we're a bit limited,' I said.

'Why?'

A pair of penetrating blue eyes stared straight into mine.

'A woman can play any man's part, can't she, Frances?'

The girl at her side smiled and nodded.

'Yes, Angela.'

'Even God?' I could have bitten my tongue.

'Especially God! Why shouldn't a woman play God?'

I shrugged my shoulders. Why not? I had no answer. The others grinned nervously. I had noticed that the two women were sitting slightly apart from the others.

'We go to Cuttlesworth,' Angela explained, as if to an unasked question. She was the larger of the two, who I realised were sisters, and there was an almost Amazon-like sturdiness in her build and open intense face.

Cuttlesworth? Oh yes, the daughter church. Peter had said something about a last vestige of traditionalism.

'We haven't seen you there yet,' Angela said, weighing me up out of the corner of her eye.

'Not yet,' I hedged and cursed the need to be political which the clergy-wife role and Angela's teasing manner had imposed.

'Well,' I said, returning safely to the matter at hand, 'we could all meet fortnightly if you like.' 'Once a week'll be fine,' Linda said, looking round at Jan and Dorothy, who had been silent so far. They nodded in agreement.

'You see, Tuesday night's been our night out for years, long before we started coming to church. A woman needs a night away from the kids. We go to the Anchor or the Duck and Partridge, so instead we'll come here. There's no problem. Our men know we're out Tuesdays. And this is what we really want to do.'

I was terrified. In a week I read all I could and tried to drag the rest out of the furthermost recesses of my brain. Their sacrifice and enthusiasm deserved a bit of effort on my part. But I was not prepared for their ingenuity and natural talent. Linda, Jan, Dorothy and I were all still at the baby and nappy bucket stage and arrived exhausted, having cleared up and put the children to bed. Ian was a nurse and worked very long shifts. None of us had done any drama for years, if at all. As we warmed up, the hall was filled with the sound of moaning, groaning and creaking, cracking joints. Games left us lying on the floor in a panting heap, especially Dorothy, who struggled with a little more weight than Jan or Linda.

'No more, no more,' she cried, 'I can't stand it.'

'Come on Dorothy, it's doing yer good,' Linda shouted.

But when we turned to improvisation, clever, creative ideas poured out, as if they had been buried inside for years, and were waiting to be released. And I learned more about life in Grimlington in an evening than I had learned in weeks.

The first simple sketch we put together was based on the parable of the sower.

'What's the story about?' I asked them, as we lay on the floor, our open Bibles in front of us.

'Productivity,' Angela said.

'So where would you set it?'

'In the mines,' she said.

Linda laughed. 'Well I like the idea, and I don't mind playing a miner, but since no woman's worked down pit in recent years, don't you think it would look better in a factory?'

'And we all know what that's like,' Jan said.

The others nodded, all except Ian. Factory work was 'women's work', poorly paid and often available as a temporary measure.

'I don't think I'll ever forget it,' Frances said. 'Nine hours a day sewing elastic into hundreds of pairs of underpants. It nearly drove me mad.'

'By the end of the day the noise and routine make you feel you've become part of the machine,' Jan said.

'What noise does the machine make?' I asked them.

They began to whirr and grind and click, gradually blending the sounds into a steady, monotonous rhythm.

'That's it,' I shouted. 'Keep going. We'll use it as a background.' After a few minutes their faces began to register boredom. Their eyes became vacant and they assumed the mindless expressions of zombies.

'Does this look right?' Frances asked. 'Because it feels right.'

'All we need's the patter now, girls,' Linda said.

And that was no problem.

Ian was the factory manager.

'Good morning, girls.'

'Good morning, Mr Heseltine,' they drawled together, turning up their noses behind his back.

'A fat bonus to any girl who can increase her productivity substantially.'

'You're too nice,' shouted Frances.

Ian looked puzzled.

'You're the politest manager I've ever come across,' she said.

'We're only factory girls remember.'

Ian tried again with a bit of a snarl.

'Who does 'e think 'e is?' says the first. 'If 'e thinks I'm killing myself for 'im 'e's very much mistaken,' and she goes to the toilets for a fag. The 'seed' is devoured by birds before it has time to grow at all.

The second girl starts well, then remembers the cream bun and flask of hot coffee in her bag. She slowly grinds to a standstill. The 'seed' has fallen on rocky ground and has no root.

'Well, I'm going to get that bonus,' says the third girl. 'I could really do with it,' and she works at a great pace, until she remembers her boyfriend waiting for her at the gate. Should she meet him or work late? Blow work, she's got to see him and the 'seed' has been choked by thorns.

The fourth girl works on. This 'seed' has increased production by a thousand per cent. She earns the fat bonus and the commendation of the boss. She seems a bit too good and prissy, but then that's how Christians are seen in the town, I was told.

We were excited and apprehensive about our first performance in public. The open air ecumenical service had been the Council of Churches' only contribution to the town Gala for years. It was conservative enough for those who thought a small dose of formal religion was right on special occasions and dreary enough to confirm everyone else's expectations of what that religion was like. We wanted to invest the service with life, to say that our faith was our life and not just an occasional courteous but cold bow before the Almighty. So we worked hard and had at the end a reasonably polished performance.

The Gala weekend was wet. In fact it was a wash-out. Friday evening's excitement as everyone put the finishing touches to their floats and costumes, was carried away in Saturday morning's torrents. By midday the High Street was full of people and still it poured. The street streamers snapped beneath the weight of the downpour and bits of flag hung limply down on to the pavement. The floats were ruined. Crepe paper awnings drooped limply and dripped into scarlet and turquoise pools. Dozens of fairies and elves were smeared up their legs and down their arms in rainbow colours. The rain brought down the soot in greasy black spots and soon everyone looked smutty, dishevelled and irritated.

We turned out in mackintoshes and wellingtons to watch the procession, but the Mayor took one look at the shivering brass band and bedraggled majorettes and cancelled it. The stalls were moved from the park to a piece of wasteland by the station in order to tempt Saturday shoppers to buy.

It was a great disappointment. The Gala is one of the high spots of the year, an old mining tradition. But more important, since Council money is short and there are no grants available, local charities rely on this occasion to raise vital funds. Lucy had been preparing for weeks, collecting toiletries and making gift baskets with them, often out of her own wages, to raise money to provide temporary accommodation for the elderly. In Grimlington the Old Folks' Home is a last resort, there only for those with no child to care for them. No one complains. Looking after elderly parents and relatives is an accepted way of life, part of being a community. But despite the enormous saving on Council funds, there was no provision for caring relatives to have an occasional rest or holiday. Lucy was involved in a project – funded by charity alone – which hoped to provide that desperately needed break. They had managed to buy three large terraced houses, but each needed a fortune in renovation and the money came in very, very slowly. Lucy loved old people and dreamed of the day there might even be a job for her. No more packing fruit and vegetables, or being sent out to sweep the yard or wash the boss's car because there was nothing else to do. She would work for the minimum wage just to feel that her life was useful to someone.

There was rain dripping from her plastic hat, down her glasses and from the tip of her nose, but she was as cheery as ever.

'We've not done too bad,' she called to me, then slipped something into the hands of a child who had stopped to stare at the stall with large, round eyes.

'If you didn't give so much away you'd make more,' I shouted back.

'Yer know I can't resist a child.'

The other stalls were a quaint mixture of raffles, hula-hoop, pick-a-straw and luscious home-made cakes. There were mounds of second-hand clothing, books, ornaments, bent lamp-shades and the inevitable red and white striped satin curtains. The second-hand trade in West Yorkshire is big business. Every market, as well as every fete and gala seemed to have dozens of white elephant stalls, filling the air with that unmistakable smell of age and use. I found one or two welcome bargains, a curate's salary not stretching as it might, but I could not help but wonder who would be tempted by the shoes. Better than none at all, I supposed.

By the evening the rain had tailed off to a drizzle and the whole town turned out for the firework display. From the top of the hill in the park it was an impressive sight. The children had never seen anything like it. Their upturned faces, lit up in the darkness by the sudden bursts of light, were a mixture of pleasure and wonder. Then, as the last explosion died away, the fair opened at the bottom of the hill in a riot of noise and a blaze of flickering, coloured lights. Children dragged their unwilling parents to the magic sight.

On Sunday the rain began again and the ecumenical Gala service was moved indoors into the Baptist Church. Numbers were depleted, but at least there was no competition from the fairground. The Drama Group waited in an agony of nerves. Only Ian looked calm. He always did. His nursing experience probably. Linda wriggled on her seat and Jan and Dorothy chattered like a pair of parrots. I fidgeted about, then went to find a toilet. Linda grinned at me as I shuffled past her.

'Hey,' she said when I got back, 'I used to think you were a right flash piece. I thought you'd got it all together, and never worried about anything, not the type I'd ever make a friend of. But underneath you're just like the rest of us, aren't yer?'

She winked at me and the service started. Suddenly it was our turn, then it was all over, without a hitch. As we slumped back into the pews with relief, Mo and Eric got up and went to the front. They were new to our church and Edward had thought that members of the other churches would be as thrilled by their story as we were. He was wrong. They told how they had lived together for some years and had two children, and then how they had moved to Grimlington, his home town, where their relationship began to fall apart. She was a southerner and lonely. He was out every night with his mates. They separated, and Eric went to live in Ossleforth, each knowing it was not the answer and feeling as desperate as ever. Without any consultation, hardly knowing why, both were drawn to church, though not the same one. Apart, each struggled with Christianity and what they saw of the foibles, yet obvious warmth, of its followers. Independently both clutched at the last straw, then discovered with amazement what had happened to the other and that they had a basis on which to rebuild their relationship.

'And I'm going to marry 'er,' Eric said, turning to Mo and smiling. She started in surprise at so public a proposal, then blushed with pleasure.

'Disgusting!' said some of the congregation. 'What a display!'

'What was?' we asked in innocence.

'All of it,' they said. 'Drama an' all.'

We were crestfallen, until the Lady Mayoress came and put her arm round Linda. 'That was wonderful, dear. I was a factory girl a long time ago and it took me right back.'

'Well, you can't please everyone,' Linda said ruefully to the group, as we gathered in the porch.

They were still a little deflated.

'You did well,' I reassured them.

'And anyway,' Ian said, 'it's those outside the Church we want to listen, not those inside.'

Everyone nodded and their faces brightened.

'If we can't take a bit of criticism we're not worth much,' Linda laughed. 'And anyway, it'll do us good. Too much praise would only make us big-headed.'

'See you Tuesday?' I asked.
'See you Tuesday,' they all said together.

Chapter 9

'It's a plot, that's what it is,' Ian informed us the following Tuesday night, when we were trying, vainly, to fit in an extra rehearsal. No one had any free time. There seemed to be church meetings for almost every night of the week.

'Keep 'em all so busy,' he said, 'that they've no time to get up to mischief. So much for converting the natives. It's so long since I've seen me mates they've forgotten who I am.'

'Your mates?' Jan said in her slow drawl. 'It's my husband. He can't understand how I can find so much to do. He swears the church is taking me away from him.'

'Well Joe still goes to his club on Friday nights and I'll not stop him,' Linda said, compressing her lips the way she did when she had made up her mind about something. I was learning to respect her determination. She was always fair.

'So I'm sorry everyone but I can't rehearse on Friday night. It's my turn to babysit. I'll not spoil his night out. You see, Michele,' she explained to me apologetically, 'round here you're born into a club, usually your dad's, and it's like belonging to a big family. It's an old tradition, dating from time when houses were so tiny, living rooms weren't big enough for the whole family, especially when pit clothes were hung to dry over oven. And they were there all the time, since sons didn't always work same shifts as their fathers. The women were glad to see back of their menfolk. It meant they could get tin bath down and soak in peace! The men still love their club. They 'ave a laugh together, let their hair down. If yer stop going all of a sudden just because yer go to church it looks as if yer think yer a cut better than rest. Yer can't mix any more, only with yer own sort. Religious people always seem to live in a kind of a...'

'Ghetto?' I suggested.

'That's it. It's not natural. Jesus would 'ave gone into the clubs and mixed, wouldn't he?'

She looked round for approval, then decided it wasn't necessary.

'Anyway, Joe and Eric go down on Friday nights. They get some stick, but that's what it's all about.'

Kelly, Ian's wife, arrived to collect him. They had only been married a few months.

'And I thought the Church was in favour of marriage,' Ian said, as she came into the room. 'Well, it's not doing much for ours. We haven't had a night in together for weeks. We haven't had the chance to get to know each other yet. Imagine how it would sound in a divorce court. "What would you say was the major factor leading to the breakdown of your marriage?" "Please your honour, it was the Church."'

Kelly took his hand coyly, and suggested gently that it was time to go home.

'A-aaaaa,' sighed the assembled company.

'Remember those days eh, Jan?' Linda said, smiling.

'That was a long time ago,' Jan said sadly.

'Come on,' Linda said, throwing her her coat, 'we'd better go home, or we'll all be in trouble.'

The following evening, Wednesday, was the mid-week meeting.

'You go,' Peter said. 'I'm not needed and it'll do you good. Besides,' he said, a mischievous twinkle in his eye, 'why must the clergy always be there and the poor little wife be stuck at home? Let's create a precedent.'

'My, two evenings out in a row,' I said sarcastically. 'Be careful, I might begin to enjoy such freedom.'

'That's all right,' he said, 'I might just enjoy having a

night in. At least it's a chance to watch the news and catch up with the world.'

'In that case, you won't mind doing the ironing will you?' I called out as I dashed out of the front door.

'Having a night off, is he?' Frank asked when I appeared at the parish hall. Substituting for my husband at a meeting was obviously quite a novelty. As he stooped to hear my reply, I noticed that Betty was right about her husband. 'Not a grey hair in his head,' she said, 'and no Grecian 2000 either! Makes yer sick!' He did look surprisingly youthful.

I refused to apologise for being second best.

'No, I'm having the night off. He's working tonight, putting the children to bed.'

Frank's face broke into a smile. The point was taken.

Despite shifts, and the strange hours many worked, there was a surprising turn-out, about a third of the congregation. Such was the sense of anticipation that it took Edward some time to call the meeting to order, struggling to make himself heard above the laughter and chatter. I had the distinct impression that for the rest of the evening his hold on the situation was completely arbitrary and might disintegrate at any moment. His topic was 'giving' and he gave himself to the subject with his customary force. But no amount of force or fire was going to impress this audience one bit.

'Give now,' he shouted, 'your money will be no good to you once you're dead.'

'You'll get it all then, Vicar,' Albert said quietly.

The meeting dissolved in laughter. Notwithstanding being cut off in mid-flow, Edward tried again.

'Dear old Lucy here...'

'Less of the "old", if you don't mind,' she said.

And so it continued. Edward rose to the challenge, cut, thrust and parried and, like a black preacher, began to use the participation to drive his message home. He enjoyed every minute of it. I had expected the meeting to be sober, restrained, dignified, as so many I had attended in the past in my non-conformist days, where the expounding of the word of God was a solemn, serious business and to speak out of turn might be seen as a breach of respect. Given the increasing informality of the Sunday services and the tendency of the congregation to reply to rhetorical questions from the pulpit, I should have known what to expect, but the entertainment factor was an unanticipated bonus. I only hoped Peter would be able to develop the taste and wit for quick repartee. His teaching experience would help.

He studied my face as I walked into the sitting room.

'Well?' he said, smiling, but then he knew my taste for the slightly unconventional. I kicked off my shoes and dropped onto the settee.

'Well, it's certainly not like any meeting I've ever experienced before. But I like it.'

He grinned. 'I thought that was what you'd say.'

'It was . . . real, I suppose. No masks or pretence, no disguising their real feelings with a show of piety. Mick was feeling lousy tonight, a failure, so he said so. People prayed just as they spoke, an odd sentence, sometimes just a word. It reminded me of when Joel learned to speak.'

'"Sock",' Peter mimicked, 'and "sick".'

We laughed, remembering. Poor Joel had been a very sick-y baby. Hardly surprising it should be his first word.

'Most of the time only we knew what he was saying, but it didn't matter. We were so thrilled. Maybe God feels like that when he hears those prayers.'

'It's a frightening experience,' Peter said, 'especially in a culture where people are not encouraged to take the limelight. That's management's job. So the sound of your own voice speaking out in public can be a shock.'

I sat back for a while. Peter watched me.

'Something's buzzing around in your little head.'

'Yes,' I said slowly. 'Yes. It's just dawned on me what we're doing to people when they become Christians in a town like this. No matter how much the church seems to us to reflect the way of life here, it's still a total change of culture.'

'And that's something you understand,' Peter smiled.

'Yes, it is.' I began to feel excited. 'At least it's very similar. We don't exactly tell them not to go to their clubs, but we don't give them enough time. We expect singing hymns, praying, Bible studies, and saying the liturgy to come naturally, as if they had always done it. But it's another world. It must be as foreign to them as it was to me.'

'It is, if you're not used to reading. I visited a chap the other day who kept insisting he couldn't come. I suddenly realised it was probably because he couldn't read and he didn't want to look daft in front of all those people. The sight of all the books we hand out must send some people into a state of paralysis.'

I got up to go to bed and could not help laughing.

'And to think,' I said to Peter, 'I thought God had got his wires crossed. What use was I, a Jewish clergy wife in a mining town? Maybe it's not as silly as it seems after all.'

I climbed the stairs to bed, congratulating the Almighty on the ingenuity of his arrangement.

I lay awake that night, a thousand thoughts rushing through my head, such a mass of different impressions, yet overriding the rest the sense that I had caught a glimpse of something very special, yet also very vulnerable. Mick's words came back to me with all the pain and frustration they expressed.

'They think there's something wrong with yer at work if yer don't join in all the grumbling, cheating and plotting. There's no trust. I hate the atmosphere. It pulls me down.'

What was it that he stirred up inside me? It was more than sympathy. A certain wistfulness? A sense of awe perhaps. Here was someone not cossetted, protected and safe, as I was, but out in the real world, where it was hard grind, yet still preserving a child-like trust, a faith that was simple, accepting and as tough as the old boots he had to wear. I never accepted anything. I questioned everything, argued with everyone, from God himself to my own shadow. My mother always warned me it would get me into trouble, and when Peter decided to become a clergyman I began to think she was right. Not that questioning is wrong. I had half a suspicion that the Church might not have become so culturally out-of-date if we had questioned our idiosyncrasies a little earlier. But there is also a time to accept, a time to believe and rest in that belief.

'I've let yer down again God,' Mick said. 'I'm sorry.' And that was it. He was ready to face tomorrow.

That treasure we were promised before we came to Grimlington was there all right and I had barely had to dig to find it. With the realisation that night that I might have something to give came another just as certain, that I would receive a thousand times more.

We discovered quite soon that almost every meeting that took place in the church, however resented, from PCC to the Fabric Committee was invested with the same banter and humour. In fact Mick and Karen's home group sounded so entertaining through the breeze block wall that their neighbours thought they must be missing something, and joined them.

There were eight home groups and although they had been meeting for some time they never really seemed to flourish as well as they might have done in an area inclined to more cerebral activity. One difficulty was that people felt extremely anxious about going into each other's homes. That, of course, was the problem on our estate, why no one came to our door. We were clergy, the professionals, and tradition had long dictated that a working man should know his place. But we never anticipated how lasting and widespread the attitude was. The church members were so generous in their hospitality that I had not cooked a Sunday lunch for weeks and I presumed that was the norm, the usual northern warmth I had enjoyed as a Geordie. And I rejoiced that I had fallen on my feet. Then on his visits Peter picked up a constant refrain: 'I won't go to any meeting in a home. I've never been one for going into other people's houses and I won't start now.' And I began to realise that my Sunday lunches out were not to be taken for granted. It took courage to let go of a privacy which had become a way of life. In the back-to-back terraces people had shared their homes and lives, but the tradition died with the houses and fierce Yorkshire pride took over. No one could see your house unless it was perfect. Those lunches were a sign that Christianity was beginning to cut across the self-reliance and independence which masked much deeper, more sensitive feelings.

As people shed their layers of self-protection a great deal of pain and hurt was exposed, and the home groups bore the brunt of it. Many individuals had been treated as if they were of no value and now they believed it. Grimlington had had a large grammar school of reputation. Children came to it from miles around. It offered unlimited opportunity and a golden future, escape from the pit and inherited drudgery. But if, with the failure of one exam, that opportunity seemed to be destroyed, then a sense of failure hung around ever after, dogging the steps of its victims. At eleven, or sooner, a man's destiny might be made final. If it was not, his self image certainly was. How hard it then was to convince people that they were loved, wanted and valuable, especially when everything around them, from their wages to their conditions of employment, often said the opposite.

From experience Peter and I were both convinced of the healing potential of groups. He warmed to the idea of leading some basic training in group dynamics, and when the first meeting in our home was a training session for home group leaders it seemed his time had come. But this was Grimlington and we had not yet learned that all the best-made plans had a strange way of going awry.

I had invited Mary round for a chat that evening. 'Are you settling down? Are you happy here?'

It was strange how everyone asked us that from the first week we arrived.

'Yes,' I said doubtfully. It was hard to tell. 'It always takes me a while. That's my fault, not yours.'

She looked at the For Sale sign through the window.

'Any sign of a buyer?'

I shook my head.

'Can you blame them? We'd like to move too, somewhere bigger on the new estate. We've our names down on the Council list, though there's not much chance.'

I groaned inside. Another church family wanting to leave this estate. Then I remembered how Mary lived. I visited them once in August in a heatwave. A roaring fire was blazing in the hearth and Phil was sitting in his favourite armchair, the beads of perspiration pouring down his face. Mary had caught my quizzical expression and explained, 'We've visitors coming to stay. We need hot water in case they want a bath.'

My face was still a puzzle and she laughed, caught my arm and gave me a little shake.

'We use coal for everything round here you idiot.'

It clicked.

'No immersion?'

'Just as well, we couldn't afford electric anyway.'

No, I could not begrudge Phil and Mary what I wanted so much for myself.

'We need the space,' Mary said, 'with the children growing up. Teenagers need a bedroom each, especially with Cheryl coming to live at home. She can be hard to handle.'

'How did it happen?'

'Cheryl? It was a hard birth, me being so small. Hospitals have improved in the last fifteen years, but there were more mistakes then. She were brain damaged. She's God's gift to us all the same, though she drives me mad at times. I tell yer what though, if I had a nervous breakdown, Council would have to find us a bigger house.'

'Any chance of that?' I asked.

'A lot,' she laughed, then our conversation was totally drowned by the sound of raucous laughter coming from the next room. We could not hear each other.

'What did you say they were doing?' she shouted.

I tried to lip read. 'Peter said it was some kind of group exercise.'

'Well there's not that much noise in our street when the pub's just closed.'

'A good meeting, was it?' I asked Betty, as I opened the door for her a couple of hours later.

She stood on the doorstep giggling, waiting for Frank.

'Ooooh, 'e's a one, that man of mine! Frank, where are yer? Get a move on.'

'I'm out here, waiting for you to finish gassing,' came a voice from the darkness beyond the front door, 'and I have been for the past quarter of an hour.'

'Ooooh 'eck,' she said, and Frank walked back up the path, took her by the arm and without a flicker of an eyelid, escorted her firmly towards the car. He turned for a moment and we caught his wink just before we closed the door.

Peter sat down on the stairs and roared with laughter.

'Well, I wonder what that achieved? It was a shambles. I deliberately refused to give a lead, not even to open with a prayer. Alicia, bless her, played straight into my hands. She got quite uptight and said it wouldn't be a proper meeting because we'd missed out a vital piece of ritual. Then everything seemed to disintegrate all at once. Frank and Betty had a private row in one corner, everyone else talked at cross purposes and Rick tried in vain to call things to order. At last I managed to shut everyone up and tried to make them see what happens when everyone comes with their own expectations and no one dares to take the lead. I think they got the point because Rick said, "Now I see what happens in my home group." But then, just as I thought we were getting somewhere Alicia unwrapped one of those mints of hers. It was supposed to be surreptitious, but we could hear the paper crackling all around the room. As she popped it into her mouth, thinking no one had noticed, Frank said, "Alicia, if that had been Jesus he would have shared it with us all." And that was the end of my training session!'

We sat on the stairs laughing for some time.

'I can't see us losing our sense of proportion round here, can you? Betty told me that when Alicia enthused to Frank about the eagle she'd seen when she was last up in Scotland, he said, "Yer've been to Edinburgh zoo, have yer, Alicia?"'

'The PCC's the same,' Peter said, 'so good humoured, not a sour note. It's great to have such support and fun. But occasionally, just occasionally, I wish they'd get down to making decisions of real importance.'

Peter's wishes were to be fulfilled sooner than he ever anticipated, and with a pain and cost he never anticipated either. That was the night they decided to disband the choir. Only then did we understand why the PCC had been constantly postponing major decisions for so many years.

Chapter 10

Nowhere in England do the old and new coexist in such perilous tension as in the Church. It stands on the one hand as one of the last surviving British institutions, an essential part of our history and heritage, and on the other as the symbol of fossilised religiosity, relevant only to a tiny, dwindling initiate. Its members polarise into those who attend because they always have and find comfort in the old ways, and those whose faith is new and see that tradition means little to the secular masses.

Grimlington was no exception. The feeling in the town was that the parish church was 'not for the likes of us'. Its traditions were the traditions of the professional classes and tradespeople, the posh, the nicely dressed and politely spoken. Their attitude was justified by long, painful memories. Legend told of a previous vicar who would cross the road rather than say good morning to a miner. Only twenty years before the church had still catered for the needs of a sizable, social elite, performing plays and playing whist. The grammar school headmaster had his own pew and read the lessons. Women wore hats. A strict silence was observed at all times. The church was fairly full, but then propriety required attendance. Once that was no longer so, the decline began.

Working men and women were never allowed to mingle their praises with those of management. The majority were nonconformist. The rest attended one of the three daughter churches, less threatening and more like chapel. Subsidence finished what changing customs had started and two closed before they collapsed. The last remaining daughter church, Cuttlesworth, struggled on, a tiny congregation in a dismal Edwardian building, clinging desperately to the comfort of their childhood memories.

By the time Edward's predecessor arrived the church had become an anachronism. It belonged to another age, long since a dream, before the soft green hills became a tangled mass of iron and steel and the trees were engulfed in waste and slag when the farmers had farmed in safety, and the church was an integral part of rural life, following the rhythm of its seasons. Then the industrial revolution stretched its grip across West Yorkshire. Birdsong gave way to the whirr of the pit and the constant shunting of the steam train. Men came from miles around to find work. The Irish asked for Tommy Cox's Catholic coal factory. They thought coal was manufactured. The Polish went there too. Nonconformists mined at Pope and Pearson's, and the rest at Dom Pedro's and any other pit that would have them. They worked on their backs, their bellies and their knees, hacking the black treasure out of the earth, to fire trains, mills and factories. Women thought themselves lucky to find work in the woollen mills. It was better than pulling trucks of coal underground. Men, women and children worked twelve hours a day, in work that robbed humanity of health and daylight and made them old before their time.

And over the years more and more trees were razed, the fields churned, the natural landscape destroyed to make way for row upon row of tiny terraced cottages with no garden, no green and one lavatory for every dozen houses, all in the name of the Christian principle of prosperity. Pope and Pearson were chapel men. Coal owners went to church just as the landowners had. They were benevolent. They were philanthropists, providing schools and public facilities, but it did not occur to their Christian conscience to improve their employees' conditions of work. In industrial England, as in rural England, all life had its order and the Church upheld it.

But then the Church had no competition in those days; no one questioned its absolute authority. It never had to fight for its life, not until the old ways began to crumble. The great depression of the thirties took its toll. Coal was mined more cheaply abroad. But still the owners refused to modernise. Industry no longer made them rich, so they fled south with what fortune they had left, and the men who had made them rich were left to starve. War provided employment, at least temporarily. But if the first war had made men question, the second confirmed their doubts. The national crisis called for coal. The men worked on Sundays to provide it and never went back to church.

In the forties and fifties the nation took over the mines and hope died as the railways, pits and stations began to close. Communities were rehoused in the name of progress and many of them died. There were pubs, clubs and the cinema for solace. And, more devastating for the Church, there was the television. A man need never be bored or wonder what to do with his leisure time again. And the Church never even realised it had a rival or asked where three quarters of its congregation had gone, until it was too late. But as it had been in the beginning, so it went on, singing the same old hymns, saying the same old services, while most of the town agreed, 'It's just not for the likes of us.'

Edward's predecessor courageously carried his church kicking and screaming into the twentieth century, but, on his own admission, only as far as the nineteen sixties. Then his energy ran out and exhaustion forced him to give way to a man with fresh, vigorous ideas. For a few months Edward waited and watched. The new prayer book was introduced, even at the eight o'clock Sunday morning Communion, lest that service become a stronghold of reactionary feeling, and the church be split into two separate congregations. But as Edward watched and listened it became apparent that far more sweeping changes would be necessary if the town was ever to be convinced that Jesus spoke for the working man of their day and not for the respectable people of previous generations. One major change would affect that most cherished of institutions, the choir!

No one doubted that Grimlington's choir had seen better days. Bob, the organist and choirmaster for forty years, did his best, but it would have taken little short of a miracle to produce anything approaching a reasonable performance with the handful he had left. The four or five remaining stalwarts, whose numbers swelled to nine or ten on great occasions, appeared to rattle round the empty choir stalls. Their robes, colourful and dignified in former years, now looked out of place in a congregation wearing jeans and dungarees. And they no longer made sufficient sound to beat the organ to the back pews. No one expected the standard of a great cathedral, but one night they were reduced to one solitary bass singing his heart out in splendid isolation. He would have had to be little short of superman, or bionic woman, to manage tenor, alto and soprano too. The days of our choir were numbered.

What hurt some of the last remaining choir members was the sudden, rapid growth of the new Music Group. Rick, who had started it, learned his love of music from the Salvation Army. At the turn of the century 'the Army' in Grimlington had a congregation of five hundred, one of the largest in the town. Now, they no longer had a Citadel and Rick and Julie had been going to Ossleforth to worship. The transference of their allegiance to us was not without a great deal of heartache. Julie was horrified when Rick first told her of his urge to visit the parish church and the increasing feeling that that was where he ought to be making music. Her whole family were Salvationists. The rigid formality of the Church of England left her cold, and one visit confirmed her worst impressions. Little short of divorce crossed her mind. Reason told her it was foolish to split the family and reluctantly, against all the instincts of her upbringing, she followed her husband. Rick began the music group and she began a playgroup.

It was probably not the first time that the Church of England was indebted to the Salvation Army – though there were some who would question that debt, when roused from their slumbers after the sermon and prayers by Rick's trumpet accompaniment to the final hymn.

Reading music was not a vital prerequisite to joining the music group, otherwise there would have been no candidates. In fact, unlike the choir, there were no conditions of entry and no audition, so Rick could only hope for a group of people who could sing reasonably in tune. And he found them. Some had not sung since they were at primary school, but it was a start and they loved it. By the time Edward arrived they were confident enough to make quite a contribution to the Family Services. There were rumbles of disapproval at the appearance of guitars, despite the fact that for years everyone had been happily chanting psalms about praising God on stringed instruments. Reading about it was one thing, doing it was another.

So when, during our first autumn in Grimlington, the PCC met to discuss the choir's final demise, feelings were running high.

'We've got to do it, there's no question.'

'But they'll be so upset.'

'They'll say it's that new vicar again.'

'Well they're wrong. We're going to make the final decision!'

'Yes, but I'm frightened. Me Aunty Gladys'll do 'er nut. She's fond of choir. They sang at 'er wedding thirty year ago.'

'Ay, and she 'asn't been since!'

'But what about Bob?'

Bob's feelings were a source of major concern. Not all churches are blessed in their organist. We were. It was impossible to think of hurting him. For forty years he had played the organ at three services every Sunday, sometimes at as many as six funerals a week and fifty weddings a year, forgoing holidays and weekends away. Such was his stamina that one Sunday evening, after he

86

had sliced his finger on a razor blade in his pocket, he played on, the blood oozing out over the keys. The squeals from the Music Group had alerted Peter to the problem. He sidled over and suggested that Bob pop over to the vicarage to let Anna dress it. With a wad of bandaging round his finger he was back in five minutes, ready to play the next hymn.

There were times when his playing seemed inspired. As he played the old familiar hymns so lovingly and sensitively during the administration of Communion the congregation had started to hum or sing along with him.

'When the wife died,' he said to me one day, 'I thought all joy had gone out of my life for ever. Then I remembered God had given me music too.'

Bob was a convinced teetotaller and appalled by the amount of beer consumed in the town. 'I 'ad a mate,' he said to Peter one day in the vestry, as they were waiting for a wedding, and lamenting the effects of too much alcohol, 'who drank eight pints a night. His stomach was out 'ere. He drank that much that 'e went out in the dead of winter in only a T-shirt and never felt the cold. Mind you,' he said, wagging a forefinger, 'it killed 'im in the end.'

'How old was he?' Peter asked.

'Eighty!' Bob shook his head knowingly. He had proved the evils of drink to his own satisfaction.

No, Bob must not be passed over or ignored. So late one night and looking haggard, the PCC decided to disband all present musical enterprise, both choir and Music Group, and form one new team, under the joint direction of Rick and Bob. Bob bowed graciously to this new development. It was a blow, but inevitable. Besides, as the younger people sought out his help and advice he confessed he had never felt so appreciated and it was altogether a very pleasant experience.

One or two choir members followed his lead and made the transition. Others could not. The pain of seeing their beloved choir pass into history was altogether too great. Ernie Fanshaw, who had been prepared to sing alone in the choir stalls, said he would never come to church again. Ernie fitted quite well into the stereotype of a Yorkshireman, dour and abrasive on the outside, and all soft and sensitive on the inside. As a farrier he commanded respect throughout the entire district. There was nothing he did not know about a horse's anatomy from the knee down. Vets called on him at all hours, seeking the wealth of his expertise. We would miss Ernie very much. Change was more painful than we anticipated.

The local *Gazette*, ever ready to rise up in the cause of the oppressed, took up the story. Angry letters accusing the vicar of iconoclasm filled half a page. One of Grimlington's great traditions had been done to death, wrote some who had not come to hear that tradition for a very long time. 'Modern music is not the same. It won't last,' they said. Who could disagree? But the church was meant to be a living organism and not an academy of ancient music, nor a repository of ancient traditions, preserved in a kind of ice age by the present membership for those who never came.

Edward responded graciously and explained that this was a communal decision, not just his own, made thoughtfully and carefully over a period of time. But the correspondence continued for some weeks and I saw how the personal attack wounded him and the criticism wore him down. Such is the vulnerable position of the clergyman. Unable by the very nature of his job to please all men and fulfil their expectations, he becomes the butt for their frustrations. Marjorie went beyond the duties of a churchwarden and shielded him in every way she could, deflecting every attack on to herself and the PCC. Gradually the hullaballoo died down and the town settled down to its usual indifference to all matters concerning the church.

One Sunday night Ernie Fanshaw and his wife were back in their usual pew for the evening service. Everyone tried to behave naturally, but their pleasure was obvious. Ernie left early. He could not countenance too much of the new music at once. And a man has his dignity when all is said and done. But he came back every week until he was rushed into hospital with a ruptured ulcer. The Sunday after he came out, he asked if he might have the opportunity to say a few words to the congregation.

'If you'd seen the buckets I brought up...'

'Yuk,' Jan told me later, wrinkling up her nose, 'it made me feel funny!'

'Well, all I want to say is that I felt yer support and yer prayers and I'm grateful.'

There were those however who would never accept change, and could not countenance the disappearance of the church's aura of middle-class respectability. I was rushing to the service one Sunday morning, marginally late, having miscalculated the time as usual, and as I passed the vestry door I noticed Peter, surplice half-way over his head, talking in a clipped, controlled voice to a rather smart-looking woman. I recognised the signs of pressure and annoyance in him. He hated interruptions just before a service, and so many people barraged him with requests and grouses, not realising how easily it destroyed his concentration. So I went to see if I could assist.

'Oh, yes,' the woman said, recognising at once that I belonged to the curt, unhelpful cleric, still struggling into his uniform.

'I only want to find my aunt's grave.'

The tone was aggrieved.

'We're just visiting the town you see.'

I did not hold out much hope of finding it, but escorted her round the cemetery, making helpful noises.

'By the way,' she said, a little apologetically after about fifteen minutes of unsuccessful hunting when I was beginning to wonder whether I would miss the entire service, 'I am sorry I can't come into church, but I'm not wearing a hat.'

Neither was I. Or did she think I was hiding one somewhere.

'We don't wear hats here,' I said. 'You can wear what you like. Most of the congregation come in jeans or dungarees.'

She stared at me for a moment, took a deep breath, spat 'Disgusting!' at me as if I were a worm which had just crawled out of the soil and marched off down the path.

As I went into church it occurred to me that hats had become such an expense that if they were regulation uniform half the congregation would have to be expelled.

Despite opposition the gradual metamorphosis continued and the new music team blossomed. Chris joined them with his violin, and then, with a nobility of spirit to which I could never rise, began a music group for children. Mary dug out her tambourine and plucking up all her courage, tried it out, faintly, in an evening service. No one complained so she became a little bolder, grinning shyly at first, then growing in confidence. One or two tentatively tried to write their own songs and then there was a sudden upsurge in composing. It became quite common to fall over someone lost in their own little world, humming away happily to themselves. It did little for conversation.

'Don't speak to me, I've got a song, and I have to find Rick or Chris to write down the notes, before I lose it.'

Woe betide him or her who had the misfortune to come upon a song first thing in the morning. It had to be sung all day until Rick or Chris came home from work.

It seemed as if latent creativity, stifled and checked for years, yet never completely destroyed, was only waiting for a new birth to ferment and explode. Julie gathered a group of banner makers together, Kelly started a dance group, and the Drama Group continued to stun me with their ingenuity. It all happened so fast it took my breath away and did more than anything to make me feel that I had at last become part of the scenery. But the greater marvel was that as our creativity expanded, confidence grew, uncloaking a talent undreamed of by those who visited the town.

'The sin of the monied classes in the palmy Victorian days was to condemn the working man to ugliness, ugliness, ugliness. A man needs beauty more than he needs bread,' said D. H. Lawrence. It may not have been in their surroundings, but they had had a glimpse of real beauty all the same. Their eyes had been opened to another world not seen with ordinary human perception and it was that beauty which so inspired them that they could not keep it to themselves. That they could reproduce it in music, dance and art work, creating something of lasting value, was a healing process in itself. Never before had I been so aware of the vibrant, life-transforming nature of Christianity. It was never meant to stifle or strangle personality, as I had seen so often in other places and other people. It made men whole. It made them free. It made them sit more easily in their human skins.

Rick and Kelly visited other churches 'of reputation' in order to glean new ideas. They came back depressed and encouraged all at once.

'They're very professional. We've a long way to go.'

'But we're not them, we're us, and for us, we've gone a long way.'

'It's a beginning.'

It was a beginning all right and in an environment where words like 'talent' and 'individuality' were almost forbidden, it was much more than a beginning.

Chapter 11

We were never given a list of parish addresses and telephone numbers. There wasn't one. It would have been superfluous since all vital information of that nature was stored in Alicia's head. Peter felt at times that he was using a computer.

'Where will I find the Studleys, Alicia?'

'Calderdale Street, off Windermere Road, just past the chip shop. I can't remember the number, darling, but it's fourth or fifth on the right, a bright blue door, you can't miss it. Oh, by the way, if you go during the day you're more likely to find her at her mother's, which is one of the old folks' bungalows on Ashfield Walk, the one with the pillar box outside.'

She was always right.

Walking round the supermarket with her was an experience.

'Hello, dear, feeling better?'

'How's Tommy settling at school?'

'So sorry to hear about your father. It was so unexpected.'

'Which ward is your Gran on? I'll see her on Thursday, that's my day for hospital visits.'

After an hour there was very little in her shopping trolley.

'Smile dear,' she whispered to me. 'You may not know who they are, but they know who you are. You represent the church.'

I groaned inwardly. That was what came of having our smiling faces plastered on the centre pages of the *Gazette*: 'Grimlington gets new curate'. Still, I suspected that I could probably get away almost incognito if it were not for Alicia. Everyone knew who she was, and that the community had taken her to their hearts, as she had taken them to hers, there was no doubt. They were proud of her too. She was known to have an aristocratic pedigree, and an aristocrat could get away with anything. Sometimes Alicia did!

Staff lunches at her house were a treat. She, Anna and I took it in turns to make lunch on Mondays for the five of us and our children. Eating together meant that Anna and I could at least keep abreast with the parish news our husbands had forgotten to tell us. This was fairly vital since most of the parish presumed that we had a hot line to the clergy, knew everyone's problems and were a source of all wisdom. In fact we were usually the last to know what was going on. Our husbands fell into bed exhausted when they came in at night. They certainly did not want to talk shop. Without our Monday lunches we would have continued to live in blissful, total ignorance.

Alicia spoiled us. There was turkey, or a roast joint, with mounds of vegetables of every kind. An inventive cook, she was generous with herbs and spices, especially if they grew in her back garden, beneath her imported Scottish thistles. It was not unusual to draw a whole sprig of rosemary from your mouth. And then a meal might be crowned with lemon cheesecake, or 'super-vommer' pudding, a recipe to end all recipes, handed down by a previous curate, consisting of coffee, chocolate, breadcrumbs and lashings of cream. By the time the smell of freshly-percolated coffee wafted in from the kitchen, Peter would be feeling slightly liverish and on the verge of dozing off in a corner by the fire. Farewell to an afternoon's work! And no need to feed him again before Wednesday.

Because Alicia's spondylitis impeded her movement and because the house was small, we all tended to get under each others' feet, so we fetched and carried for her, acted as her legs and moved at her command.

'Plates, dear. Place mats. Glasses over there.'

On my first visit I went to what I assumed was a china cabinet to look for some more of her favourite stoneware. I opened the cupboard door, and there, crammed on top of each other in a vast pile were hammers, screwdrivers, saws, chisels, clamps, drills, anything but crockery. I looked round and everyone else was grinning.

'Just because you don't know one end of a screwdriver from the other,' Peter said, 'don't imagine all women are the same.'

'Alicia has a certificate in mechanical engineering,' Edward said, with a hint of awe in his voice. Mechanics were as much of a mystery to him as they were to me. 'In fact, when the church boiler played up the other day, there was quite a race. I think Alicia got there before Peter.'

'She carries the necessary tools around in her handbag,' Peter said, barely disguising his pique. He had trained as an engineer, graduated during an industrial slump, then went into teaching after several months of unemployment. But he never lost his deductive skills in diagnosing the faults of a dud machine.

'So, you have a rival,' I said to him, 'and a female one at that.'

I caught sight then of a vicious looking instrument and drew it out.

'This wouldn't by any chance be the mallet,' I asked, 'the famous one which slew a mouse?'

The others examined it at a distance, then turned up their noses. The mouse incident was legend in the church. It was rumoured that Alicia was entertaining the sister of an Archbishop to tea, and who could doubt how lavish the fare, when a mouse ambled across the carpet. Indignant at this interruption, but not alarmed, she ran to her china cupboard, returned with the mallet and landed the creature such a blow on the skull that its tea-party days were over, for ever.

'Is it true?' I asked her, but she refused to comment and disappeared back into the kitchen.

We all drank our coffee huddled over the fire as Alicia's house was cold and in desperate need of renovation.

'How could the church let the house fall into a state of such disrepair?' Peter asked.

'It's not their fault,' Alicia said. 'You must remember that most people don't like to come into our homes. They don't know what they're like. That's pretty typical of the Church of England, or at least it was. The life of the clergy is supposed to be a bit hair-shirt. I don't mind the spartan life. This house is a lot better than many round here. Besides, the PCC did offer me central heating once.'

'You didn't refuse?' Peter asked incredulously.

'The cold doesn't bother me darling. I always sleep with my bedroom window open anyway, summer and winter. You remember how cold January was last year? When I got up one morning my bedroom was full of snow. I had to shovel it back out of the window before I could get to my clothes.'

Peter stared at her in disbelief and she smiled benignly back. There was no reason to suppose she was not telling the truth.

'Speaking of the cold,' Peter said, turning to a subject which had been bothering him for a few weeks, 'how do you keep warm when you do a winter interment?'

Alicia looked at him in amazement. The problem had evidently never crossed her mind. Peter looked to Edward for help, but none was forthcoming.

'The weather is getting colder and colder,' he said, by way of explanation. 'You may think it's a silly question, but I'm a cold-blooded sort of chap and I don't function at my best if I'm perishing. We wear the same gear in the dead of winter as we wear in the summer heat waves. The wind already howls right round that cemetery and blows my cassock up like a balloon. I've tried thermal underwear and it doesn't help. I feel like wearing a parka over my surplice.'

There was a moment's silence.

'Speaking of interments,' Edward said, in a tone of voice that suggested he was not going to be drawn into trivia, 'the undertaker rang this morning with the date of Nellie Hepworth's funeral. Do you want to do it, Alicia? I gather you visited recently.'

'Yes,' Alicia said, apparently quite stunned. 'I visited on Friday. I had such a strong feeling I was to tell her to set her life in order and be sure of God's forgiveness before it was too late. But I never thought it would be so soon. Did I do the right thing?'

'Would we had your courage,' Peter said.

'Well there was such tension in the family, so much to sort out, but I wouldn't want to precipitate anything. This is always happening to me.'

'I should regard yourself as a prophet of . . . I mean a warning angel.'

'You think so?' Alicia smiled, then her brows knitted again. 'I only hope she was ready.'

We left her that day to wonder and hope, marvelling at her concern for so many people.

'How does she manage to give such individual love and attention?' Peter said wistfully. 'With so many funerals it takes me all my time to fit in the visits.'

Michael O'Connor, the undertaker, rang early on Monday morning to deal with the weekend's business. Well might he advertise a lovely chapel of rest. It struck me he must take little himself. With an average of a hundred and seventy funerals a year, give or take an intemperate winter, and that at the Anglican Church alone, without Catholics and nonconformists, Grimlington had a track record which left many other places behind. Fellow curates from college days, with whom we still kept in touch for an occasional commiseration, were staggered at the number. Peter was taking two or three funerals a week before they had done their first.

'It's the air round here,' we joked, 'even the sparrows have to clear their chests in the morning.'

The truth of the matter was that Grimlington was a static community with little new housing until recently, and a high proportion of elderly people. But nevertheless bronchitis and other chest diseases undoubtedly took a heavy toll. The local newspapers informed us that inhaling coal fumes was a hazard. Sulphur dioxide burnt holes in the lungs. Our councillors were concerned. The area had fallen way behind. Something must be done. But nothing ever was. Grants to convert fireplaces to smokeless fuel cost a great deal of money and there was none to spare. The Coal Board could not convert their free coal allowance for pit workers into gas, even for the retired. So new council houses and old people's bungalows were still built with no heating other than coal fires. The elderly humped their coal or froze.

Because of the death rate, visits to the bereaved were often short, hurried affairs and totally inadequate. Peter was frustrated. He could not fulfil his own expectations, let alone other people's.

'It shouldn't be like this,' he said. 'I planned and hoped to continue visiting for at least a year to provide the sort of comfort and counsel which is really necessary.'

The only consolation was that in a town like Grimlington, family and friends usually took over where the clergy seemed to fail. And they were probably more acceptable. Not everyone was glad to see a clergyman standing on their doorstep. He almost had to batter the door down on one occasion.

'Who is it?'

'The curate!'

'What do you want?'

'To come in.'

'What for?'

'Because I'm burying your father on Wednesday!'

But the clergy were gladly received in most homes. After all, a man could cry in front of them. They were different, not like other men. They would not think it sissy.

'I shouldn't cry, I know.'

'Why not?'

'Because men don't.'

'Who says?'

Peter found himself constantly giving families permission to express their grief naturally. We were a nation, it seemed, which released our emotional energies at football and rugby matches, but at funerals kept them tightly buttoned up. Everything had to be dignified and respectable. There were few areas of our national life that struck me as being so totally un-Jewish. Judaism gave space to grieve. There are seven days compulsory mourning, and most Jews take advantage of the opportunity.

One young miner that Peter visited marched round the house, swearing and cursing.

'I loved me dad. Why did 'e 'ave to die, the stupid old sod?'

'Sssssh,' whispered his mother out of the corner of her mouth, smiling at Peter, 'don't swear in front of parson.'

'Let him swear all he likes,' Peter said. 'It's one of the healthiest expressions of grief I've seen in a long while.'

The saddest visits were to stunned and lonely spouses, who sat vacant and alone in their misery.

'We kept ourselves to ourselves. We never bothered anyone. We never went into other people's houses, never mixed. We were happy just with each other.'

And now there was nothing to fill the gaping, empty void the partner had left behind.

Peter often felt the inadequacy of his own words. The Christian burial service seemed almost meaningless and out-of-place for those who had had no interest in Christianity in their lifetime. But there was no secular alternative. He did not like eulogies. Coming from the mouth of someone who had never known the deceased, they sounded hollow. Instead he preached as forcefully as he could of his own certainty of resurrection for those who followed Christ. And he grieved for the many who still walked away, locked in their own despair, unable and unwilling to reach out and take hold of the great hope he could offer.

Most mourners gave no instructions about the service, but left it to his discretion. However, one or two were quite specific.

'None of them futuristic services,' said one man, once a regular church member.

'I don't understand,' Peter said.

'No guitars and that. She didn't like 'em when she were alive. She certainly won't like 'em now.'

Peter did not know how he could be so certain, but assured him that we had not yet introduced guitars into the funeral service.

One woman was so determined that every detail should be perfection itself that she rang several times to check. Unfortunately for her, on the last occasion I answered.

'I wanted the curate, but you'll have to do,' she said.

I was beginning to get used to being a disappointing second best.

'Your husband is burying my mother.'

'Oh!' I said. Well I could hardly say, 'Good!' or, 'I'm sorry!'

'Could you tell me what comes after the anthem?'

I faltered. It amazed me that while a person would never dream of consulting their bank manager's wife about the state of their financial affairs, or the doctor's wife about the state of their health, yet the clergyman's wife is presumed to be a repository of wisdom in all matters clerical.

'I don't know,' I said. Then thinking it best to be honest, 'I've never been to an Anglican funeral.'

Honesty is not always the best policy, for it almost begged the next question, 'What kind have you been to then?'

'Jewish!' I said.

There was a moment's silence.

'Could you get your husband to ring me then? It is your husband, I presume?'

Given the number of funerals, it was inevitable a mishap should happen at some time or another. We were all enjoying a staff lunch at the vicarage one day, tucking into one of Anna's speciality Bakewell tarts, when all went dark as a funeral cortege slowly passed the dining-room window. Edward, Alicia and Peter watched it in silence. The Catholic Church was in the other direction. So were the Methodists and the Baptists.

Edward swallowed hard and cleared his throat.

'Whose was that?' he asked, as casually as he could.

Peter's eyes suddenly looked twice their size.

'Mine!' he said with horror, rushed from the table, and out of the door. The last we saw was a human whirlwind, chasing a hearse down the street. Fortunately there is a short-cut through the cemetery. So by the time the procession drew up at the church gates, Peter had opened the church, put on his gear, put out the hymn books and service sheets and was waiting graciously at the doors as if he had been there for at least the last twenty minutes.

So all was well. At least that was what he thought. But unfortunately one of the town councillors was there and he complained to the Council, who told the mayor to do something about it. So he instructed the town clerk to write to the vicar to tell his curate that the church doors must be opened at least half an hour before a funeral. And the vicar replied that any criticisms of his curate should be made direct and was the Council stuck for pressing business!

Peter laughed in disbelief when he saw the letter. The councillor lived nearby.

'Couldn't he come to me himself and tell me face to face? I could have at least had the chance to explain. I know the doors should be open earlier. Can't a man make a mistake?'

'Definitely not!' I said. 'Only perfection is acceptable, and especially from a clergyman!'

Peter never forgot to attend a funeral again, although there was one where he forgot something else and the response was just as unforgiving. The autumn continued bitterly cold and the nip in the air became a sharp penetrating bite, with no respect for several layers of underwear.

'For this funeral I am going to wear my parka over my cassock,' Peter muttered, tearing round the house in his usual hurry. The ground outside was covered that morning in a sparkling white frost. 'On second thoughts, I'd better not,' he said, as he got to the front door, then rushed back to the bedroom and put on another vest. It was a fight to fasten the buttons of his clerical shirt. He was so well padded he could have rolled to the cemetery. Half-way through the service, as they were gathered around the grave he noticed that the mourners appeared to be staring at his feet. He followed their gaze and saw to his horror that he had forgotten to change out of his new, luminous red shoes. Being size tens they refused to disappear under his cassock.

'That'll teach me to worry about the trivia of this life,' he groaned. 'Perfection is just out of my grasp.'

'Don't worry, love,' I reassured him, 'I don't expect anyone will have noticed.'

I spoke too soon. The following night was drama night. Linda was barely through the door when, with a huge grin stretching from one side of her face to the other, she said, 'Hey, what's 'e been up to now?'

I couldn't guess. 'What now?'

'Well, I was in the newsagents at the top of the High Street yesterday and I overheard the woman who was serving telling another woman in the shop that she'd just come from her cousin's funeral and you'd never guess, but the vicar was wearing bright red shoes. "No decorum, these days, the clergy," she said.'

Linda giggled, so did the others.

'It's about time someone brightened up the church's image,' Jan said.

'His reputation ruined and all for a pair of shoes,' I said ruefully.

'Take heart,' Linda reassured me. 'Clergy have lost their reputation for less. Just tell him to be 'imself.'

'Just being yourself' was something for which Grimlington people had a great capacity, a state of existence we were to see in its most uninhibited form in the very near future.

Chapter 12

November was heralded in with great excitement, not just because of bonfire night, but because that first weekend by long tradition was the parish weekend away. Peter and I had been on church houseparties before, and enjoyed them enormously, but none of them had ever been quite like this.

In Grimlington church outings of any kind were always a problem, as we never had enough cars between us or at least enough that were on the road. Conveying one hundred and fifty people to Filey was therefore a mammoth headache.

'I want to go with me mam.'

'I can't sit in back, I'll be sick.'

'Me shift doesn't finish till seven.'

'I'm not going with him, 'e kicks.'

Eventually, by squeezing three adults with children on their knees into the back of every car, no one was left behind.

Despite all pleadings that luggage be kept to the minimum, suitcases were the largest I had seen, bulging with enough clothing and provisions for a trip to the Himalayas.

'I thought we were going to Filey, not the Antarctic,' I said to Peter as he wrestled with cases, rugs, tins, flasks, guitars, projector and screen.

The sarcasm was noted. He threw me a withering look.

'It can be cold,' Lucy said, obviously feeling that Peter needed moral support.

With every stop to collect more people, the contents of

the boot had to be rejuggled, with loud expostulations from Peter which I hoped none of them would hear. Then at last we held our breath as the final bag was stowed away and the boot slammed shut. We were off. No we weren't. Gladys had forgotten her mac, her slippers and the plastic bags, just in case. Back we went and her neighbours appeared at their sitting-room window to wave us off with as much excitement as they did the first time.

Then, as far as any vehicle is able, struggling under such a weight, we raced with twenty or so other cars down the A62. Not one treasured moment in Filey was to be lost. About a third of the party had set off early in the morning, taking a day off work and keeping the children off school, to have those few extra hours eating mussels and candy floss on the sea front. After all, for some it was their only annual holiday. If it was not, it was certainly their only experience of staying in a hotel and a rare chance of a weekend away. And they had been saving up for months, putting away a few pounds a week in the envelope in the kitchen drawer marked 'Filey'. There were lots of envelopes in the kitchen drawer, marked 'coal' or 'electric' or 'milk' or 'rent', and though mother added to them every week from the contents of the pay packet, they were never very full. But once autumn came round again those marked 'decorating' or 'kids' shoes' would have to stay empty. It was a difficult choice. Shortage of money imposes many hard decisions. The soot in the air meant that houses really needed to be decorated every year and the children's feet would keep on growing. But for that weekend in Filey you could put up with a sooty house, boots that pinched and leaked, and tights with darns in them for that matter.

And if, when the time came, despite the sacrifices, there was still not enough in the envelope because of other unforeseen necessities, the money could sometimes be borrowed from Mum and Dad. Or a smile might just melt the heart of Bill, the treasurer, and he might give a few weeks' grace.

'Come on, Bill, only nine weeks to Christmas. I'll get lots of overtime and soon pay it off.'

'My cash flow! I don't know how we run this church!' He would lift his eyes to heaven in mock despair, and the matter was settled.

Poor Bill had just cause for alarm. We were already dipping into our special discretionary fund for families such as Phil and Mary and their children. Phil was an attendant at the swimming baths and his income was incredibly low. Although he and Mary cleaned the church every week, which helped, there was no possibility of a family of five on Family Income Supplement affording a weekend away. Several families were in the same predicament, but we insisted that financial hardship should not prevent them from coming. So the settling of our hotel accounts could be a little wearing on the treasurer's nerves.

Our debts were not his only source of concern. Tradition had somehow forced him into the unenviable position of chief organiser and it was his lot to ensure everyone had a bed for two nights. We fought our way into the hotel through a lobby piled high with high chairs, push chairs, hiking boots, guitars, suitcases and stray children, all abandoned in the hunt for a bedroom.

'My key doesn't fit in the door.'

'My room doesn't exist. There's no number ten.'

'Yer on the wrong floor, yer wally!'

'Somebody's in our room already!'

'Just pray they don't snore!'

'Thanks!'

Standing in the hall like a traffic warden, Bill dealt patiently with the mounting racket of complaints and misunderstandings and pointed people in the right direction.

Above all the other din a voice was heard.

'Who wants my gezunder this year?'

'Your what, Alicia?' I asked naively.

'What goes under the bed, darling,' she explained, then seeing my surprise, 'These corridors, dear, they're so long and draughty. Someone usually needs it.'

I looked round, but no one came forward.

'Looks as if it might be yours this year!'

My first sight of the upper floors of the hotel confirmed her words and I was in half a mind to go and take her up on her offer. When I had been told with great excitement, 'We stay in a hotel with a swimming pool', I never for a moment imagined the London Hilton, but nor was I prepared for this vast, old-fashioned building with its art-deco furnishings and corridors so gloomy that they seemed gas-lit. They were silent and empty and I marvelled that they seemed to swallow up over a hundred people, turning the raucous noise into a few eerie, floating sounds. But we soon realised that the bedroom walls were often plaster-board and paper thin, putting paid to any privacy. Before long people were discovering all kinds of things about each other they never knew before. But then that is what a weekend away is all about, or so I gathered.

The swimming pool turned out to be a sort of nine foot by six foot brownish green hole, filled with tepid, steaming water and surrounded by murals of golden beaches and palm trees. But it was wet, so the children loved it. So did the one or two who succumbed to the suggestion that this might be the Canaries and donned their bikinis. This was a feat of some daring, since the pool was on full view to the hotel's main corridor and thoroughfare through a large glass window. And no detail, however personal, ever escaped frank comment!

We all spent the first evening putting our children to bed, then putting them back to bed at half-hourly intervals. Some of the spouses, coming because it was a family occasion and not because they anticipated any involvement in the more spiritual content of the programme, had found the bar and sat giggling like a gang of naughty schoolboys who had dodged an RE

106

lesson and dreaded being caught. We joined them after the first talk and the atmosphere relaxed considerably, especially as night wore on into the small hours of the next morning, and the combination of time and the beer loosened many tongues.

We regretted our folly at five-thirty, when Joel and Abby bounced out of bed, demanding towels and swimming costumes. At seven we finally let them loose on the world, with everyone else's children. Alicia had by then been in the pool for some time. Parents arrived for breakfast, their hair uncombed, their eyes half shut. A vast mural of Filey in Edwardian days, yellowing with age, as if Edwardian itself, filled an entire wall. The women were dignified in their long skirts and bonnets, the men stiff and erect in immaculate suits, as they supervised their offspring on the Yorkshire sands. As we launched reluctantly into the kippers, they seemed to mock us with their eminent respectability and the discipline of their well-ordered world. For some time I glowered back at a particularly smug-looking gentleman with a curling moustache, the conversation floating around me as in a mist.

'Guess what I heard last night?'

Grunt!

'Well I never thought those two rowed like that. It just goes to show, we're all the same really.'

With our stomachs full of toast and hot coffee we began to wake up. In fact the morning's discussion about our involvement and potential influence in the Grimlington community became rather animated. It was a subject which touched some raw nerves. We had little influence in the town, we were forced to confess. We showed little practical concern for the council estate. Even the curate was pulling out, if the house ever sold.

'Typical,' the inhabitants said, and they were right. As a missionary church we were a damp squib. If we cared about our town then it was time to show it.

Ideas were batted back and forwards across the room,

run the playgroup more often, start a toddler club on the council estate, expand the youth work, which was virtually non-existent. They were all exciting possibilities, but each ended in a blind alley. Our buildings were inadequate, our manpower already stretched to the limit of its resources. Then Linda launched an attack which left us temporarily in a state of uneasy silence.

'The real trouble with the church is that it's too middle-class,' she said, and there was a cutting edge to her voice I had never heard before.

I felt a thud in my middle. I had been unaware of her pain. I had thought, naively I suppose, that what I was enjoying was working-class warmth and spontaneity. But it was not enough, as far as Linda was concerned. These were superficialities which solved nothing. They merely masked the real problem, which was apparently much deeper.

I looked around the room. A few people were nodding vigorously. Some smiled uncertainly. Others wore the set expression of those who have retreated in hurt self-defence. It was almost time for lunch. Since food for the body usually wins any battle with food for the mind, the meeting stopped. Where it would have gone had it continued I would never know. I was left guessing what Linda meant, but one day I would find out. Of that I was determined.

The children had been swimming for most of the morning and were exhausted and ravenous. But feeding a child is like putting petrol into a car. By the time their parents were ready to sink into an armchair for a snooze they had mobilised themselves into an army and armed with buckets and spades, commandeered us all on to the freezing, windy beach.

Saturday's climax was the Grimlington Follies, awaited all year with avid anticipation. Every joke, foible and funny had been stored up for this one-hour cabaret of all-round entertainment. No one was spared, churchwarden or vicar and certainly not Alicia, who was played that year by a man. After that it was even harder to settle the children in bed and almost impossible to concentrate on a speaker.

Later, yawning, I suddenly remembered I had been invited to room nine for coffee and against my better judgement, made my way there. There were people crammed into every available space.

'Always room for another one,' they said and shuffled along the floor.

'Oh heck,' said Pat, our hostess, as she moved several disjointed legs to get into a cupboard, 'I've remembered the milk and the coffee and the tea bags and the sugar, and I've brought some home-made biscuits, but I've forgotten the electric kettle. This is the first time in eight years.'

'Now don't worry,' Betty said, 'aren't health visitors always equipped for any eventuality?'

She produced a device which is left in a mug of water until it boils and by midnight there were only a dozen of us still waiting for a drink.

The highlight of the whole weekend was Sunday morning's Communion service. The lounge seemed very hushed and still, especially after the noise and the laughter of the night before. It was not a heavy silence, imposed merely by a sense of the occasion, but one which made me feel deeply at one with God, myself and the world.

As the bread and wine was passed from one to another I looked around the room. The children sat at their parents' feet, quiet for once. The spouses who had refused to come in to any other meeting, sat beside their wives or husbands, relaxed and at ease. The service said we were 'one body', a meaningless platitude in so many churches, where people were alienated from each other by indifference. To be one body was to be bound by a blood tie, more family than family. And this was one of those rare occasions when we knew it was so. The Jew in me always participated in this moment with a sense of wonder, that those whose paths might never have crossed, who might once have had little in common,

109

separated by race, culture and prejudice, now belonged to each other because of all that this act symbolised. But that morning especially so. What if I had never come to Grimlington, never known these people? It seemed unthinkable. How much I would have missed. Now their hurts, struggles, hopes and fears were mine and mine were theirs. We were relatives, whether we liked it or not. We were stuck with each other for the rest of eternity. But I did like it. In fact I was very, very glad.

Chapter 13

It was a source of immense relief to me that Grimlington
Parish Church was not a monstrous Gothic barn, built
by the sentimental Victorians, who raised monuments
to the glory of God that were cold, austere and
inhibiting all human contact. After the beauty and
colour of the synagogue my Jewish nature rose up in
protest at such icy sobriety.

But Grimlington was passably pretty, small, cosy and
part Norman. On a board at the front of the church,
beside the old stone altar, which had been smashed in
half in Cromwell's day, vicars were listed from 1180.
Every time I went out to take Communion my eyes were
drawn to it. For hundreds of years men and women had
worshipped here, standing on the same flagstones, when
there were only hills and fields and they had brought the
first-fruits of their crops and cattle. The world changed,
generations came and went, but the Church remained. I
had a powerful sense of my Christian, as well as my
Jewish heritage. Like the rest of humanity, I would
vanish, but others, belonging to another age, would take
my place.

The church was even mentioned in an encyclopaedia
of Britain's treasured heritage for its beautiful Flemish
glass. When the sun streamed in through the windows
the building was fused with a myriad of coloured lights.
Banners now hung gaily from every pillar and children's
artwork, friezes and collages, decorated the bare stone
walls. This was home. We loved it.

But any building is a burden and one of historical
interest carries its own penalties. Woe betide us if we

suggested the slightest alteration. We were pursued with all the fury of the preservationist societies, who were more interested in the authenticity of the building than the comfort of the congregation. It was all right for them. They never turned up for a service. And when it came to the constant losing battle which so many churches face, against damp, dry rot and woodworm, with the added problem of subsidence, there they were again, aided and abetted by the Town Council, urging us on from behind, with support that was often moral rather than financial.

Not that we were happy to stand back and see our building fall apart. We were not. It was simply that there were so many other, vital demands upon our spending. It was hard to get our priorities right. The average income of the congregation was so low that if every member gave a tenth there was still nowhere near enough to meet the annual budget. As unemployment rose, and employment became a matter of desperation, so wages could be kept to a bare minimum. Many church members would have been better off on the dole, but they had their pride. Any work was better than none at all, and Family Income Supplement or long hours of overtime could make the basic wage enough to live on.

And yet they would give away all they had, without a thought, to a mate in need. In fact, their attitude to money was refreshingly novel to me. When I first became a Christian I was amused at how embarrassing most non-Jews found the subject. Like death it was taboo, never discussed by nice people. The only thing to do with it was to amass it slowly and carefully, then hide it away for as long as possible. Peter was already trying to do the same, without much success. 'Otherwise,' he said, 'we shall never be able to afford our own house in retirement.' Saving was the cardinal virtue, more than that, the cardinal Christian virtue, at least I thought it must be, until we came to Grimlington. Then I realised that it was a middle-class tradition and not Christian at all. It may have grown out of the Protestant emphasis on hard work and thrift, but when I thought about it, the New Testament did seem to me to encourage giving away rather than storing away one's surplus.

In Grimlington what a man earned by the sweat of his brow he was entitled to spend with equal gusto and as much pleasure as possible. And spend he did! He could be as rich as Rockefeller on payday and poor as a beggar for the rest of the week, but what did it matter if he had enjoyed the spending of it? The town suffered a minor epidemic of videos, microwaves, expensive toys and all the other symbols of the materialistic age. In some cases it was a sign of prosperity, in many it was not.

Most of the church members were unaffected by it. Some were still without fridges, washing machines and other modern conveniences which I took for granted. I felt rich by comparison, uncomfortably so at times. Owning a car suddenly seemed a luxury, not a necessity and a right. Yet what little they had they gave to the clergy. Our car and petrol allowance was such that we were able to live on Peter's stipend without being worn down by continual scrimping like so many other clergy we knew.

'But you can't afford it,' we said to Bill, the treasurer.

'We're only being realistic,' he said in his matter-of-fact way, and that was that.

So the church budget was incredibly tight and Peter and I laughed when we saw the Church newspapers extolling the virtues of a parish administrator – it was the only way to cope with the idea.

'What wouldn't I give?' he said wistfully one day. 'Imagine being free to pastor, counsel, visit, do the job I'm paid to do, I long to do, instead of moving chairs, laying out hymn books and . . . and this lot.' He waved at the mounds of letters and papers, littered all over his desk, correspondence and lists of telephone calls about broken boilers, damp rot and repairs to vandalised property.

'And somewhere beneath that lot is my sermon

113

preparation,' he groaned. 'There seems no justice. We, in a church most needing administrative help, are least able to afford it!'

The idea of an administrator was a beautiful dream, and that was all it was. So was more secretarial help. Peter was forced to admit it every time he trailed five miles into the diocesan centre for a few handouts because we had no photocopier of our own.

Early in November the PCC met to discuss our financial difficulties and the approaching annual Gift Day. Edward stopped the usual speculative ramblings on how much we might get by asking them how much they intended to ask God for. Ask God! Everyone looked sheepish. Consulting the Almighty about matters financial, much as a businessman might consult his bank manager, was not what anyone had had in mind at that moment. They turned to Bill. He had the treasurer's knack of bringing matters down to earth. He consulted the books and cleared his throat.

'We usually get about a thousand pounds on a Gift Day,' he said, with an impassive face, which in fact hid the driest wit this side of the Pennines.

There were smiles of agreement.

'And how much do we need?' Edward asked relentlessly.

The smiles melted on the spot.

'Well, what exactly is the debt on the renovation of the parish hall?' Bill consulted the books again and without looking up muttered, 'Six thousand pounds.'

An uneasy silence fell.

It had taken the PCC some time to adjust to Edward's revolutionary attitude to the budget. Church funds, he maintained, were a family affair, not to be requested, raised, or earned outside. For too long the Church had appeared before the world as a charitable institution, always in debt and always on the scrounge so that its real ministry had been totally undermined. It appeared to prefer a man's wallet to his person. With their cardboard barometers out in the porch and their 'Please save our roof' appeals, churches looked like discarded, unwanted relics. Besides, fund-raising could become a clergyman's full-time job and an unpardonable waste of time and emotion.

Edward had only been in Grimlington a few weeks when he suggested that twenty per cent of the church's annual income be given away to missionary work, on the basis that their need was always greater than ours, however it might appear. That would be increased to thirty per cent when the congregation could stand the shock. Then he suggested that the proceeds from the annual church fête, the main fund-raising event of the year, should henceforth be given away to deserving charities. The PCC had been wondering what he would suggest next.

'We haven't got six thousand pounds,' someone whispered loudly, 'because we keep giving it away.'

The laughter died down when Mick began to speak. He said little as a rule, but what he did say was always worth hearing.

'Well,' he faltered slightly as he realised everyone was watching him, waiting for a pronouncement. He did not enjoy the limelight. 'It's like this, right. We've no money. We need six thousand pounds. We can talk all night, but that won't get us it. So let's ask God. He'll show us what to do.'

For a while everyone looked at everyone else, until someone said, 'You mean now? This minute?'

'Yes,' Mick said, 'now.'

So they sat in silence for some time, a heavy, uncertain silence. The minutes ticked slowly by and then gradually, imperceptibly, the atmosphere began to change. Silence gave way to an expectant hush. The room became charged with such a sense of God's presence that they caught their breath. Confusion and scepticism melted away and excitement took their place. Unable to contain himself any longer, Frank said, 'If he's our God and the whole world is his, what's a mere six thousand pounds to him?'

He looked around and this time everyone was nodding enthusiastically.

'If he's our Father 'e'll give us what we need.'

'Right,' said Edward, 'how much do we expect then, three thousand?'

'No,' everyone shouted.

'The lot!' said Frank, speaking for them all. 'Our faith could do with a bit of stretching.'

On the following Sunday Edward climbed into the pulpit, cleared his throat and informed the church in a matter-of-fact kind of way that in preparation for the Gift Day we would be praying for and anticipating six thousand pounds to clear our debts. A ripple ran through the congregation and he started his sermon. But everyone was ready to express their opinion as soon as the last amen of the service was said. An older woman in front of me was indignant.

'The PCC must be mad,' she said. 'This is Grimlington, not flippin' Brighton an' 'Ove. Who's got that kind of money round 'ere?'

Frank was at her side and he put a fatherly arm around her shoulder.

'Yer haven't, love, yer haven't. I haven't. No one has. That's the point. But he has.'

He pointed to heaven. Her eyes followed the direction of his finger and she stood looking up at the ceiling for some time, then went out shaking her head.

I felt a certain sympathy with her as I looked around the congregation, most still in their pews, stunned by the announcement. There was Mary, talking animatedly as she usually did, tossing her head as she spoke. How far could her Family Income Supplement stretch? Jan was kneeling on the pew, her head resting on her arms, chatting to a new family behind her. Like so many others who could not share their faith with their spouses, she would only be able to give a tiny proportion of her housekeeping money. Joe, Linda's husband, was standing at the back with his hands in his pockets, deep in conversation. He was small, with a heart so full of

116

kindness, that it more than compensated for what he lacked in height. He enjoyed a good chat, but his smiles could barely conceal the lines of worry and tension which had suddenly appeared around his mouth and eyes. There were rumours of huge redundancies in the iron and steel industry and the only craft he knew was welding. There was a mortgage to pay. Things were very tight as it was.

Everywhere I looked it was the same story. There was no way our congregation would find six thousand pounds between them. I shook myself, feeling slightly ashamed of my rationalism. After all Peter and I had survived two years at theological college with no fixed income at all, and still had some savings! God alone knew how. But this was different. The people were so vulnerable, so unspoiled in their faith. Was it right to put that simple trust to the test? What if the six thousand pounds did not come?

'Stop it!' I commanded myself as I made the long walk home. 'The truth of the matter is that they are just as excited as Edward and the PCC. It's you, you cynic, who has the problem. You can't believe and have to justify it.'

My mother was waiting for me at the front door, arms folded, looking as smug as a businessman who has just clinched an important deal. It was my parents' first weekend with us. We had converted the tiny dining area of the kitchen into a bedroom by hanging old sheets over the glass partition. It was hardly private, but they had made themselves quite cosy and at home. It amazed me how happy and amenable they were, especially after all the threats never to come and stay with us once we lived in church property.

'So!' my mother said. 'Aren't you going to ask me what I'm so pleased about?'

'Mum, what are you so pleased about?'

'I thought you'd never ask. I've sold your house for you, that's what.'

'What?'

'You'd barely set off when the doorbell rang. It was a woman asking to see round. So you take your chances when you can, and I showed her round, using my best sales technique. And, I think you've got a buyer.'

My father nodded happily. He was looking so frail these days, and he had become very forgetful. I felt uneasy, but pushed it to the back of my mind.

'So you see,' my mother said, following me into the kitchen and obviously waiting to deliver her punchline, 'even the Church of England has to send for the Jews when it wants to sell anything.'

I hardly dared to hope that my mother was right. I was beginning to feel we would never move. The longer we stayed the more disheartened I felt with the temporary nature of our housing. It was not home. I could not relax. I was not an especially private person, but being constantly overlooked began to wear me down. I was becoming quite tense and the children bore the consequences.

'Oh, Mum, I do hope you're right,' I said, then felt ashamed. Who was I to grumble when so many of the church families lived in conditions far worse? If we thought we were cramped, it was nothing compared to Paula, one of the young people. Peter suggested in a sermon one morning that people would find it helpful to begin the day with quiet and an opportunity for prayer and meditation.

'I'd be lucky,' Paula chuckled, digging him in the ribs as she often did on the way out, 'with all my sisters.'

'You share a bedroom?' Peter asked.

'We share a bed, you mean! Never mind, as each one gets married it leaves more room.'

Privacy was a luxury all right. There were Phil and Mary in their tiny, damp two-and-a-half bedroom house with three teenage children and no prospect of a move. I had to admire Mary's simple acceptance of her situation.

'I want to move so badly. I pray for it every day, and

118

for one for you too. But meanwhile we're still here, so this is where we're meant to be and I shall have to be contented with what I've got.'

She was right. There was no point in getting into a state about something outside our control. Even if our house sold there was nothing else in the town to buy. Most of the houses were too small to provide a clergyman with three bedrooms and a study. Anything larger was a rarity and snapped up almost before it was vacated. Since most of the larger sized housing belonged to the older members of the community there was some discussion about how long it was likely to be before a house appeared on the market. It was a wonder there was no queueing at the doors. Still, my mother's news made me feel that a move was a little more imminent. It was as well that I had no glimpse into the future. Patience is not one of my qualities.

Gift day Sunday was a bright, crisp November day. Peter and I walked home from the morning service at a brisk pace in an effort to ward off the icy chill of the wind and our own anxiety.

'One thousand five hundred pounds isn't bad,' Peter said, more to himself than to me.

'No, no, it isn't,' I reassured him, 'especially for us.'

'But it isn't six thousand,' he said, and my heart sank.

We stopped and waited for Joel to catch us up. It was hard work on his little two-wheeler bike.

'That means there has to be four thousand five hundred in the collection tonight.'

'I know,' I said, 'I still remember how to do subtractions.'

Peter drew a long breath. We had even left Edward chewing his nails in the vestry.

It was a long Sunday. We could settle to nothing.

'You go tonight,' Lucy had said to me, 'I'll sit for you. Dad doesn't always appreciate that I could do with some time alone.'

Evening came at last and the church seemed

unusually full. The chatter was louder and more excited than ever. The atmosphere was charged. It reminded me of a first performance or the opening night of a West End play. The service seemed agonisingly long and once over, Edward gave the blessing and dismissed the congregation. No one moved. He looked round, unsure of what was happening or what to do about it.

'Yer don't think we're going home now, do yer?' someone shouted. 'The counting's only just begun.'

Everyone nodded happily and made themselves comfortable. They would wait all night if necessary.

Bill appeared at the office door and asked for more help. It was a good sign and the excitement mounted. Dorothy leant across and whispered to me, 'I hadn't anything else so I put me milk money in.'

'What'll you do when the milkman calls?' Jan asked from the row behind.

'Worry about it then! I'll make it up somehow. Cut back on the electric or summat. The kids have put their pocket money in too. It was their idea. They wanted to.'

'My husband would go bananas if he knew how much I'd given,' Jan sighed. 'He reckons ten pence a week is more than enough for any church. Anyway, he won't know. I'll just have to do without those new boots this winter.'

One or two people started to hum, then sing. Others joined in until there was such a loud noise that I wondered how Bill and his helpers were managing to concentrate. The office door opened and as if it were some magic signal, the singing stopped instantly. Edward emerged and with every eye marking his steps, made his way slowly into the pulpit. His face gave nothing away. There was no trace of a smile and my heart sank. I could hear the blood pounding in my ears and noticed that Dorothy's knuckles were white as she grasped the pew in front. There was a hush such as I had never known in Grimlington before, not a cough, creak or a rustle.

As Edward made his announcement the suspense was almost unbearable.

'With various covenants and promissory notes...'

'Get on with it,' I whispered.

People began to fidget.

'... today's collection amounts to... nine thousand, nine hundred pounds!'

There was a moment's stunned silence as the news sank in. What did he say? Was it good or bad? Then suddenly he shouted, 'Hallelujah!' and the place erupted. People were clapping, cheering, laughing, crying and hugging each other. Edward leapt down from the pulpit, ran to the bell tower and rang the bells. Alicia hobbled up and down the aisle, waving her arms in a dance of victory, like Miriam, the sister of Moses in the Old Testament.

'Eeeeeh, but this is better than being in club on New Year's Eve,' Marjorie shouted as she was lifted off her feet. 'Give up will yer! I'm not as light as I once was. Yer'll do yerself a mischief!'

'I bet the noise can be heard at the other end of town,' I said to Mick, who was suddenly caught in a bear hug, which temporarily winded him.

'Dance, Mick,' the people shouted.

He looked round and blinked.

'Me? I've only just become a hugger!'

No one wanted to go home, so eventually, at about ten o'clock, Marjorie and Brian, the other churchwarden, shouted, 'Time please,' in a good humoured sort of way and ejected everyone out into the cemetery. Some of the young people set off down the street singing loudly.

'If they don't get arrested for being drunk and disorderly tonight, they never will,' I said to Peter. We watched them for a while and laughed.

'Come on,' he said, slipping an arm around my waist and looking up at the stars, 'there's a full moon. May I walk you home?'

121

'Should a clergyman be so forward?' I said archly, looking up at him out of the corner of my eye.

We set off towards the estate. Peter breathed in deeply.

'You know,' he said, 'there are times when this job has its rewards and I wouldn't swop it for any other, not if they made me the richest man in Britain.'

'You're sure about that, are you?' I asked.

'Well, the temptation might just overcome me. That's why it's never likely to come my way.'

We giggled like a pair of teenagers, all the more so when our island home came in view.

The Church First School was buzzing with the news when I dropped Joel off the following morning. A large crowd had gathered for a chat as it usually did, only it was larger than ever.

'Nine hundred pounds in one collection,' Milly said, impressed. 'That is good.'

'No, no, it was nearly £10,000.'

That was more than good. It was unbelievable.

'Where the 'eck did you get that lot from?' Milly asked, suspiciously.

'We've got a rich Father!'

The crowd dispersed reluctantly to the shopping, cleaning and washing with much laughter and shaking of the head.

A few days later Peter came home from staff prayers with the news that in the extraordinary and apparently coincidental way these things happen, Edward had just received an estimate for repairs to a crumbling wall in the parish hall. It was much higher than estimated, almost £4,000.

'So that's why we needed the extra £4,000,' Frank said the following Sunday. 'It's a good job God sees our bills before we do.'

That night the phone rang. It was a friend, a curate in Sussex. Still in the first flush of excitement, Peter poured out our news. I watched as his face slowly fell.

'What's the matter?' I asked as he put the receiver down and shook his head.

'Well, he wasn't exactly impressed. It seems they received over fifty thousand pounds in a night for their new hall.'

'But love,' I said, 'that was Sussex. Let them have their plush new hall, just like that. It doesn't detract from what's happened here.'

Peter smiled. 'You're right. You know it reminds me of something.'

I nodded. The same thought had occurred to me.

'You mean a certain parable about a widow who put two coins into the collection?'

'Yes. Jesus commended her, not the others who had put in more, because those two coins were all she had.'

Chapter 14

Discovering wildlife on or in the human body always comes as a shock, no matter how common the experience may now be. Like a prophet of doom, Betty warned us about the inevitability of head lice, rampant in the schools, but she never alerted us to certain other hazards.

Joel had been complaining of acute itching for some time. Since, taking after his mother, he always had a flair for the dramatic, we ignored his antics, the jumping, screeching and leaping up and down. Until one day, for a bit of peace, I went to apply some zinc and castor oil cream and could not ignore what I saw wriggling defiantly before my very eyes.

Shaken, I called the doctor's surgery immediately, fighting to control the tremor in my voice.

'Worms?' said the receptionist cheerily. 'Oh yes, there's a lot of them about. Can you come and get a prescription straight away?'

Could I? I could not collect it fast enough. I rushed to the chemist, where the assistant impassively handed me a large white paper bag. I had hoped for some glimmer of sympathy, a sign of commiseration, but she was well trained.

Abby got away lightly with a teaspoon of medicine morning and night. Our treatment and Joel's became a rugged endurance test. Six of the largest tablets I had ever seen had to be chewed and swallowed every day for a week. The taste was passable at first – a sort of combination of raspberry sherbet and vitamin C – but the initial flavouring quickly wore off, leaving the sickening bitterness of the drug. The aftertaste was unbearable. I was not sure whether it was me or the worms in my intestines which were being poisoned. But we persevered.

The following week I popped down to our Wednesday afternoon toddler club as usual, and by some strange coincidence Betty and Penny, her fellow health visitor, were there, delivering their annual talk on bugs, lice and nits. As always I underestimated the walk down from the estate and was a little late, so I crept in unobtrusively and squatted down at the back. Betty saw me.

'Come in, love, come in,' she shouted. 'I'm glad you made it. But what a shame, you've just missed the bit that's relevant to you.'

So now I could be sure that by four o'clock the whole of Grimlington would know our guilty secret. The joys of living in a small community! Wherever I went for the rest of the afternoon there were shouts of, 'Unclean! Unclean!' Fortunately there was no longer any real stigma attached to our condition. As Betty and Penny reassured us with graphic descriptions, colourful illustrations and great relish, we would all succumb sometime or another to head lice, body lice, bed bugs, fleas or scabies. We scratched our way through the tea and biscuits.

The fortnightly toddler club was known as 'Mums and Babes', though it always struck me that 'Babes and Mums' would be far more appropriate as there was no doubt to whom the afternoon belonged. Some Wednesdays as many as thirty toddlers – it seemed like many more but they were never still long enough for us to count them – piled into the parish hall, trod on and tumbled over mounds of toys and several intrepid helpers. Screams of pain, pleasure, anguish and frustration split the air and shook the walls. The main hall was packed with bikes, pedal cars and scooters and in pride of place stood Alicia's home-built wooden slide. She explained to me in detail her problems of design, the angles of the hinges, the added safety devices, but it was

125

all a mystery to me. All I saw was the terrified pleasure of an eighteen-month-old, whizzing past us at incredible speed on its nappy-padded bottom, making joyful gurgling sounds all the way down.

The mums themselves huddled in a little room, as far away as possible, vainly trying to follow a speaker, despite the din and constant interruptions. In the few months I had been in Grimlington the programme had been varied and imaginative, tempting the wider community in. There might be anything from flower arranging or dental hygiene, to family planning or delousing your pets, or children! A demonstration of economy cooking provided the opportunity to sample tuna pizza and bean sprout casserole at three o'clock in the afternoon. Bean sprouts had only just arrived in town and were still an object of some suspicion. As were courgettes, and avocados.

'But what do you do with them?'

'I don't know if I fancy them.'

'Are they nice?'

Jan, who with her international experience, was giving the demonstration, shook her worldly head and sighed.

An afternoon of book reviews lacked a certain sparkle. The stories were told from cover to cover and I decided gratefully that there was little point in buying the books. But the effect was soporific. We semi-slumbered, until Cynthia, whose taste is a little more intellectual than the rest of us, reviewed *The Great Divorce* by C. S. Lewis.

'Hell', she said, and we stirred, 'is a depressing, grey town, where it rains all the time and the inhabitants keep falling out with each other and move further and further out into the suburbs.'

There was a moment's pause as we absorbed this information, then it became apparent that we were all thinking the same thought.

'In fact,' she said, grinning suddenly as the thought occurred to her too, 'it's just like Grimlington.'

126

'Let's face it, it's much like anywhere,' Linda said loyally, as the laughter died down.

'Well, I think I'll stick to me Mills and Boon, thanks,' said Pam, a divorcee, struggling to bring up two children alone. She could be relied on to say exactly what she thought. 'I need a bit of romance and light relief in me manless life these days.'

Jan nodded. 'Linda and I like a good "bodice-ripper" every once in a while, don't we Linda?'

We watched Linda with interest, but she refrained from comment. Cynthia sat with her C. S. Lewis on her knee, looking a little crestfallen.

The afternoon which caused the greatest hilarity was a lecture from a member of the St John Ambulance Brigade on First Aid.

'Next time there's a death in the family,' he said, 'your mum, dad, aunty or whatever, go and have a good look and familiarise yourself with a dead body.'

We all swallowed hard. Yorkshire bluntness can go a bit far, even for a Yorkshireman.

The life-size resuscitation model he had brought with him was laid out on the table in front of him in a grotesque pose.

'I,' he said, 'shall now demonstrate the mouth-to-mouth technique and simultaneous cardiac massage. I shall then be asking for volunteers to do the same.'

'That's all right,' Pam called out, leaping to her feet, 'I've kissed far worse than that.'

But none of us anticipated the antiseptic solution he kept sloshing over the dummy's mouth between volunteers. It tasted more like the kiss of death than the kiss of life, and lingered for ages after.

'I can't decide if it spoils or improves the taste of the tea,' Pam said.

At three-thirty the schools finish, and most of the mums disappeared in a flurry of buggies, baby bonnets and mittens, leaving the parish hall looking like a bomb site. Bits of toys and games were strewn from wall to wall

127

and the last few valiant helpers collected them together and played at doll's house, jig-saw puzzles and post-box toy to make sure everything was complete and ready for the playgroup on Friday morning.

It may have seemed like madness, but we longed to be able to meet every week, or even twice a week. Facilities in the town for young mums were hopelessly inadequate. Betty was always telling us how many were lonely and trapped, with nowhere to escape from the screams of a demanding toddler, and no one to talk to when post-natal depression descended in a frightening cloud. Some were desperate. In Manchester, where we had lived when Joel was small, there were council-based toddler clubs in every local park and they saved my sanity. Grimlington relied on self-help and voluntary groups, but it was not an area where they were likely to be very forthcoming. It was an unbelievable opportunity for the church. We enquired about the possibility of starting a toddler club on our estate, but the only location we were offered was the library and we were asked to give assurances that the children would not touch the books. No one was prepared to give assurances of that kind, and even if we were, the real problem was that we did not possess the manpower to run it.

The toddler club was an arm stretched out into the community. It met a need, and it also provided a safe way of observing the church without coming too close. Linda first went when she was suffering from post-natal depression herself. For the sheer relief of getting out of the house it was worth putting up with a bunch of religious weirdos.

'I laughed at them. I called them a load of nuts behind their backs. Well, I knew deep down that for all their funny language and quaint ideas, I was the mug. For them life was really worth living. But I wasn't going to let them get to me. At least, that's what I said.'

But before long her Tuesday nights out with the girls had become an endless heated argument about the existence of God and the merits, or defects, of Christianity, with Linda, to her surprise, vehemently defending the cause.

'She's got it bad,' they said, seeing the single glass of lager untouched on the table and Linda waving her arms around, too absorbed to remember her drink.

'I can't explain it like they do,' she said to her friends, 'so you'll just have to come with me. It's better than being stuck in at home.'

So they came, Katie, Carol, Wendy, Dorothy and Jan, Jan whom Linda met at an ante-natal class, lonely, homesick and still suffering from culture shock. She was married in Canada to a Grimlington lad and he promised he would never want to go home again. But the firm for which he worked closed down and she was pregnant by then. It was a case of follow him or lose him, so she left her family, friends and furniture and followed him. Not to the quaint little Yorkshire cottage, which she saw in her dreams, but to his parents' house, the end terrace next to the gasworks, with a caravan in the back yard. Soon they had their own business and a house, but part of her always yearned for Canada, even after their second child was born. In the town she was always, 'that foreign woman' or 'the Canadian'. She never felt she fitted, not until Linda half dragged her to 'Mums and Babes.'

From there to the church was a natural progression, like caterpillar to butterfly. Alicia saw to it that it was. Dorothy's husband began to come with her; so did Joe, Linda's husband, looking around uncomfortably at first, then growing in confidence when he realised he quite liked the place and that we had taken to him.

But still the toddler club met only once a fortnight. We lacked the necessary leadership. Many of the women went back to work as soon as they possibly could to supplement the family income. To stay at home was a luxury, not a choice. Others were stretched to the limit, involved in countless other activities and caring for relatives or their children. Those at home with pre-school children often felt too diffident about their own abilities.

'I'll help, but I won't run it.'

It was always the same story. It amazed me that so many gifted, creative people could not believe in their own gifts. But false assumptions enforced by years of experience could not be driven away overnight. Self-confidence is a tender plant which grows very slowly.

At first I could not accept that we could do nothing but stand back and watch such potential pass us by. I felt like a child whose bag of lemon crystals has burst. Try as she might, she cannot prevent the precious golden powder from slipping through her fingers. 'We must do something,' I insisted.

Peter smiled. 'Oh? What have you in mind?'

'Pay one of the mums to be a community worker. Then she won't be forced to find work elsewhere.'

'With what?'

My frustration was acute.

'With anything! Many churches are managing to employ an extra worker these days. Just think what we could do with a youth and community worker.'

My imagination began to run riot.

'A playgroup every morning, toddler clubs or a day care centre for the elderly in the afternoons and a youth club in the evenings.'

Peter took a deep breath, then shook his head sadly.

'Carry on dreaming, but we still have to be realistic. This is Grimlington. Even the Gift Day money was swallowed up the moment we got it.'

'Manpower Services?' I tried.

'You have to be unemployed for six months to qualify. So many of our women get temporary work here and there that they're never technically unemployed for long enough. Besides the grant is meant primarily for retraining and I don't know if we could justify it. And what if it were stopped after a year?'

The urgency of the situation was compounded by the

fact that the playgroup which Julie and Karen had started was heavily over-subscribed with a long waiting list. Gone were the days when a social priority area could expect nursery places for three-year-olds and ours was one of only two playgroups in the town. It was only open for one and a half hours two mornings a week and the other catered mostly for children outside the town. But Julie and Karen were teachers and both wanted to go back to work. In the event, teaching jobs were hard to come by and Julie stayed in charge, though there were times that winter when she lived to regret it.

One such occasion was the day Tracy disappeared. Tracy was Linda's youngest, a bright-eyed little monkey and far too canny for a three-year-old. By the time she could walk she had developed an insatiable passion for hide-and-seek. No one noticed her absence from the playgroup that morning, not until Linda, who had just slipped out to the High Street for a bit of shopping, arrived back to collect her.

'Where's our Tracy?' she asked, as all the other mums were buttoning their offspring into their coats.

'She's here somewhere,' Julie said breezily, looking around the hall.

Karen sidled up to her and smiling at Linda, muttered under her breath, 'Julie, I've not seen Tracy for ages.'

'Oh,' Julie said. 'Anyone seen Tracy?' she shouted above the din.

One or two people heard and peered at the children at their knees.

No, Tracy was not one of them. The realisation that this might well be a crisis dawned slowly. But once it did the atmosphere became charged with a sense of barely-controlled panic. They scoured every room, every corner, every space large enough for a child to squeeze into, but there was no sign of Tracy. Linda bore it all with a certain stoicism. She would be rational, sensible, but then someone appeared from the cloakroom with a mackintosh and a small pair of shiny red wellington boots. Her bottom lip trembled and all noble resolve crumpled in that instant.

'My baby,' she sobbed, pointing to the glass doors, 'she's out there, alone, without a coat and nothing on her feet. She'll die of frostbite.'

By then several people had rushed past her and out into the street. Weeping bitterly and too distressed even to bother with a handkerchief to catch the drips, Linda trudged up to the police station. She must have moral support. So pushing one child in a buggy with one arm and carrying another kicking and screaming under the other, the tears pouring down her face too, Vicky went with her.

'Please, God,' they both wailed all along the main road, 'let her be safe.'

Grimlington's entire police force, all four of them, heard them coming, stopped what they were doing and were waiting for them when they arrived.

'Now then, lass,' the sergeant said, 'don't you worry. She'll be all right. She wouldn't talk to strangers, would she?'

'She'd talk to anyone!' Linda howled.

One policeman rushed to his panda car and issued a description. Another leapt onto his bicycle. The search was on in earnest.

Karen alerted the Church School headmistress in case Tracy had gone to find her big sister. Half the staff ran out to their cars to join the hunt. Dorothy informed the vicar through his sitting room window as she crawled on hands and knees through the undergrowth in his garden. His meeting disintegrated in a moment. Peter, who was in the kitchen washing up the coffee cups, came back and found everyone had gone. Sue unrolled the carpet in the parish hall normally reserved for the tiny babies of the Sunday morning creche. She felt a little stupid, but with Tracy, you never could tell. Carol ran on to the High Street and checked every shop. Business came to a standstill. Jan ran half a mile home for a car, but it broke down on the way back and none of the passers-by would stop to give her a push. They were all too busy looking for a missing child.

After an hour or so, overcome by exhaustion and the urge to spend a penny, Julie went back to the parish hall. In a fit of despair she flung open the toilet door, and there before her, knickers round her ankles and singing happily to herself sat one little girl.

'I counted to ten,' she said, 'but yer didn't find me.'

Chapter 15

No one ever discovered how it was that Tracy was not in the toilets, nor anywhere else for that matter, when the parish hall was checked from top to bottom. But it turned out to be an experience which drew the women into a closer camaraderie than ever. Motherhood was a common bond which made them stick together. They all understood about teething problems, nappy rash and sleepless nights. But for Julie, Linda and the others that was not a lasting basis on which to build relationships. They were more determined than ever to share their faith with their friends, but how? That was the problem. Such was their alienation from the church that persuading them to come was a minor miracle. And besides, every now and then, in order to please the older members, the service was more traditional. What if the women said, 'Come to church. It's not like you think, it's changed,' and then it was exactly what their friends imagined. All would be lost. They would never dare ask them again.

So a Guest Service was planned, with all the words and hymns printed on a sheet. That way no one need feel embarrassed that they could not follow the liturgy or find the place. Anyone who found reading a trial was sent into a panic by the mini library of service and song books heaped into his hands as he came in through the doors. And we would not invite an outside speaker. We had Edward and after all there are some advantages in the familiar.

The Drama Group began to rehearse in earnest. This was to be our first performance in the church itself and

134

we felt a little daunted. We chose a piece called *The Long Silence*, not original, but we had not yet branched out into script writing. A group of angry, belligerent people gather on a great plain at the end of time and accuse God of being ignorant of the depths of human suffering. He lives in heaven, untouched by pain and misery. In his absence they put him on trial and condemn him to a terrible death, despised and betrayed by his friends. Then there is a long silence as they realise that God has already served his sentence. It was powerful stuff, at least it would be if we could do it justice.

We congregated in church for a rehearsal one Tuesday night late in November, oblivious of the fact that it was vestry night and that one of the clergy would be available for consultations in the next room.

'Let the legitimacy of his birth be doubted,' Angela shouted from the pulpit.

Next door a couple were asking about the baptism of their baby. Alicia's head appeared round the door wearing an astonished expression.

'Sorry, Alicia, I'll keep my voice down,' Angela apologised.

The door closed and we giggled.

Angela took a breath. 'Let him,' she shouted, then remembering, lowered her voice, 'let him be born ... a man.'

She paused for a moment. 'Couldn't I say, "let him be born a woman"? It would mean that God had a much richer experience of human suffering.'

'Get on with it,' I snapped and to my surprise she was about to obey, when we were interrupted by a loud hammering on the vestry door.

'I think you've locked me in, or out,' Alicia shouted.

I groaned and picked up Peter's vast bunch of church keys.

'Which one is it? Anyone know?'

After fumbling for a few minutes we found it and Alicia appeared, brandishing a flask and half a quilted sleeping bag.

'I always come prepared for the cold,' she beamed. 'This is my leg warmer. Anyone want a cup of coffee?'

'Ooooo yes,' they all said and that was the end of the rehearsal.

'We'll never be ready,' I moaned at Peter, when I told him what had happened.

'Yes, you will,' he said soothingly and I privately lamented the fact that so few really appreciate the trauma of those involved in the creative arts! He was far more concerned about the number of people coming to the vestry to ask for the christening of their baby.

'We're going to have to do something,' he said.

I looked at him quizzically.

'You mean because there's such a superstition attached to it?'

'Yes, but that can be a good and a bad thing. On the one hand it does mean we have contact with families we never normally see. On the other hand...'

'It jars to hear them make vows in public they have no intention of keeping, though they don't realise they're doing it,' I finished for him.

My non-Anglican background made me suspicious of indiscriminate infant baptism and less sympathetic than Peter. If the parents had no faith, it seemed as meaningless a ritual to me as the countless enforced baptisms of Jews during the Crusades and at other inglorious times in the Church's history. It was supposed to make them Christians but it achieved nothing because baptism without faith is meaningless. Grimlington was a God-fearing community on the whole, fear rather than faith being the operative word. Many people were genuinely afraid that if their baby died unbaptised, it would not get into heaven. I could not conceive of that kind of a God and felt sad that they could.

'We've so many christenings now,' Peter continued, 'that quite a number of the congregation are making noises of protest. They feel it's all a bit of a mockery. And you know what it's like round here, they vote with their feet.'

I had noticed, how could anyone not, that attendances at the monthly baptismal services had dropped dramatically. But that was also true of the formal civic services. On Remembrance Sunday earlier in the month, when the Mayor and other town dignitaries had processed down the aisle with their wreaths of poppies, very few regular church members had been there at all. For some reason the brass band did not think it necessary to come into the service either. Instead they sat, crushed together, in the doorway of the parish hall, out of the rain and under the feet of the parents leaving their tinies at the crèche.

The service seemed to lurch from one mishap to the next. Our MP stood to read the lesson and announced four chapters of the Old Testament. The congregation groaned. Lunch would be more than late that week! Then he read the wrong lesson anyway. The two minutes silence lasted at least three or four, as we all waited for the bugler, who was sitting happily in his pew, apparently unaware of the fact that everyone was waiting for the reveille. In the end Edward announced a hymn instead.

Every formal service seemed to be blighted in some way. We were simply not given to slick professionalism. The human factor disrupted every attempt. But no one seemed to mind. There were no angry recriminations. In fact it was a source of some amusement. A man was allowed to make a mistake, wasn't he? Perhaps it was God's way of stopping us becoming smug. Mistakes were forgiven, hypocrisy was not.

That was why the membership resented having their services taken over by those who never normally came. They would have welcomed visitors, but this was different. The guests imposed the form of service and made them feel like the visitors. Their church was no longer recognisable. They felt they were conniving in a downright dishonesty. And the Yorkshire temperament is given neither to subjugation, nor dishonesty.

And then sometimes the guests complained. That hurt. That was rude. No one would come into our homes and criticise the amount of dust or our choice of decor, or our manners, but in they marched in finery fit for a wedding, tutting at our jeans and casual clothes, moaning about the new services and grumbling if we used guitars or tambourines. They felt it to be a personal slight that 'their' church had changed in the twenty years since they were last there. Many of the regular congregation were new members. Such criticism came like a slap across the face. It was hard to swallow. They could not understand that the visitors were probably feeling threatened by an alien environment, which they thought should be familiar and were embarrassed because they could not distinguish between the Old and New Testaments, let alone follow the service. Church members got up and tried to help them find the place. They had struggled once too. For some the Bible was the first book they had read from cover to cover, 'The only thing I've read apart from *Daily Mirror*,' someone said. It was an achievement.

Sometimes, usually at christenings, their help was refused. The baby and only the baby was the centre of attention. Relatives clucked, cooed, chattered and giggled their way through the service. One zealous mother decided to change her baby's nappy during Peter's sermon. Unfortunately she was not too well equipped. With their usual spontaneity and generosity the congregation rose to the occasion, passing handkerchiefs and tissues along the pews. But the baby, aware that it was the centre of some great commotion, yelled with a fury that brought the service to a temporary halt.

'All right, Margaret,' Peter said. He had been trying desperately hard to concentrate and continue whatever the distraction, because it was important that people should not feel unwelcome because of their children. But

138

he knew when to admit defeat.

'We'll just wait for you to finish.'

No one minded a disruption like that. Everyone understood the horror of handing the clergyman a dirty, smelly baby at the great moment. What jarred were comments such as, 'Thank God that's over and we never have to come again,' made loudly on the way out. And just a quarter of an hour earlier everyone had heard vows made to the contrary.

'Well if that's all baptism means,' Rick said, 'I'm not having my two baptised.'

Several other families agreed and a state of mini-mutiny was declared. How else has change of policy come to the Church of England down through the years?

'What do we do?' Edward asked.

'We haven't much choice,' Peter said, and so did the PCC. Edward agreed. He respected Rick and was not a man to feel threatened when his congregation came of age and expressed their own opinion. On the contrary, people were used to doing what the boss told them and it was an exciting moment when church members no longer deferred to the clergy. Besides they were only pushing him towards a crisis he wanted to tackle anyway, but had postponed.

But whatever decision was made, poor Edward would alone bear the consequences. People saw a strong, confident leader, not a sensitive, vulnerable man, already bruised by the struggle to bring change. The constant barrage of angry letters and phone calls accompanying any change upset him. But he refused to give in and took the responsibility for all unpopular decisions, even when they were not his own. It was the same for Anna, who had to stand by and watch. Sometimes she herself was a more accessible target. I wondered how Peter and I would react when our turn came. The job of vicar was not for the man who coveted popularity or the quiet life.

So Edward suggested to the congregation that it was

neither polite, nor charitable to withdraw their presence from formal services. They were missing a golden opportunity to demonstrate the real life and warmth of the church. On the other hand, he conceded that those services should reflect the more normal Sunday worship and not seem such a performance. And he promised that the PCC would look into the whole question of baptism when it met the following Monday.

That Monday night the new 'baptismal policy' was born. It sounded very grand, but simply meant that couples could have an immediate Thanksgiving service for their baby on request, but baptism only after a course of four one-hour sessions. It was not very onerous but the repercussions resounded through the town.

'Do you know what Vicar's done now?'

'No more christenings!'

'Whoever heard of such a thing?'

'Go into someone else's home, not likely!'

'Why do I need a course anyway? I was baptised, so I'm a Christian.'

'No you're not,' Edward said. 'That's why you need the course.'

The great controversy once again filled the letters page in the local *Gazette*. At least the church was providing a story, even if it was built mostly on rumour and hearsay. In a week, custom at the vestry hour was halved. Every couple that came received a visit as before.

One night Peter went out at seven-thirty and was still out at midnight. I began to feel a little uneasy. He said he was going to do a baptismal visit and would be back within the hour. Perhaps I had misunderstood and he had several visits to do, but who could he visit at that hour? At about twelve-thirty I heard the key in the door. The door slammed shut and Peter's footsteps were heavy on the stairs. He came into the room, saw that my eyes were still open in the darkness and snorted loudly. He kicked off his shoes and they landed on the floor with a thud.

'Never,' he growled, taking off his clothes and flinging them into their usual heap in the corner, 'have I met such a belligerent pair in all my life.'

He sat down on the end of the bed.

'They argued about everything. If I'd said the moon was made of blue cheese they'd have insisted it was green. He said he believed in God, like most miners, and that made him a Christian. "No it doesn't," I said. "Anyone can believe in God." Then he said he didn't have to go to church to be a Christian. I agreed, but told him that 'if he was a Christian he would want to.' 'No he wouldn't,' he said, "because they're a snooty lot." "How do you know?" I said. "You haven't been." Even his wife agreed at this point. We've been going round in circles for four hours,' Peter groaned, 'and my head hurts. I hope I don't get any more like that in a hurry.'

Peter snuggled down in bed that night, little guessing that from such inauspicious beginnings, special relationships are sometimes born!

The following day was one of those days when I wondered why I had bothered to get out of bed at all. Joel ripped the knee of his brand new jeans, the vacuum cleaner exploded in a cloud of black smoke and the television played up just as the children's programmes were about to begin. We were calming them down when the phone rang. It was Anna. Edward was running a high temperature.

'Don't worry,' she said, 'it's probably a twenty-four-hour chill and I'm sure he'll be fine for the Guest Service on Sunday.'

Peter felt chilled too.

'I hope he's all right. We can't cancel now.'

But when he was summoned to the bedside the following afternoon, one look at the coughing, shivering form was enough to confirm his worst fears.

'Edward,' he said nervously, 'what about Sunday?'

Edward laughed hoarsely.

'Oh help, but I've never thought that kind of preaching was my gift.'

'Well now's your chance to find out. You'll be given the words.'

Peter nodded and walked home through the cemetery with a new confidence. Hadn't John Wesley said that every Christian should be prepared to preach, pray or die at a moment's notice? He had only been asked to preach. Things could be a great deal worse! Then he bumped into Dorothy.

'Is it true that Edward's ill?' she asked him.

'Bad news travels fast around here.'

'Well, who's going to preach on Sunday night then? I've invited me Aunty Maisie, and she hasn't been for years so it had better be good.'

'I am,' Peter said confidently.

'You!' she said with such incredulity that Peter decided to ring the Bishop the moment he got home to see if he was free.

He wasn't. So the preparation began and for two days the children and I crept around the house like mice. I was glad when Sunday came.

The Drama Group was in a worse state of nerves than Peter before the service began. Stationed at different corners of the church they nibbled their service sheets all through the hymns and readings. Then the great moment came. They leapt to their feet where they stood and railed at God for his heartlessness and cruelty. In a moment it was over. Some people were obviously moved. Others were not.

'When I heard you shouting your heads off like that in God's house, I got down on my knees and asked him to forgive yer,' Nancy said later, as we were drinking coffee in the parish hall. Jan and Linda were crestfallen, then suddenly they saw the funny side and tried to hide their grins behind their coffee cups.

'I suppose it was a bit shocking, us yelling like that from the pews,' Linda said, 'but they'll get used to us.'

I left Peter to come home on his own as so many people were waiting to chat to him. When he finally arrived he was tired out, but very happy.

'So many people said they were helped,' he said with disbelief. 'One woman had tears in her eyes as she thanked me. It never ceases to amaze me when my preaching has that kind of effect.'

'Was it that bad?' I asked.

'Oh you!' He grinned, then the smile died away. 'I've been thinking. A Guest Service is all very well, but it isn't enough, is it? One or two people understand what Christianity's all about for the first time in their lives and we're beside ourselves. But it's a drop in the ocean in this town. Why should we expect people to come to us? There's such a gulf between us. Despite the new music and easy atmosphere, church is alien territory. It's terrifying to walk through those oak doors. We're expecting people to make some great cultural leap.'

I could not help but smile to myself. This was familiar territory to a Jew who had come into the Church, with so many cultural boundaries to cross.

'So where do we go from here?' I asked Peter.

'Jesus never stayed cocooned in the safety of a religious establishment. He would go into the market and the clubs, meet people where they were. They came to find him once the word got round that he had something to offer. We must go out into the community with our playgroup, toddler club and whatever else we can manage to offer. And we work at developing a church that meets the needs of the people here.'

'Joe keeps inviting you to go to his club,' I reminded Peter.

'I'll go, I'll go', he laughed. 'It would do me good. One thing I miss is a large group of colleagues. You have no mates in this job. It's a lonely life. Maybe that's why so many clergymen become eccentric. There's no one to point out their foibles.'

He got up to go to bed, then suddenly turned to me.

'If I do begin to go a bit eccentric, you would tell me, wouldn't you?'

'What do you think? Oh go on with you,' I laughed. 'You've had too much excitement for one day.'

Chapter 16

By the beginning of December the shops were full of fairy lights and cardboard Father Christmases. Every organisation, great or small, had its carol service and expected a clerical presence. We almost drowned in sickly sentimentalism. But several events prevented that Christmas from becoming too glib and saccharine.

Joe received his redundancy papers. He was simply handed a letter one morning which thanked him for his years of service, but in the light of the present economic climate . . . And that was that.

'Thank you and goodbye,' he said. 'After all this time. No job, no future, no nothing, all there in those few typed words.'

He folded the piece of paper and tossed it onto the table. 'Funny, isn't it? That's all it takes to get rid of a man, that tiny bit of paper.'

Reluctantly he picked the piece of paper up, unfolded it and read it again, as if by magic the words might have changed in the last few seconds.

But they were exactly the same and he shook his head. 'Don't mind me, I'm just being morbid. We've enough redundancy pay to see us until after Christmas, if we're careful, and on Monday I'll go up to the job centre. I'll soon be fixed up, you'll see.'

On Monday morning Joe leapt out of bed and went down to the Social Security offices to sign on.

'I was feeling cheerful and hopeful, but they soon knock that out of yer. I mean, couldn't they treat yer like a human being? I just seemed to become a number. No one had a smile or a hello or a kind word. They made me feel it was all my fault and I was a nuisance. I suppose they were just doing their job, and being efficient like. But that was to file me away as quickly as possible! It's bad enough being in a place like that. It's daft. You know everyone else is in the same boat, but yer say to yerself, "What am I doing in a place like this? I don't belong 'ere. What must they all think of me?" It does terrible things to yer pride. Going to Social Security's like begging. Yer asking for a hand-out.'

'You've earned it, Joe,' I said. 'You've been paying your taxes and National Insurance for long enough.'

'Ay, but yer don't see it like that. The' give yer all these papers to fill in, hundreds of 'em and some of the questions are right personal. I felt like a convict. I don't see any man has the right to know those things about me. I felt ashamed. If it wasn't that I needed money for mortgage I'd 'ave walked out.'

Joe began to pace the room. His Marx Brothers moustache seemed to droop more than ever now that his smile was gone. He was a gentle, sensitive man and I felt angry at what the experience had done to him.

'And then,' he said, shaking his head at what was totally beyond his comprehension, 'the questions are all in fancy language and they treat yer like an idiot if yer can't understand them. They pass yer from counter to counter like some kind of garden gnome on a conveyor belt.

'And what about a job?' I asked him.

He stopped pacing, smiled at me sadly and shrugged.

'Not much hope. But I'll not give up. I'll keep looking. Maybe it'll be better after Christmas when things get back to normal.'

Linda brought two mugs of hot tea into the sitting room and sat down.

'It's funny how yer world can be turned upside down overnight,' she said. 'Here I am wearing exactly the same clothes as I wore two days ago and I suddenly feel shabby. Maybe it's because I'm frightened there'll be no more. I feel as if everyone is staring at me as I walk up town, and whispering, "See her, poor soul, her husband's unemployed." I know they're not, but it's just how I feel.'

'That kitchen yer've been wanting, love, it'll have to wait,' Joe said apologetically.

Linda laughed, but it was forced. 'Oh that, it can wait.'

'It can't, yer know it can't. There's no room to turn round in there. But I'll make it up to yer one day, yer know I will.'

She nodded at him and blinked back the tears.

'I dreamed of central heating too. This place is freezing. Ah well,' she said and tossed her head. 'For the moment the State seems to own us. Joe thought about making wrought iron gates for some of our friends, but they'll only deduct whatever he makes from his unemployment pay. From now on we're trapped, our income's fixed. The State doesn't allow for any hard-earned extras or life's little treats.'

The tears welled up again and she bit her bottom lip.

'Well,' she said, shaking herself, 'we've a lot to be thankful for. We've our kids, we're fit and healthy, and God'll take care of us. Though I sometimes wonder what he's up to!'

So did the rest of the church that Christmas, for a situation developed which was to stretch our faith to its very limits. The first I learned that anything was wrong was the beginning of November when we went to lunch at Mick and Karen's. They were both unusually tense and were struggling to make polite conversation. It was unlike them.

'Do you mind if we get dinner over as quickly as possible?' Karen asked, laying the cutlery on the table in a jumble and disappearing back into the kitchen.

I followed her out.

'It's just that we have to go up to the vicarage to see Edward and Alicia. It's about Paul, my sister's little boy. You've seen him at church, haven't you? The Sunday School teachers know him very well. He's a character! He's never really been well. Janice took him to the doctor's on Friday and the doctor could feel a lump just above the groin. He's going into hospital tomorrow for tests.'

We sat in silence while Karen was busy in the kitchen. There was nothing to say. I wondered how I would be feeling if it were our Joel. Mick sat in the armchair playing with their little boy in a distracted kind of way. Karen brought in the roast meat. There were no serving mats and the table was still only half set.

'I'm sorry,' Karen said, 'I don't know where I am today.'

We ate half-heartedly. No one had any appetite.

For ten days there was no news, just tests and more tests. Every morning, after the mums had dropped their children at school they congregated in the church to pray. Anyone working a late shift joined them. It was a large group. Little Paul was an appealing child with an elfin quality and was greatly loved.

Then suddenly one day he was rushed to Leeds and a malignant tumour the size of a large grapefruit was removed from his liver. For some days it was touch and go whether he would live or not. He had been weak for so long that he had little fight left. If he lived there was no certainty that the cancer would not form elsewhere.

The group at church went on praying, longing for God to heal little Paul and let him grow up to laugh and play like other children. We were novices in the whole area of prayer for healing. We knew God could do miracles and heal people for whom the doctors held out no hope. But sometimes he did not. How could we know in this instance which it was to be? We wanted Paul to get well so badly that it was impossible to be objective.

Mick and Karen sought out all the help they could get and with Edward's support, contacted a community of Sisters, known to have experienced healing in many amazing ways. One of the Sisters was absolutely convinced that Paul was going to be healed and we all took fresh confidence from her faith. We were certain. It seemed an affront now to suggest there might be any alternative. And then Paul began to get better. It was slow at first, then with every new day there was a fresh marvel. He spoke. He sat up. He ate fish and chips. He played with his toys, got out of bed, walked, ran and was stronger than he had ever been. He would be home for Christmas.

Amidst the many other frantic activities which increased with every successive day as Christmas drew nearer, the headmistresses of the town organised a 'Search for the baby'. Just as the shepherds and wise men had followed the star, one class from every primary school would follow the clues left all around the town, until they found the baby Jesus. Their final destination was not to be a stable, but Grimlington Parish Church, a much grander substitute.

The headmistresses met there the night before the event to finalise the plans. For six headmistresses to agree requires an exceptional amount of goodwill, but after lengthy debate about where Joseph would stand and the shepherds would kneel and what the wise men would do, the Christmas spirit finally prevailed.

'Oh yes, dear,' one of them said, turning to me at last, 'what we want you to do is announce all our honoured guests, a bit like a TV presenter.'

'Like Jan Leeming?' I asked hopefully.

'Well, you'll have to wear the dress of the time.'

'They didn't have TVs in those days,' I pointed out. 'I'd rather wear modern dress.'

'Couldn't you dress up as a Jew?' another headmistress suggested, then suddenly realised what she had said. 'Oh, I'm sorry, I didn't mean...'

'That's all right,' Miss Murdoch, the headmistress of the Church School said, with a wink at me, 'she'll just be herself.'

It was all a huge success. By the time the children arrived at the church door they were breathless with excitement. When they saw Mary holding a real baby they found they had enough wind left to make such a din that I could barely make myself heard. The public address system was not yet ready for use. Mick had been working away, night after night in his spare time, but each piece of equipment was so expensive. He kept asking the PCC for money, but we suspected that in the end he resorted to his own pocket and had to wait until he could afford the next precious part.

So I shouted until I was hoarse. 'Look, children, see who's coming, special visitors from the far corners of Grimlington, all bearing gifts for the baby. Here are the shepherds!'

I suppressed a smile as Peter walked past me, wearing our best bath towels. He hated dressing up and at six foot three was hardly inconspicuous. Someone had persuaded the vicar he would look more authentic if he rolled up his trousers under his tunic. I was distracted from the sight by the arrival of Betty and Penny.

'And here are our health visitors, bringing tins of powdered milk and strained apple and packets of liver and bacon. Just what a baby needs to help it grow big and strong.'

Betty winked at me as she passed. I suddenly remembered her telling me that she and Penny made up the packets of baby food and ate them for lunch when they had nothing else. They could have been giving away their own dinner!

'Who are you, the librarian?' I whispered to a striking-looking gentleman at my elbow, who was carefully balancing a large pile of books.

'The Director of Education,' he said curtly.

'The Director of Education,' I announced hastily.

'The Mayor and Mayoress!'

The photographer from the *Gazette* started flashing his camera.

'Get those legs,' Betty shouted at him, pointing at the vicar, 'for posterity.'

He did and for a while pandemonium reigned. Only

the baby was quiet and dozed happily, oblivious of all the fuss. The teachers ushered their children out.

'Phew!' the headmistresses sighed. 'Thank goodness that's over. The children seemed to enjoy it.'

'It was certainly unforgettable,' I agreed.

Then, as I thought about it, it seemed to me that it had made its point quite forcibly. Every member of the community had an offering to bring to the Christ-child. Gold, frankincense and myrrh were fairly meaningless, but books, baby food and toys the children understood. No, they would not forget it.

But whether I would have a chance to catch my breath and remember was another matter. The parties began. Alicia was as excited as any child.

'Come on, Edward, do get a move on,' she said, dragging him out of a staff meeting. 'We'll be late for Father Christmas at the nursery.'

'But we haven't finished planning the services yet.'

'Yes, but they're expecting us. They'll be disappointed if the clergy aren't there.'

'Since when did Father Christmas need a chaplain?' Edward asked wearily, but too late. Alicia was out of the door and half-way across the road.

Frank gave three annual performances as Father Christmas for the Church School.

'I always take time off for the Lord's work,' he said.

And Alicia watched all three and the children's faces with unconcealed delight. I must admit it was one of the most convincing performances I had ever seen. No wonder Frank's son was an actor. The talent was inherited. With a tinge of regret I had to keep reminding myself that I did not believe in Father Christmas any more. Alicia obviously did not bother and I envied her capacity for child-like enjoyment.

'Hello, children. Did you see them hailstones? Rudolph thought it was icing sugar and tried to eat them.'

The children loved it. He invited them out to tell their

favourite jokes, gave them their presents and had a special comment for each child.

'Now then, children, it's a funny thing. On our birthday we get presents. And on Jesus' birthday we still get the presents. Well, that's just like him. I know that because he's a special friend of mine. So then, children, teachers, and mums and dads, you won't forget whose birthday it is and why he came, will you? Now then, Miss Murdoch says you lead her a bit of a dance. So I'm going to lead her in one now. Music please!'

And out they danced.

Then there was the staff tea and after that, on a stomach full of trifle, chocolate gâteau and wine, carol singing by torchlight round the parish. We visited the elderly and shut-in and everywhere it was the same, nightclothes and supper had been laid out ready by their children. Some were still there, caring for their parents, washing them, tucking them up in bed and seeing they were locked up for the night. And woe betide us if all was locked up. No amount of carolling on our part would move the bolts. We sang three verses of 'Angels from the realms of glory', outside one house and although there was a light on and a shadow behind the curtains, no one came to the door. The TV had won. Undaunted, Betty had an idea. She nipped into the call box opposite and we heard her shouting down the phone, 'It's us, love, from the parish. We've just sung yer three verses of a carol. Do us a favour and come to the window for the fourth verse.'

The curtains were pulled back and a beaming face appeared. Then, our fingers numb and our voices cracked, it was back to the parish hall for hot soup and mince pies.

That was a quiet evening compared to the Christmas girls' night out. We met at the brand new pub, built just off the motorway at the bottom of the town. It was called, euphemistically, 'The Hamlet', because it stood where once there had been a bustling community of tiny, cobbled streets, which had sprouted around one of the pits. The pit closed. The old 'hamlet', all buckled and cracked with subsidence, all but demolished itself. A whole way of life vanished and in its place was built a large, lavish red-brick palace, with a glass sun lounge, filled with palms and cheeseplants, offering a scenic view of the main road into town!

For Linda, Jan, Dorothy and Carol this night out, or 'fuddle' as they called it, was a long-standing tradition. Everyone brought a small present, numbered it and put it in the centre of the table. Then we each drew a number out of a glass and took the corresponding present. Mine was a piece of rock with plastic eyes in it.

'I thought someone would like it,' Jan said.

Linda shrieked with laughter and held up a frilly suspender belt and a pair of black fishnet stockings.

'Good grief,' she said, her eyes as wide as beermats, 'what will Joe make of these?'

'Cheer 'im up no end, I shouldn't wonder,' Dorothy said.

As we sat among the palms, watching the lorries trundle past, giggling like a gang of teenagers, the responsibilities of womanhood and the tribulations of motherhood were temporarily suspended. All girls together, we could say anything. We were young again, joyous and carefree. It was a marvellous, heady experience. And we went on shouting and giggling all the way home.

Peter was snoring gently as I snuggled down in bed in the small hours of the morning.

'Oh by the way,' I whispered to the Almighty under my breath, 'wherever you take us in the future, let it be somewhere where the people can laugh. I couldn't bear it otherwise.'

Christmas coincided that year, as it often does, with the Jewish feast of Chanukah, the Feast of the Dedication of the Temple. The night before Christmas Eve I took down our brass menorah and gave it its annual polish.

When the children gathered around the table we told them the story of how Solomon had built a great and wonderful Temple in Jerusalem. Then in 169 BC the Syrians desecrated it by offering pigs upon the altar. But Judas, the Maccabee, drove them out and they rededicated the Temple to God. There was only enough sacred oil left to burn the eternal light of the presence for one day. But a miracle happened. It lasted eight days, until more could be made.

Joel watched me wide-eyed as I lit the small 'servant' candle at the front of the menorah and used it to light one other candle. Tomorrow two would burn, the next night three, and so on until all nine were ablaze, and it stood on the window-sill, letting its light shine out into the darkness, reminding us of a very special miracle.

Long after Joel had opened his Advent calendar and disappeared munching his chocolate money, I sat on, gazing at the single flame and enjoying its symbolism. The similarities between Chanukah and Christmas became more significant to me every year. Christ was God's Temple who came into the world, and would never be destroyed. He came as a Servant. He came as light too. His coming at all was the greatest miracle of all time.

All the celebration and the laughter were fun. But celebration without meaning was artificial, a cheap cracker full of promise, but empty after the bang. For many, Christmas was like that, all noise and festivity and a bitter disappointment. And seeing it, Christians were often restrained. Christmas was too secular. It was an embarrassment. But when celebration and worship were intertwined, then man and God could enjoy each other to their fullest capacity. It was a delicate balance, but for me, Grimlington came very close to getting it right.

The Christmas Eve Christingle service had a special magic.

'Who's Chris Tingle?' people asked.

They knew Fred Tingle, the local plumber.

'What's a Christmas tingle?'

We explained that the Christingle was an orange, symbolising the world, the candle being Christ, the light of the world and the red ribbon, encircling the orange, Christ's blood, shed for the world.

'Oh!' they said uncertainly, but still they came in their hundreds. We packed the people into every available space until it seemed that the church walls might bend. Each child received a Christingle and at last the great moment came when, beginning with one candle at the front, the light would be passed down the church. Some child picked that moment to be violently sick and the proceedings were disrupted by mops, buckets and the smell of disinfectant.

The little boy in the pew in front of me was wracked by spasms of coughing. Every time he coughed, out went his candle. How this happened was a total mystery to him. He kept looking round to see if he could catch the villain who had the effrontery to blow out his candle when he wasn't looking.

At last every candle was alight and out went the church lights. A hush descended. I looked around at the extraordinary sight of hundreds of tiny flames, flickering in the darkened building, casting shadows across the ancient stonework. The children sang 'Away in a manger' and there was wonder on their faces as they glowed in the candlelight. A lump rose up in my throat.

'The light shines in the darkness and the darkness cannot overcome it.'

I thought of Joe and I thought of little Paul and his parents. It was the year of the bomb in Harrods in London. And I looked again at the single flame in my orange, bright, alive and inextinguishable. None of us knew what was hidden in the year ahead. But one thing was clear. Because of Christmas, Emmanuel was with us and we would not have to face it alone.

Chapter 17

The snow came, covering trees, rooftops and the distant slag heaps with a delicate, crystal-white coating. On a picture postcard Grimlington might almost have passed for the Yorkshire Dales, but for the lack of trees. I walked to church in the strange, eerie morning silence which always accompanies the first snow. There was no sound except my own breathing and the gentle crunch-crunching under my feet. It seemed as if the whole town were in hibernation.

Then gradually, as I crossed the cemetery, the sounds of children's voices floated through the gravestones, distant and distorted. By the time I reached the church all solitude and quiet meditation was rudely driven away by a hail of snowballs. Along with everyone else I ducked and ran for safety, and we stood in the porch shaking the snow off our coats and stamping our feet.

Inside all was warm and cosy. Seeing the first snow-flakes the night before, Peter had had the presence of mind to alter the clock so that the heating came on early. He thought of things like that.

'People are miserable if they're cold,' he said. 'It kills the spirit of worship. They don't feel welcome. They stay huddled in their overcoats, unable to relax and meet each other.'

By some strange irony, his sermon that morning was about manna, that strange powdery white substance which the Israelites found covering the ground when they woke up one morning. They collected it up into jars. I wondered whether it ever occurred to them to roll

155

it into balls and throw it at each other... probably, knowing my ancestors!

As soon as the service was over, the congregation rushed out into the cemetery, drew up battle lines, and the fight continued. Alicia had a lethal right-hand volley. I surrendered and we put the children on the sledge and towed them home for dinner. Not before one old lady had complained bitterly that the pathway had not been cleared.

'Dreadful, isn't it?' Peter said with a twinkle in his eye, 'I quite agree.'

She nodded, then stopped, realising that her veiled criticism was having no effect.

'Sorry, but in Grimlington at least, the days of the verger are over,' Peter said to me on the way home. 'I've done two services this morning and clearing paths will have to wait.'

On Monday Peter again had cause to lament the passing of the verger era. The snow had fallen all night. The wind caught it up and swirled it round and round the cemetery, then blew it in mounds up against the church's old oak doors. But Peter was oblivious of the fact as he prepared for a lunchtime funeral. He let himself in through the vestry door at the side, checked the heating dial, robed, laid out hymn and service books and unlocked the front doors from inside. He was all ready, or so he thought. It was only when he was leading the procession up the church path that he noticed the one foot drift piled up in the porch. In normal circumstances it would have been manageable. In a cassock and surplice and for six pall-bearers it was an undignified climb.

Just as the service was over, Alicia arrived with an ingenious home-made plough. She dragged it along the ground and to the astonished and admiring gawps of a group of onlookers, soon cleared a path right round the church. Unfortunately, by the time the schools came out, the temperature had dropped below freezing and it became an ice rink. Grannies, mums, teenagers and tinies staggered along or clung to each other in a desperate attempt to stay upright, some laughing helplessly as they found themselves prostrate on the ground.

Within another day the banks of snow on either side of the pathways, the thick white carpet on roof and garden, were covered in tiny black speckles. Wherever it was trodden underfoot, the snow had turned grey. What soot and litter failed to spoil, the dogs completed. And soon any illusion of living in the Dales was gone.

One afternoon in that freezing January week, I trudged through slush and ice to collect Joel from school. Linda was there, waiting for Kathy as usual, but her face was very pale and her eyes were blotchy as if she might have been crying. I said nothing. Neither did Jan, who was waiting for her little girl. We just stood there, wondering what to do.

Suddenly, without looking at either of us, Linda said, 'I've a lump.'

I felt as if someone had dropped a piece of ice down my back. No need to ask where the lump was. Every woman lives with the same dread.

'I thought it was nothing,' Linda said, trying to force a smile, 'so I didn't tell anyone. I was sure the doctor would tell me not to be so silly and send me away. But he didn't. When I went this morning he just said I had to see a specialist, straight away. He was so abrupt it frightened me. He wouldn't say any more.'

'You know that the vast majority of breast lumps aren't cancer?' I said to her.

She nodded, without expression, probably thinking as I was, that there was still a chance she was one of the minority.

'You know, it's funny,' she said, staring at the ground, the tears welling up into her eyes, 'I was just thinking that God was good, a real father. Since Joe was made redundant we haven't missed out at all. We've been

157

given food and all we've needed just at the right moment. Christmas was great. We even managed to buy presents for the kids.'

She stopped for a moment, fighting to regain control. It was hard to talk in such a public place.

'But this! This is far worse. It's the not knowing that is so awful. I keep saying "Why?" over and over again. Don't get me wrong, I'm not afraid to die. It's the kids,' she said, looking up as the school doors opened and out poured a tangled mass of arms, legs, boots, mittens, hats and scarves. 'They're still so little. They need me. And I do so want to see them grow up.'

I forced back the glib and easy words which came so quickly to my lips. 'Don't be so premature. Stop talking about death.' Like the advice of Job's comforters, they would have been a rejection of her honesty and a reflection of my inability to cope. She was not being morbid. I loved Grimlington people for saying what they felt, and not what they thought they ought to say or what others wanted to hear. It was better for Linda to express her fears and face them, than for us all to connive at sweeping them under the carpet. Out of sight was not out of mind in this case.

So Jan and I were lost for words. There was nothing to say. We simply stayed close, to let her know that she was not going to face this ordeal alone.

At home that evening I tried to keep myself busy and fill my mind with anything but Linda's lump, but it would not go away! I resisted the urge to check myself at first, then gave up. What must Linda be feeling?

'Haven't they got enough on their plates?' I shouted at the ceiling, but my question hung round in the air, unanswered.

She went to see the specialist the following week. She waited several hours, naked from the waist up, and was shivering by the time he came into her cubicle.

'If this is just an ordinary cyst,' he said to her, wielding a syringe, 'I should be able to draw off some fluid.'

It was painful, but none came, which was worse.

'I'll have to have you in, I'm afraid,' he said, 'and as soon as possible. And I think you would be well advised to sign a consent form agreeing to a total mastectomy if it turns out to be necessary.' He left quickly with a friendly smile and she found herself alone, feeling dazed and slightly sick.

'It's all so easy for a man,' Linda said to us later. 'It doesn't seem to mean anything to him. Well, to be honest with you, apart from feeding babies, they were never much use to me before either. Then someone said to me, "It doesn't matter, you can just have them lopped off," like pruning branches of a tree. And I realised how much I wanted to keep them. It's an amputation and it's gruesome. I'm only twenty-eight. I don't want to be half a woman.'

She shook her head. 'Poor Joe, as if he hasn't enough worry.'

Joe had applied for dozens of jobs. It was always the same. He set off in such high spirits, then slouched home and sank into his armchair when he received yet another rejection. It was a terrible blow to his self-esteem.

'We'll let yer know,' he mimicked, then groaned. 'If I hear that again I'll go mad. Why don't they just say, "On yer bike, lad." I'm always too young, too old, underqualified, overskilled. What do they want? Yer can't win.'

When a job was advertised for a caretaker-cleaner at the Post Office, Joe was among the first to apply.

'I've always wanted to work with people,' he said and I understood. He did love people. No favour was too much trouble. But there were twelve other applicants for the job and Joe heard nothing more.

One night, while Linda was still waiting to be admitted to hospital, my mother rang in some distress. My father appeared to have had a kind of stroke.

'I'm frantic with worry. He can't walk, he's totally disorientated, he talks such nonsense and he seems to be incontinent. I can't bear to see him like this.'

When Peter and I got to Newcastle he was already in

159

hospital, frail, but shuffling about. What was un-bearable was his apparent inability to interpret what he saw, so that he thought my white anorak, rolled into a bundle, was a baby.

'Will things get any better?' I asked my mother.

She shook her head. 'Apparently not. The scan shows a great deal of brain damage. Things can only get worse.'

I felt numb as we travelled home. It was like a recurrent nightmare I had had as a child. People that I loved the most had changed so much that I no longer recognised them. How was it possible that this fine and dignified man should come to this, the one thing he had dreaded beyond all others.

'I never want to be a burden to you,' he had always said. But he wasn't a burden, just a terrible, terrible ache. It seemed so cruel. Why couldn't we have our allotted years in full command of our faculties? The more I thought about it the more I saw how helpless and insignificant human beings were. In one way it made me angry, in another it was almost a comforting thought. I could not accept that God was a callous ogre, destroying what he made. He had reversed the cruel destiny of man, not condemned him to it. To decay might be an inescapable part of our lot. But it was progress to a new beginning, not an end in itself.

Linda was admitted into hospital, smiling and at peace, but feeling 'a bit like a jelly'. I could not apply myself to anything the day of the operation, but wandered round the house with the vacuum cleaner in a half-hearted kind of way, muttering semi-prayers. I was doubly anxious because Peter had received news that little Paul was very unwell again.

At four o'clock I could bear the suspense no longer and rang the hospital. Of course all the efficient nurse would tell me was, 'Mrs Jameson is back from surgery and sleeping.'

I rang Joe.

'That's all they'll tell me,' he fumed, 'until I go in at seven for visiting.'

'Ring me as soon as you know anything.'

'I will, love, I promise.'

It was nearly ten when he rang, but he was elated.

'She's OK,' he shouted, trying to control the tremor in his voice. 'It's not . . . I mean she's still got her . . . Oh, yer know what I mean. I was beginning to think nothing was ever going to go right.'

'Thank God!' I said to him.

'I am. I am.'

A few days later Linda walked into Drama. I stared at her as if I had seen an apparition.

'Are you all right?'

She grinned.

'A bit washed out, but fine basically. Anyone want to see? It's very pretty, every colour of the rainbow. They didn't use stitches. They used a laser instead.'

She opened her cardigan and we all gawped at the top of her chest. As she had said, it was a colourful sight. We ooohed and aaaahed appropriately, while Linda smiled and blushed.

'Wait while I tell yer what happened.'

We listened with the ghoulish fascination which hospital stories always seem to create. Besides, Linda was a wonderful storyteller.

'I came round from the anaesthetic,' she said in a hushed voice, 'and slowly remembered what I was in for. I groped around frantically, but with all the bandages it was hard to tell what was what. When I realised I was all there, I wanted to cheer. But then I found something else lying on my chest. It was an open hymn book. A nurse came over and she told me I was fine. There was no cancer. "What's this for?" I asked, picking up the hymn book. "Oh, we thought you might be needing it. You've been serenading the entire ward with your hymn-singing for the last hour. It's been better than *Songs of Praise*." Well, did I feel stupid! But the

161

nurse said, "I shouldn't feel embarrassed if I were you. You should hear what some people shout as they come round from an anaesthetic. I'd like to think my subconscious was as pure and holy as yours."'

'When I got out of bed a while later and staggered down the ward to the toilet, everyone was shouting, "Hallelujah, Linda!" "Praise the Lord, Linda." I nearly died! I laughed so much I almost burst the wound.'

'Well,' I said to her, 'I kind of hoped you'd be a comfort to others, but that's ridiculous.'

We never did do any drama that evening. Angela and Frances had come prepared for the occasion. I was about to begin a rehearsal, when they interrupted the proceedings.

'Do you mind if I take over?' Angela asked.

'Be my guest,' I said, 'I'm getting used to it!'

'It's just that we've planned a little something, haven't we, Frances?'

She gave her sister a knowing wink, then delved into her bag and pulled out a bottle of wine. Frances opened hers carefully and took out a chocolate cream gateau, paper plates and cups and plastic forks and spoons. We were stunned into silence for once and just gawped as Angela poured the wine and Frances shared out the cake. She had even remembered serviettes.

'Well,' Angela said, 'shouldn't we give thanks?'

So we did, joining hands.

'Thanks for Linda, for looking after her and keeping every bit intact. And thanks for the cake and wine.'

'Cheers!' we all said, raising our glasses. 'Here's to you, and her!'

Chapter 18

Although February is the shortest month in the year, it always seems the longest. Each grey and bitter day drags on from the next as if winter were interminable and spring will never come. There was a weariness about the town. No buds had yet appeared on the few trees to give a semblance of life to their tired-looking spindly branches. The first crocuses had sadly surrendered to the mounds of black mess the snow and slush had left behind. A selection of unwelcome viruses left people looking wan and drained. They trudged up the High Street, heads bent, with heavy step.

But it was not the time of year which cowed their spirits and thrust them into such a heavy gloom. Winter came and went every year and life continued. But this winter the news was ominous. The Coal Board announced more and more pit closures. The talk was of mass redundancies, unemployment and men of thirty who would never work again. A strike began to look inevitable and everyone knew what that meant. The women faced it with dread.

Every morning they clustered together on the High Street corners or in the supermarket.

'I knew it would come to this, I knew it. All over again! We nearly starved the last time. How the hell will we manage?'

'What else can we do? If they're made redundant it'll be as bad. Our Keith was hoping to start when 'e finished school in summer, but there's no 'ope now. What's 'e goin' to do?'

'They say there's plenty work in Selby.'

'Ay, but for 'ow long? It'll be just like last time. They moved me Uncle Wilf not two year since and now they're shutting that pit too.'

'Well I'll not go to Selby. I've all me family 'ere. Better starve together than survive apart.'

'But what good will a strike do, I ask yer? Since when do they ever listen to likes of us?'

'They don't. But we'll stand by us men, like we always do.'

A strike would affect the entire community, and so the church experienced its share of anxiety too. The congregation was made up of people who depended on the mines in some way or another for their livelihood. They employed electricians, engineers, carpenters, and plumbers. Every shop, every small business needed the custom the pits provided.

But at that time the major anxiety was not the strike, although it was there at the back of everyone's mind, it was the fact that little Paul no longer seemed to be improving. He had appeared at family services, bright-eyed and alive again, but now he was listless and constantly complaining of pains in his legs. When he drew pictures of himself, he drew a little boy without legs. Not given to hiding their emotions, the congregation expressed their heartache and bewilderment quite openly. Some broke down and wept during the time of intercession.

Mick and Karen took him and his parents to see the Sister at her community again. She anointed him with oil and reassured them that she was as convinced as ever that Paul would soon be strong and well.

Many church members felt the same. Others were not so sure. It created a problem for the clergy.

'How do we counsel everyone?' Peter said one evening, his head in his hands, resting his elbows on the kitchen table. He had been sitting there for quite some time after he finished his evening meal. 'More than anything I want to believe that Paul will get better, but there's a constant niggle of doubt which won't go away.

So many people have pictures in their minds of Paul at school, or Paul running and playing, that I don't know what to think. If we try and prepare everyone for his death, we're accused of having no faith. But once our emotions are involved like this, how can we distinguish God's will from our own wishful thinking? I feel utterly at a loss.'

'Do we need to know the future?' I asked Peter.

He looked at me blankly.

'Isn't that God's prerogative and not ours? I thought faith was to do with not knowing, yet still trusting.'

He nodded.

'I suppose all we can do is wait, and trust. But I have the awful feeling that we're shirking our real responsibility.'

There seemed to be an increasing number of evenings when Peter felt angry or helpless. Any illusions I had had that he would slip into the life of a clergyman with the rapture of someone who finds the job he has seen in his dreams, were rudely shattered. He often felt controlled, even driven by his work. It was endless. It was a yawning pit and no matter how much he poured in, it never began to fill up. He could never sit down at the end of the day and say, 'I've finished.' There were always mounds of papers lying on his desk – unfinished administrative business, the half-written sermon, notes about repairs left unmended, visits not made, counselling postponed and the relentless forward planning, that needed time and creative thinking. And he was still only the curate. Edward never treated him as the 'junior boy', yet he was aware that the vast majority of emergencies never came his way. Nevertheless, all his best plans to change the basic work patterns of the clergy and have reasonable time off began to disintegrate under the pressure. And at the end of the day there was still nothing to show for his labour, no sense of completion or satisfaction.

'I take no exercise,' he growled, pacing the house. 'I have no leisure activities. Soon I'll have no conversation either. I'll be boring. How did I get like this? I promised I'd take an evening or an afternoon off a day, like most civilised human beings.'

'I don't see how the clergy dare work a six-day week anyway in a time of unemployment,' I said, trying to be provocative, which was not altogether helpful.

'If the three of you did a five-day week it would provide three days employment for someone else.'

'Tell that to the powers that be,' he barked. 'Most clergy won't let go anyway. They're driven by guilt. I know now why so many become workaholics. It makes them feel better, I suppose, as if they must be achieving something. At least they can't be criticised for sitting around. It's easier to give in to pressure than fight it.'

But as he prowled round the house like a bear with a sore head things became clearer. He was someone whom pressure drove into reverse, rather than the opposite. His whole body and mind resisted it with fury. He would not give in.

'I will fight it. A clergyman must be able to experience a certain measure of normal existence. I know one thing, if I don't, I'm not going to survive in this job for long.'

I had my struggles too. I missed the relaxed, easy routine of the teacher's wife, when every week was gloriously the same and mine to arrange. I had started to write and I resented the constant interruptions, Peter's to-ing and fro-ing which unsettled the children, the physical restraint required to keep them out of his way, and the stopping to make lunch when I had just settled Abby in bed. Many wives would be only too pleased to have their men around all day, I thought guiltily, especially those whose husbands worked long hours and were rarely there. And here was I suffering from over-exposure! But he was around, yet not around, because he was always on duty. Sometimes I felt like a glorified housekeeper, seeing to the curate's every bodily need and sending him on fit and fed to fulfil the next demand.

There was that inevitable loneliness too. Some of our deepest heartaches over people we loved could not be shared lest we breach their confidence. If one of the children were ill, or it was my turn on the crèche rota and I missed the morning service, I missed church altogether that week. I sometimes went for weeks without being able to take Communion and it was a loss. Grimlington, being a static community with its close ties and inbuilt support system, did not identify easily with those who were forced to be mobile and found themselves without loved ones and family nearby. We missed our friends from Manchester and Nottingham. We no longer had weekends off to see them and they were working on Thursdays, Peter's day off. Many precious friendships were left unnourished and began to wither and die.

Frank Field, the MP, published his report on the plight of divorced clergy wives. We were saddened by the high clergy divorce rate, but not surprised. The Church promised to do more for the destitute, disenfranchised clergy wife. That was something but I still felt uneasy. Wasn't it dealing with a symptom, rather than a cause? As a doctor's daughter I knew the best medicine was preventive. Would no one ask why it happened? Perhaps not, because the clergy knew that a solution would have to be so radical that the behavioural pattern of years would have to change. And the clergy wife had no voice.

Peter and I tried to plan our own mini-revolution. Against all the odds we would hang on to our marriage, our family life and our sanity. We also intended to preserve our creativity, enjoyment of life and our sense of humour too. Having Jewish roots helped. Judaism, with its philosophy of the joy of life, its acceptance and value of man's humanity and all that that meant in terms of the richness of family life, was the perfect foil for the Protestant work ethic. Man might well be meant to labour and toil, but the Haggadah, the Passover service, insisted he was also made for 'seasons of gladness, rejoicing and festival'. These were God-ordained, compulsory, vital for his mental and spiritual health, and not just some unnecessary extra, nice if the time can be spared, but dispensable if work makes a prior claim. That was why, for most Jews, the Sabbath was special and began the evening before.

'Everyone prays for a Jewish judge in court on Friday,' we were told by someone in the congregation who worked in the Leeds law courts, 'you can guarantee you'll be home early.'

We decided that our Friday family night, our 'Sabbath celebration' as we welcomed the weekend, should be sacrosanct too. It was a struggle. There were so many other demands on Peter. The youth group were expecting him. He would have to let the leaders down. But it was more important to say 'Kiddush' with the children, light the Sabbath candles, eat, sing and tell stories by candlelight, then take the bread and wine, reminding ourselves that Christ had said, 'When you do these things, remember me.' We tried to invite others and draw them in too.

Edward and Alicia were puzzled by the importance we gave these occasions. The home was not the traditional place for Christian worship. They were doubtful whether the Church had anything to gain at all from the traditions of the Jews.

'The Church is the new Israel,' Alicia often preached.

'Where does it say that in the New Testament?' I asked her. 'Show me chapter and verse.'

'Well, darling, you know what I mean. We are the chosen ones now.'

'And God has finished with the Jews?'

Alicia smiled graciously. She was far too wise to get embroiled in a subject so packed for me with emotional content.

But I was saddened that Christians so often dismissed Judaism which was their own heritage. It was their own loss. Christ was Jewish and the disciples and the apostles and the Church began as a Jewish sect. Then, in a fierce rise of Jewish nationalism after AD 70, the Jewish Christians were thrown out of the fold. And Christianity

168

was swallowed up in the Greek, Gentile culture where it grew and spread. It lost a certain colour and vibrancy, vigour and joy. For the Greek philosophers the human body was seen as a negative force warring against the spirit. The early Church fathers felt the same. Sacred and secular were divided and pushed poles apart, until, as in present day Grimlington, church and community seemed to have little in common. Emotional repression suited the British middle-classes with their stiff upper lip. But a working-class community was more volatile and much freer with its emotions.

The relevance of its Jewish roots for a church like Grimlington became more and more apparent to us. The Jewish culture with its sense of family and community had a lot in common with a town where everyone knew everyone else. When a man had been lying in the same position all day, digging coal out of the earth, when a woman had stood sorting nails and screws into the same little cartons for hours on end, they did not wish to stand rigidly in a church service. They needed to relax, unwind and let their hair down. Worship had to be full of colour, movement and excitement, as well as have its moments of quiet stillness. An intellectual exercise, requiring an effort in concentration, was not enough if it was to be a real reflection of the life and needs of the people of the town.

I was excited by the realisation that here was a possible key to bridging the gulf between the church and the town. We had to escape from the hidebound attitudes which had imprisoned the British Church for years. We needed to break down the cultural barriers and go free. But I could not impose my ideas by force. Peter and I could work out our own family life in terms of our Jewish heritage, but when it came to the church, they would probably say, 'Her again! She has a vested interest!' and they would have been right. I would have to wait.

Meanwhile Edward planned the Easter services, filling the week with a series of meditations, culminating in a Maundy Thursday Communion.

'I wish we could do a Passover instead,' I said to Peter.

'So do I, but be patient.'

'When are we going to fit in our own Seder night?'

It was not a proper Easter for me without celebrating the great Jewish festival of freedom which had meant so much to Christ.

'Don't worry, we'll do it,' Peter reassured me, 'and we'll invite Edward, Alicia and Anna to share it.'

'But when? They're busy all week.'

'If we have to wait until midnight, we'll do it.'

I was just about to dash out to a joint meeting of the Music and Drama Groups to plan for Easter when the telephone rang.

'It's Mick.'

The voice sounded flat, totally devoid of emotion.

'Tell Peter, will you, that Paul died this afternoon.'

I was totally at a loss for words.

'We can't believe it, we just don't understand,' Mick said and in the desperate weariness of his voice was a hint of despair.

I knew this was no time for discussion or explanations.

'I'll tell Peter,' I said, 'and Mick, we'll be thinking of you all. I only wish there was more we could do.'

Peter came into the kitchen as I put the receiver down. He sat down slowly and shook his head.

'I've been expecting it for some time,' he said, 'but I wish it didn't have to happen like this, with everyone so unprepared.'

'Do you want to go round?'

He rang the vicarage, but Edward had already gone.

'You'd better go to your meeting,' he said and I agreed, reluctantly.

My feet felt like two great blocks of lead as I walked through the cemetery and up to the vestry door. There was no sound from inside the main body of the church. Perhaps the meeting had been cancelled. Then I heard the coughing and muffled sobbing. I tiptoed in and joined the little group, huddled together in a corner with handkerchiefs on their laps. Linda followed me in, and looked at me in bewilderment when she saw the little group.

'Paul,' I mouthed to her.

She understood and sank on to a chair.

'I'm not surprised,' she mouthed, looking in concern at the little group.

We sat there for some time, perhaps half or three quarters of an hour, the uneasy silence broken only by an occasional sob or the sound of someone blowing their nose. I could not help contrast it with those early mornings when everyone had prayed with such hope and fervour. But I began to feel uneasy. There was a weeping for sheer grief and a weeping for our own disappointed hopes and at some point the latter had taken over from the former. We were teetering on the brink of self-pity. I caught Rick's eye and he was obviously feeling the same. It was time to move on.

'When we were at College,' I heard myself saying, 'one of the student wives died. She was twenty-three. We had all prayed so hard and she had been making such progress. That evening was the first Communion service after Easter. We all felt miserable, just like we are tonight. The Vice-Principal got to his feet and he said, "Of course we all grieve for Chris and her family. It's only right we should. But if all we do tonight is grieve, then we make a mockery of Easter and all this College stands for. Why train to be a clergyman, why bother being a Christian at all, if death isn't defeated for ever?"'

'This isn't the end for Paul,' Rick said gently, 'it's a beginning. His pain is over and he's safe and happy now. Whatever our questions or our confusion, that's all we can know for now and we must hang on to that. So, to work!'

Edward had to announce Paul's death to the church on Sunday morning. My stomach muscles tensed for him as he fought to keep control.

'I feel I must say,' he said, with a slight tremor, 'that this is no time for recriminations. It makes no matter now who said what and who believed what. If you want to point the finger, point it at me. I failed you in that I did not know how to advise or lead you. The whole matter of healing is a mystery. We all make mistakes. I know God heals, but for Paul, this was the best form of healing.'

Joel, sitting next to me, scribbling in a note-book, suddenly looked up. 'Has Paul gone to heaven?' he asked.

I nodded.

'The lucky thing! I bet it's got the biggest adventure playground in the world. There'll be dozens of swings and one of those pulleys that whizz you through the air. And his legs won't hurt any more. Do you think he'll find Chica?'

Chica was Granny's dog who had died a few months earlier.

'I hope he does. He can take him for walks till I get there.'

I looked at Joel and marvelled. A child had a much clearer perception of truth than the rest of us. We were simply too sophisticated.

Chapter 19

It was almost Easter when the miners' strike began. At first the effects seemed to be minimal. There were more men out shopping with their wives or playing with their children in the park. The women wore a constant anxious frown as they bustled around the supermarket, trying to make the vital cut-backs in the housekeeping. All mortgage, rent, gas, electricity and HP payments were frozen. Nothing else could be done. And life continued, much as it always had, except for a certain foreboding in the air, which everyone tried to ignore. Easter eggs were bought sparingly and handled with care. It might be the last taste of chocolate for a very long time. The future hung like a heavy storm cloud on the horizon, too far away to worry about yet, though burst it must some day soon.

Joe had found a temporary job humping boxes and crates at a local storage depot. On Good Friday he was laid off.

'Don't worry,' Linda said when she told me. 'They'll take him on again on Tuesday. They don't want to give 'im 'oliday pay, that's all. They do it with all their temporaries.'

I was incensed.

'I can't bear it,' I said to Peter, as we cleared away the tea dishes. I clenched my fists and dug my nails so deeply into my palms that I suddenly became aware of the pain. 'They just shrug it off, but I could go and throttle an employer or two. We're going back to the days of Dickens. The injustice of it. It's unfair.'

Peter nodded and put an arm around my shoulder.

'I know, love, but there's nothing we can do.'

'Nothing!' I said, brandishing the washing-up brush. 'Just let me catch any of them and I'll give them nothing.'

When it came to defending the flock I had a kindred spirit in Edward. The previous week, as we walked into the vicarage for a staff lunch, we heard him shouting, 'How dare you!' down the telephone. There was steel in his voice.

Peter flinched and caught Anna's eye. She grinned back knowingly. They were made of much gentler stuff. Edward was a wonderful ally, but a fearful opponent.

'Well!' he said, joining us in the dining-room a few moments later, 'I won't have anyone talk to Lucy like that.'

'Who was it?' Peter asked tentatively.

'Someone in the Housing Department. Lucy's been going almost every Saturday to ask for a new house. He told her to get married, or pregnant. It was the only way to get a house in a hurry. How insensitive! I won't have her hurt like that. Some officials seem to have no feelings at all.'

But no matter how loudly we shouted or how great a fuss we made, Peter was basically right. There was little we could do to protect people at the mercy of an apparently uncaring system.

On Good Friday evening the hail eventually stopped, the ice melted away and the skies cleared to give a fine, almost spring-like feel to the end of the day. Just as well, for I was looking forward to the Council of Churches torchlight procession through the town and I hate the rain. There was a spring in my step as I walked to church, enjoying the masses of daffodils in bloom in the cemetery. Stella, a friend who had come to stay for the weekend, was with me and we stopped for a moment and looked around at the familiar landscape, the higgledy-piggledy brick housing and uneven back yards, joined together like a misshapen patchwork quilt.

'You know,' I said to her, 'when I think of all the

beautiful places I could have been. Funny isn't it, but there's nowhere else on God's earth I'd rather be.'

A beautiful new banner in shades of lilac and purple was hanging above the pulpit and we sat enjoying it for some time. A cluster of grapes dripped their juice into a goblet and underneath was written. 'Yours was the suffering we see in the wine.'

It reminded me of the third cup, the 'Cup of Blessing', at the Passover service, which we had managed to share as a family with Edward, Anna, Alicia and Lucy on the Wednesday evening. That was probably the cup which Christ used to institute the Communion. 'I'm going to drink a bitter cup of suffering, so that you can drink the Cup of Blessing,' was what he was saying. Passover and Easter merged as the great celebrations of the freedom which God gave to man. It suddenly occurred to me how tremendous it was that Joe, Lucy, those caught up in the strike, all of us there in the church, were no longer victims of our circumstances. Inner freedom was far more important.

My meditation was disrupted as everyone prepared for the march, collecting torches and extra woollies and spending that last penny. With the troops assembled and our ranks swelled by the Baptists, we all set off to collect the Catholics and Methodists.

'Pssssst!' Dorothy whispered. 'Not mentioning any names, but there are certain individuals I wouldn't go near if I were you.'

She nodded in various directions.

'Last year I ended up with wax all down the back of my best coat.'

Silence fell, for us a major feat of self-control, and we marched, torches held high beneath a clear, starlit sky. Doors opened and people stood, silhouetted in the light, as we passed by. It felt strange to say so much without using words. As we reached the pub at the traffic lights two young men came out and bawled, 'Christian bastards!'

Stella looked at me, her eyes wide with astonishment.

'Did I hear right?' she asked.

'I think so.'

'I've never come across anything like that before.'

'Me neither, but it seems quite a healthy reaction.'
She nodded.

'Better than suburban indifference.'

'Oh, there's none of that around here.'

I smiled to myself as we walked along. Grimlington people can be belligerent, abrasive and maddening, but they're never bland or dull. I was to remember those words a few weeks later when an event occurred which provoked that belligerent spirit to its full fury.

It had been apparent for some years that Cuttlesworth, the last remaining daughter church, would have to close, but no one had been prepared to take that final drastic step. Even Edward kept putting it off. There was a limit to how much criticism a man could shoulder at any one time and there was no doubt that the decision would hurt. The congregation was tiny, but vocal and fiercely loyal. Angela and Frances of the Drama Group, fighters to the last, had joined them to give their moral support. It was almost a holy war.

The arguments for keeping the place open were emotional rather than rational, and had more to do with legend than fact.

'They're stuck-up at Parish. They're unfriendly, unwelcoming. They're all professional people.'

None of it was true, except of course a larger church could not offer the intimacy of a congregation of twenty. But gradually we picked up various impressions, memories and stories, which slotted together like pieces of a jigsaw puzzle to create a picture of years of division and mistrust, all rooted in the church's inadmirable history.

Grimlington's vicar was once exceedingly rich. The church had owned vast areas of land all around the town. Glebe, as it was called, was a means of paying the incumbent. All rents went to him. That made him a

176

squire of some importance, with a large staff, coach house and a farm, and not always too popular with his tenants. The system persisted as late as the 1950s, when all land reverted to the diocese and was sold. The stipend became uniform and overnight the clergy became the poorest paid of professionals, which always seemed to me far more in keeping with the spirit of Christianity. 'The Church' was no longer a career with prospects. The clergyman might still live in a semi-palace, but whether he could now afford to heat and furnish it was another matter.

However, this was not the problem at the turn of the century. Grimlington's vicar was wealthy enough to resist the division of his living into several parishes of equal size, the tendency in most fast-growing industrial towns. He could afford curates and the building of daughter churches. The Methodist threat made it imperative.

Methodism was the working man's Christianity. Chapels were appearing in every pit village so fast that it was hard for the Church of England to compete. There were almost as many chapels as there were toilets and more chapels than there were trees.

In 1903 a local squire lent the vicar a piece of land for a religious establishment and Cuttlesworth was built. Like the other daughter churches it fared well at first. Attendance at services was average, but exceedingly good at the mass of social events which quickly became its prime function. West Yorkshire never experienced the religious fervour of the Welsh mining communities. Gradually, although the Sunday School was quite large and women attended the meetings almost as faithfully as ever, the malaise set in. In face of war, pain, poverty and suffering the Church had little to say. It offered dances and social evenings to try and disguise the spiritual void, but in the end they were not enough and the congregation dwindled.

The huge social gulf between the parish and the daughter church persisted. In the 1970s whenever the

Parish Women's Society had tea together the Cuttlesworth women came and did the washing up.

'How kind!' a newcomer was heard to comment. 'And I suppose we go and do it for them.'

Her companion coughed politely.

'No, no, but we do give them a little something for doing it.'

'Did the men ever go to church?' I asked Jack, as he was sweeping the parish hall one day.

'Not really, not the working men. Not so's I'd remember,' he said.

Jack was a retired carpenter, a master at his craft. I had a soft spot for him. He was a gem. He cleaned the parish hall, checked and kept it, gave hours of his time without a word of complaint. And if anyone had cause to complain, he did. It could be left in total disarray.

He seemed to welcome an excuse to stop, leant on his broom and chuckled. He had an infectious chuckle and my endless questions about the past amused him. His body seemed a weight and he was breathing heavily. I wondered if the cleaning was becoming too much for him, but his face, though flushed, was as bright and alive as ever. He thought for a while.

'Yer see, Michele, what yer have to remember is that yer life were not yer own. Yer belonged to boss, body, soul and spirit. He were always right. And 'e could make yer work as many hours as 'e wanted.'

'Not Sundays too!'

'What! He could make yer work all day and all night if 'e 'ad a mind to it, if there were a job to finish. Yer work was yer life.'

He rested his chin on his hands, which were balanced on the broom handle, and suddenly he was miles away in another world. Then he chuckled again. 'Listen' he said, 'I'll tell yer a story which'll show yer what it were like.'

I pulled out two chairs and we sat down.

'When I were an apprentice, many year ago now, I once 'ad to build a cupboard. It were tongue and groove and every joint were done by 'and. It took me days, but when it were finished I were right pleased wi' meself. It were a beautiful cupboard. I called boss to show 'im what I'd done. He looked at it a while, then 'e picked up an 'ammer and smashed it to pieces before me very eyes. "What did yer do that for?" I asked 'im. To tell yer truth I were fighting back tears. It were a terrible feeling. I'll never ferget it, not as long as I live. "Do it again," 'e said, "and this time, 'ow I told yer."'

'What did you do?'

'What did I do? I started all over again, just like 'e said.'

He looked at me and shook his head. 'Ay,' he said, 'that world's gone and I can't say I'm sorry.'

'If the men didn't go to church, what made you go?'

'That were recent. I went as a child, then like all me mates I stopped once I were appenticed. I didn't see point. It were Madge who dragged me back. She said it 'ad all changed. New vicar, that were last vicar, were different. And then Alicia were on me doorstep, tellin' me I 'ad to go too. That were definitely new. We'd never 'ad a woman minister before and I'd never met anyone like Alicia. I certainly wasn't going to argue with 'er.

'But Madge were right. It were different. The sermons were about Bible and God and how we could know him. I could understand them. There I was, a man in me fifties, and I understood for t' first time what being a real Christian were.'

He threw back his head and laughed. 'Well at least I found out before they were putting me underground. And I'll tell yer this. One day, last vicar said, "Jack, you don't need to call me Sir, or Mr Jones. Call me by my Christian name, like I call you by yours." Yer could 'ave knocked me down. So 'ere I am now, chatting with vicar and anyone. It's a new world, it is. And last week when I went out to t' front to pray, well, that were out o' my realm altogether. Madge and I never thought we were good enough to mix with church people. But times 'ave changed all right.'

I left Jack to finish sweeping the parish hall, amazed. 'Not good enough' indeed! They had probably been shaming the 'religious' in the town for years with their self-giving. Still, I now understood why there was such resistance to shouldering responsibility and coming into the limelight. 'You must not get above yourself' was an unwritten law, buried deep in the sub-conscious.

And the Church of England made sure it stayed that way. Lay reading courses were cerebral and intellectual, requiring a large measure of academic ability. After all, the lay reader must know all about Barth and Bultmann to meet the needs of a congregation like Grimlington! Pastoral gifts and quality of character were important, but education seemed to matter more.

But if it was almost impossible for a working man or woman to become a lay reader, it was even harder for them to be ordained. Dave tried. He felt a strong sense of calling and showed real pastoral ability with the children, but he worked on a building site and had no exam passes. For Dave ordination was a dream, a distant dream, light years away in the future.

If Grimlington Church was ever truly to reflect the life of the town, then local lay leadership was crucial, and not just an optional extra. So we got on with it. Mick began to lead services. He had a liturgy all of his own, full of local colour. Marjorie preached with unusual vigour and handled the banter from the congregation as well as any politician. And yet I realised how easy it was to turn to the more skilfully articulate first, because they were not afraid to come forward. We were in danger of recreating a hierarchy based on status and often missed the treasure sitting deferentially in the pew. How I longed for that age-old tradition to go. It was British, but hardly New Testament!

Class distinction still operated in the Church all right. The Cuttlesworth congregation had a point, but it was no longer concentrated in the parish-daughter church divide. Cuttlesworth was no longer working class. It was simply dying and a poor example to the town of the life it was supposed to represent. Keeping it going required an unwarranted amount of effort. So in May the PCC finally decided on its closure. Two months' warning was given to soften the blow, but the respite was used to launch a campaign. Angela organised a petition to the Archbishop of York. Sue signed it in her corner shop. An old lady told her it was a protest against the vicar's insistence on silver rather than copper in the collection. She was outraged. It was months before she discovered the truth.

Feelings ran high in the town.

'My Granny went there for years.'

'I were brought up at the Sunday School.'

'I enjoy the whist drives.'

Some joined the protest, 'Because,' they said, 'I've never liked that vicar. He's no business changing everything.'

The *Gazette* was full yet again of outraged letters from people the clergy had never seen in the church.

Marjorie and several other people from the parish church went up to Cuttlesworth every Sunday to assure them they were loved and wanted, to listen and sympathise. Her mother had been a pillar of the congregation there once. But the bitterness only seemed to grow.

Frances rang me one night to say that she and Angela would not be coming to Drama any more.

'Well you didn't think we would continue as if nothing had happened, did you?' she said gently.

'I hoped and prayed you would,' I said. 'I hoped that knowing how much we had all come to mean to each other you would feel you still belonged, whatever happened.'

'I'm sorry. It's just not possible. We can never come to the parish church again, not after what's happened, but we will support your performances whenever we can.'

The Drama Group were sad, though not surprised.

'We'll go round and see them,' Linda said. 'They can't let this come between us.'

'They'll come back, won't they?' Dorothy asked.

But no one answered. Perhaps we knew that nothing would make them change their minds. It was a down-hearted little group who tried to rehearse that night. I gave up and we finished early.

I stayed to lock up and Linda stayed with me, chatting. The others headed for home.

'You understand about the power of feeling behind the closing of Cuttlesworth, don't you?' I said to her.

'Yes, I do. It goes back a long way. It's very deep.'

It was a soft spring evening, the kind when you want to stay out and breathe in the promise of summer warmth. I had been waiting to ask her something for months and this seemed like the moment.

'Do you remember at the Parish Weekend when you said, "This church is too middle-class"?'

She laughed.

'Yes, that's me, always opening my mouth when I should keep quiet.'

'No, you were right to say it if that was what you felt. I must say it's not like any middle-class church I've ever been in. I think I know what you mean, but I'd rather hear it from your lips.'

She knitted her brow in thought and searched for the right words.

'Well, it's not just one thing, it's lots of things.'

I waited.

'Sometimes, oh sometimes I get so angry. I want to shake people or hit out at them. I feel as if some part of me is being slowly rubbed out. And it's a vital part of me. It's what I am.'

'I know that feeling too,' I said, 'or at least I used to. I found the church a terrible shock. I felt that nobody wanted me as I was. My Jewishness was treated like theft or drug addiction. It was a habit to be kicked.'

'That's it,' Linda said, 'that's exactly it! I'm a working-class girl and that's not something to be ashamed of. I'm proud of it. It isn't all beer and pools and Woodbines. There's good things in our way of life,

182

when I was at school I 'ad a teacher who said to me, "Linda, you're intelligent. Go to university. Drag yourself out of the hole you were born into." I felt like slapping his face for patronising me like that. Who was he to say I was living in a hole? It might seem like that to him. But I thought, "If I'm as wise and contented as me Dad, then that's enough for me."'

She paused and felt for words again.

'The middle-classes think two things about the working man. Either he's unintelligent or he's miserable. We're neither. There's a great deal of natural wisdom in this community and a great deal of contentment too. That's why our lads are on strike, to fight for their families, their homes and the way of life they love.'

I looked at her for a while and could see her eyes glinting in the twilight. No one could easily cow Linda's spirit.

'You won't change, will you?' I said to her.

'Not much chance!'

We walked slowly out onto the street.

'So the church has to, but how?'

'Well for one thing, there's no point telling people they're miserable sinners when they're perfectly happy as they are.'

She laughed and I said nothing.

'Do you want a catalogue then?'

I nodded.

'Well the home groups are too intellectual, they're not about real life. The preaching's above people's heads at times. We need leaders, local people who know Grimlington and are trusted. Why must the people who take part in services have posh voices? There are too many meetings about irrelevant things. If it hasn't anything to offer someone like me Dad, then forget it. Oh, and simplify the blooming news-sheet,' she shouted as she ran across the road. 'No one can understand it. What does "Vestry hour" mean to somebody new?'

She was about to disappear down the track behind

the houses to the bottom of the town when she turned back.

'Hey!' she shouted. 'I almost forgot to tell you the best news. Joe has a permanent job, in a warehouse. Pay's terrible and he'll have to work masses of overtime, but it's a job.'

She turned again, skipped off between the houses and was gone.

Chapter 20

As spring gave way to our second summer in Grimlington, I began to find our temporary accommodation an almost unbearable strain. The curtains hanging three inches above the window sills, which had amused me twelve months ago, began to grate and annoy. Everything we needed was always at the bottom of a crate in the garage. And our sleep was often interrupted by the intimate revelations made at the bus stop outside our bedroom window.

Still, compared to the hardship the strike was now beginning to cause, it was very little to put up with. Anyway, like everything else, the house market was at a standstill. Had someone wanted our house, there was still nothing for us to buy, nothing that is except a house belonging to the diocese. The previous vicar had been a rural dean and earned two curates. That was when ours was built. The original curate's house, an Edwardian red-brick semi, had been allowed to fall into a state of acute disrepair. It was so cold, damp and miserable that the PCC refused to consider buying it and when the last occupant left, handed it back to the diocese with relief.

But we loved old property. It was sad to see the old house go to rack and ruin. Alicia's brother was an architect and when he came to stay, Peter asked him if he would mind going with him to have a look round and assess the amount of repairs and alterations.

He was delighted. As we strolled from room to room his eyes lit up. He became so excited by the possibilities that his suggestions took our breath away, especially his idea of a sun lounge extension built on to the south-facing kitchen. Wouldn't we like a little sun trap, he asked. Would we! The prospect painted a happy smile on our faces until we awoke to the reality that this was the curate's house and not a luxury villa on the Costa Brava. Besides, vista there might be, of a school playing field, one of the few 'greenbelt' areas in the town, but the tip which lay beyond it was hardly scenic, although it was reputed to be the highest hill in West Yorkshire.

With some careful calculations, Peter estimated that the church could buy and repair the old house with the proceeds of the sale of the new one. The PCC were convinced at last. They were desperate. The issue was becoming boring. And our move was on the way at last.

'You see,' Peter said to me, smiling, 'you who said we would never have the fun of doing up an old house again once I was ordained, here you are with a house to be repaired and modernised to your specification, and with an architect to command!'

What was more the church was generous beyond our wildest dreams. They would cover the full cost of a professional decorator and a hall and stair carpet. We were uneasy. Their budget was stretched to the limit. But they insisted. They had allowed it to deteriorate. They would repair it properly, even if temporary bank loans were necessary. Then suddenly our house sold and I could have wept with relief.

It was some time during those weeks that I happened to let slip to Edward and Alicia that I had not been confirmed. I knew it was dynamite, but I could not help it. Alicia was complaining about those who came to us from other denominations and did not bother to ask for confirmation. Denominationalism always jarred me.

'Well, I agree with them,' I said, 'I'm not.'

Peter kicked me, but it was too late. Edward and Alicia were staring at me.

'It's totally unnecessary,' I said, 'especially for those baptised as an adult, as I was.'

'That may be so, but it's not the point,' Edward said.

'You see, you put me in a very difficult position. Canon law requires me to urge any regular communicant who is not confirmed to do so as soon as possible.'

'Trust you!' Peter said in the car on the way home. 'Why did you say anything? Couldn't you keep quiet?'

'What's the point of making a protest if you keep quiet about it? You know I'm not an Anglican and I never wanted to be an Anglican. I'm a Jew. I was converted to Christ, not to the Church of England, or any other denomination. Denominationalism makes me sick. It's the greatest failure of the Gentile Church and one which makes it the laughing stock of every other world religion, especially the Jews. So why should your failure be imposed on me?'

Peter looked slightly hurt, then pursed his lips, as he did when he made up his mind that reason must prevail over emotion.

'You know I agree with you entirely. You know I think confirmation is a nonsense, a poor attempt at Bar Mitzvah and without foundation in the Bible, but you do see Edward's point?'

'It's the same for you. You vowed to keep canon law at your ordination.'

'Oh, don't worry about me. I can sort out 'my own conscience.'

I struggled with the issue for several days. Wasn't it enough that I was a clergy wife? Would I have to abandon my last Jewish protest in a meaningless ceremony? And it angered me that like the Communion service itself, here was yet another ceremony the Church had plundered from the Jews, and ruined! Communion was robbed of its warm family atmosphere, confirmation of its great place in the community. At Bar Mitzvah there is only one candidate, one centre of attention, as he sings the law from the platform of the synagogue and proves he is now a man. Then there is a big party. Confirmation was a poor do by comparison. There were several candidates, all put through the sausage machine at once. None were given individual attention, the chance to say what the ceremony meant to them or even read a lesson. There was no sense of their coming to maturity in the church community. And definitely no party!

Grimlington was neither rigid, nor restrained in any celebration and it was an encouraging consideration. The candidates were older, making a real commitment to the church, and that helped too. I read the account of Jesus' baptism again. He did not have to be baptised. In fact, John seemed reluctant to do it. But Jesus insisted. The law must be fulfilled. It occurred to me that there were times when, for the sake of others, we had to submit to the system. Ideals have to be slightly tarnished every now and then for the sake of relationships.

'I suppose I'll do it,' I said to Peter, with very little grace.

'Not for my sake, I hope,' he said.

'No, for Edward and his flipping conscience!'

Quite a large group of candidates were waiting to be confirmed.

'Date of baptism?' Edward asked.

Baptism was a prerequisite of course.

'Do you mean the one when I was a baby, the one when I became a Jehovah's Witness, or the one when I became Pentecostal?' Ella asked.

Edward looked nonplussed. 'The first will do.'

By contrast, Sid, who owned a fish and chip shop, which was in dire straits because of the strike, and had only been coming to church a few weeks, realised he had not been baptised at all.

'We'll have to baptise you then,' Edward said.

'Ah yes,' said Sid, 'but you will do it proper, won't you? I want it like they did it in Bible. None of your sprinkling bit, not for a grown man. They went right under and that's how I want it. God's changed me completely, turned me upside down, and if I'm going to tell everyone about it in public, I want there to be no mistake.'

Peter leapt around with glee at the prospect. Edward

discovered we could hire a portable baptistry. It was an enormous monstrosity, somewhere between an over-grown fishtank and an undersized swimming pool. It held four tons of water and took all day to fill.

'You won't forget your bathing costume tonight, will you?' Edward said to Linda, who was one of the sponsors, Sid deciding he was a bit past the godparent stage.

She giggled.

'Ooooo Edward, you are a tease.'

'I'm serious,' he said, without a flicker of expression. 'I expect the sponsors to get in with me.'

Linda sidled up to Peter and me a few moments later, an uncertain smile on her face.

'Er, what sort of a bathing costume shall I wear tonight?'

Peter and I stared at her in silence. She studied our faces, then muttered through gritted teeth, 'He's having me on, isn't 'e?'

'Don't worry,' Peter said, 'we'll get our own back.'

As they were getting ready in the vestry later that evening, Peter said casually to Edward, 'Have you by any chance noticed the new cracks in the chancel arch?'

Edward looked up, alarmed. Peter noticed things like that.

'I shouldn't worry about it. It's probably the weight of the water.'

He grinned and disappeared into the church, where Bob was playing the organ with perhaps a little more gusto than usual. He stopped and listened. The music was familiar. It couldn't be . . . Wait a minute, it was! He caught Bob's wink in the organ mirror and nearly laughed out loud. When he had jokingly suggested Handel's Water Music, he never expected Bob to take him up on it. But in seventy-five years, despite his serious love of music, Bob had never lost his sense of humour.

The significance of his playing was evidently lost on the congregation, too excited by the novelty of the experience to pay much attention to the organ. I remembered baptismal services from our Free Church days in Manchester and imagined somehow that this would be the same. They were always great occasions, moving, joyous, yet nevertheless invested with a certain seriousness and intensity. But in Grimlington intensity was doomed from the start. Finding the church as full of steam as a sauna was a source of some amusement. The Music Group could hardly see Rick to follow his instructions. The vicar suddenly appeared like a ghost out of the mist. Then, to crown it all, Sid, who was wearing an old pair of trousers he had not worn for years, whispered to Linda in a panic, 'Me fly zip's gone!'

'His fly zip's gone!' she whispered to Edward during the first hymn.

Edward raised his eyes to heaven and whispered back, 'Run over to the vicarage for a safety pin.'

Linda ran and arrived back a few minutes later, out of breath, brandishing a nappy pin. It was all Anna could find. Sid took one look at it and paled.

'I don't have to wear a loin cloth, do I?'

Linda stared at him, realised he was serious and clapped a hand over her mouth to hold her laughter in.

'Yer great wally. Just use it to hold yer trousers up.'

The rest of the service passed off without further mishap. It may have lacked a certain sense of grand occasion, but what we had was much better. It was real and just as moving in its own way. The ripples spread out into the town. A grown man was baptised at the Parish and no one had ever been baptised like that before. 'That takes guts,' they said.

As the day for the confirmation drew nearer, I felt increasingly tense and unhappy. So many conflicting emotions wrestled to take charge. It was hypocrisy to assent to a ritual in which I did not believe. Yet canon law required it. Why should the Church of England have the last drop of my Jewish blood? Yet that was nonsense. Confirmation would change nothing. My feelings were a mystery to me.

190

Sitting in the front pew with the seven other nervous candidates I had to fight down a sense of panic and the urge to run. I looked down at the Order of Service and noticed for the first time a passage headed, 'Re-affirmation of Baptismal Vows'. I jumped up, pushed past everyone else in the pew and rushed to find Peter, who was standing calmly at the back of the church.

'Do I have to say this?' I demanded, waving my service sheet under his nose.

He put an arm around my shoulder.

'Yes, why not?'

'Because,' I said, fighting back the tears, 'it makes it look as if I never meant them the first time. And you know how much it meant to me. It was the hardest thing I ever did in my life. It's all right for you and everyone else baptised as a baby. I understand why you should want to own vows made on your behalf. But I knew what I was doing. I risked everything, my family, community, traditions, culture, my very identity. Re-enacting it all just sounds sham and hollow.'

Peter smiled and held me close.

'I do understand. But don't we all need to reaffirm the vows we've made to God, whether it's marriage vows or whatever, just to remind ourselves of the commitment we once made? Goodness, I've had to remind myself of my ordination vows over and over again these last few months, whenever I was tempted to give up and run away.'

I nodded and reluctantly went back to my place, ignoring the puzzled expressions as I squeezed past yet again. Joe was sitting next to me. He touched my arm reassuringly, saying nothing, and his presence was a comfort. I noticed his clenched jaw and realised what an ordeal the experience was for him, though for very different reasons.

From the moment the Bishop appeared, large and genial, the atmosphere relaxed. The church always responded to his warmth and enthusiasm.

'I do enjoy coming to Grimlington,' he said, leaning

with both hands on his bishop's crook and a broad smile on his face. They enjoyed having him just as much. How could they not?

The knot in my stomach began to unwind. For the first time I noticed the new banners, 'the fruits of the Spirit', resplendent in crimson and gold, hanging from every pillar. The Music Group sang at times as if for us alone and I was touched by their encouraging smiles in our direction.

Then, with his ams outstretched, the Bishop invited us to stand in front of him. He knew all our names by heart. I was staggered. He bent his head to us and whispered, 'I want you to understand that when you promise to renounce evil it means no more ouija boards, fortune tellers or astrology of any kind. The Bible is quite clear about that. And no more reading your horoscope. Can we proceed?'

Satisfied with our nods, and then our vows, the Bishop laid his hands on our heads. When my turn came he called Peter out too. 'Come and put your arms around her,' he said. It was an episcopal command. Then he prayed for our family, and our home, and I sensed the loving support surrounding us. It was a privilege to belong to these people, to be part of a very special community. To commit myself to the entire Church of England would have taken more grace than I could muster, but at least I could commit myself to them.

'Do allow us to welcome you into our fellowship,' Rick said, drawing me into a bear hug during the giving of the Peace.

'And about time too!' Ian said, over his shoulder, with a twinkle in his eye.

As the Communion service ended, the Bishop finished the contents of the two wine goblets, then, presuming he had consecrated the wine in the decanter, drank what remained of that too. I watched him in awe.

We brewed our own wine, Mick, Bill and Chris taking it in turns to provide from their cellars, but replacements were not always there on time. Aware that supplies were running dangerously low, Peter went to do the eight o'clock Communion service the previous Sunday with some trepidation. But as he opened the vestry door he saw to his relief that a new demi-john was waiting for him. The writing on the label was Bill's and he blessed him as he yanked off the bung. It came off suddenly, accompanied by a loud hiss, which continued for several seconds. He peered at the dark liquid. It was a little murky. He sniffed it, but it smelled all right. In fact, apart from a gentle fizzing it seemed perfectly all right, especially at seven-thirty on a Sunday morning. He poured some into a goblet, took the service, then drank the drop that remained and cycled home for breakfast.

'Funny,' he said, as he munched his toast, 'my legs feel a bit wobbly today. I really must eat something before I do that service in future. Missing breakfast doesn't suit me at all.'

After the mid-morning service, Bill came into the vestry to count the collection as he usually did.

'Thanks for remembering the wine,' Peter said. 'You saved my neck. The older ones would have been so upset to have missed out. There's just one thing though. You don't think it could be still fermenting, do you?'

'No chance,' Bill said, with a determination that took Peter aback.

'Oh? How can you be so sure?'

'I took pains to ensure it wasn't. Communion wine has to be fortified to keep.'

'So?'

'So I fortified it, with half a bottle of whiskey.'

That was why I watched the Bishop drain the decanter with such interest. But if his taste buds were offended he had the grace to hide it. In fact he did not as much as hiccough. As Edward and Peter escorted him to his car and waved him off they only hoped he would be all right on the way home.

Unknown to me, Peter brought a bottle of wine home to keep for the Communion services he did for the elderly and housebound. He stood it on top of the kitchen cupboard. Later that week I was making a casserole which required half a pint of red wine and the open bottle caught my eye. 'Can't leave it there to waste,' I thought.

'Where's my Communion wine?' he asked, a few hours later, as he was about to go out on his visits. 'I brought it home especially.'

I thought for a bit and then my heart sank. 'Where did you put it?'

'On top of the cupboard.'

'Well there it is,' I said sheepishly, pointing to the casserole on top of the cooker.

'You couldn't take them round some boeuf bourguignon instead?'

Chapter 21

Despite the strike, despite the anger when Cuttlesworth finally closed, that summer had its share of excitement, especially when it came to creativity. The Music Group, having amassed a great deal of their own material, decided to launch out into making a cassette. I was invited along to narrate two lines of a psalm which gave me an opportunity to observe the work of great genius in the making.

One sultry Saturday morning at nine-fifteen, and that had to be a test of dedication, about twenty people, complete with music stands, musical instruments, recording equipment and a hired organ, squeezed into the cellar of a tiny terraced house. There was barely room to lift a foot or move an arm. I was not normally given to claustrophobia, but nor had I ever felt so much like one of a bag of marshmallows before. Beads of perspiration appeared on most brows. People began to undo their buttons and remove any superfluous items of clothing, space permitting.

'Open that window,' Tom called out.

He was the local police sergeant and any suggestion carried all the weight of a command. Someone obeyed and the window opened into the coal shed. There was a communal groan.

'Shut that window!' Rick shouted. 'We're about to record.'

At ten-thirty I walked out into the sunshine. It was a relief to swallow fresh air. I gathered later that the recording did not finish until seven in the evening and that apart from an hour for lunch they were all down there together for all that time.

'How did you survive?' I asked Mary.

'With difficulty,' she grinned. 'It ponged a bit.'

'A bit?'

'Yes, but what's that between friends? Those songs mean so much to us we didn't really mind. That one I wrote came to me one day when I was fed up, sick of cleaning, and the washing and of prayers that never seemed to get answered. Those words came into me head. Yer never know, maybe they'll help other people.'

Rick worked on until the following morning, putting the whole thing together. At last he was satisfied and his painstaking effort had its reward. The cassette sold better than we had ever dared to hope. Alicia almost bought them up herself and sent them to the nether regions of Scotland. It was not great music. We were neither deaf, nor that biased. But it did have a vitality that was special. The words were real, born of everyday experience. It was an offering of ourselves and, more than that, in an area such as this it represented that most priceless of treasures, a finished piece of creative work, a flesh and blood achievement.

We would have been satisfied with that, but there was more to come. One day Rick's phone rang. It was the manager of a Christian record company. Rick's heart missed a beat.

'We like your cassette,' the voice said. 'We've been looking for a new church-based group for a while. We've tried all the big, well-known churches with a reputation, but there's a freshness about yours that appeals to us.'

'Probably because most of the group don't read music,' Rick said.

'That makes it all the more amazing,' the Sales Manager said. 'Well, you're obviously prepared to work. Your songs have great potential. How about our coming to see you with a view to your making a record with us?'

Rick was almost at a loss for words. It was more than he had ever dared to hope.

But there was yet more excitement on the creative front in store.

'Brother Christopher would like to know if we fancy a weekend of dance at Frankhill Abbey,' Linda said, in such a matter-of-fact way that it sounded as if she was inviting us out to the Wilton Ballroom rather than a monastery.

'Well, he said he's going to ring you about it,' she said, noting my astonished expression. Frankhill Abbey was usually recommended for silent retreats, not dancing.

Then I remembered that Linda had gone to something similar there the previous year, with Kelly and one or two others, and they had come back with an urge to dance and a great enthusiasm for Brother Christopher.

'He's a lovely little mover,' she giggled, reminding me of their previous visit. 'No, seriously, he really can dance. He says it's not easy to live in an all-male community, but whenever it gets on top of him, he goes into a little chapel with his cassette and dances his heart out. Once, he didn't bother to switch on the light and it was only when he switched on the cassette and they started groaning that he noticed the two Brothers prostrate on the floor.'

I could hardly believe the Brothers there would want us after that, but Brother Christopher assured me that they were all agreed. Would our church welcome the idea of a weekend of dance? There was room for twenty-five but which church could muster an entire corps de ballet? Not Grimlington!

'We've only three or four dance enthusiasts,' I said, 'I think it would be a bit of a waste of your time.'

'Wouldn't some of the others come and have a go?'

I tried to imagine Mick or Frank or Tom leaping gracefully through the air. 'I don't think so,' I said, 'but we do have a Music and a Drama Group. Could we have some sort of creative weekend with workshops, and could the Brothers provide some input with guidance on creativity and contemplation?'

'I think so' Brother Christopher said. 'Yes, it should be possible.' And so was born the idea for the most extraordinary weekend I had ever spent.

The organisation was a nightmare. No one ever signed lists and I could not find out how many people wanted to go.

'Why are the people of this parish allergic to signing pieces of paper?' I said to Peter.

'Because they're not used to planning so far in advance.'

I had the faint suspicion that it was also something to do with the number of notices which bombarded them every week. It was apparent that the notice-sheet was not always read, let alone digested, and I remembered Linda's comment.

Finance was a real problem, but, to my astonishment, the PCC offered to cover the cost. There was the feeling in the air that people needed a change and at last I gathered twenty-four names.

We set off one evening in a flurry of great excitement and arrived in time for Evensong. We had to sit a long way back from the Community, as did all the visitors. The heady smell of incense and the sound of the distant chanting made the Grimlington gang goggle. For a horrible moment I thought one of them might let the side down. Anything was possible! But we all fumbled our way through the old prayer books, disintegrating with age, and pretended that this was how we did it every week. Once we gave up trying to find the place and follow, something of the awe and silence which seemed to hang in the atmosphere touched and stilled us. Even the children of the theological students who were present sat perfectly still. We were amazed. None of us had ever seen a child sit through a service without uttering a sound before.

Later that evening, after tea and a chance to meet some of the Brothers, Christopher explained the ground rules, silence in the corridors, promptness at meals and the like. 'Some hope,' I thought and so evidently did Rick, as he chose 'Let there be love shared among us' as our opening song. Everyone held hands as they usually did and gazed rather sheepishly into each other's eyes.

'You call that love, do you?' asked Brother Marcus, who had joined us to talk about contemplation, 'It was nothing but sentimentality.'

We shuffled on our chairs.

'Love is doing good to those who hate your guts.'

His words cut through any illusion we might have had that this weekend was going to be happy and comfortable. He was right. It was too easy to substitute sentimentality for Christian charity, but he also underestimated the importance of feelings of solidarity and mutual support in a mining community, and just how much real support there was behind the gesture.

'We won't be singing that again in a hurry,' I thought, 'at least, not without thinking carefully about the meaning of the words.'

Brother Marcus spoke to us of the mystery in God, the days of darkness when he seemed unknown and unknowable and all we seemed to have were so many uncertainties. His words mirrored my experience of the last month, when I had longed to say to Peter, 'Leave this silly job and go back to something sensible with routine and long holidays,' but could not; the times I had cried out to God about the estate and how to get close to the people there, but no answer came and soon we would be moving; the days when the darkness of the area felt as if it rested on my shoulders like a leaden weight and I could not shake off the sense of weariness.

'But if we're in darkness all we have to do is switch on the light.'

Ian jolted me into realisation that some members of the group were struggling with a very new idea. Or perhaps the words were the problem. Brother Marcus knew what he meant by the 'dark night of the soul', but was not aware that they had never heard the term before. We were talking at cross purposes.

'But we can know God,' someone said indignantly.

'Yes,' I reassured them, 'but that's not what Brother Marcus is saying. Look, when Paul died, how did we all feel?'

The silence that followed was oppressive. I knew I was taking a risk. Paul's death had become a bit of a taboo subject which no one wanted to discuss. But at some point we would have to face it and then seemed as right a moment as any. No one spoke for ages. Everyone stared at the ground, as if it might suddenly split open and spare them this ordeal.

Eventually Rick said quietly, 'Well, I can only speak for myself, but I think I was confused at first. Then it seemed to me I had been trying to push God into a box and he just wouldn't fit. He was far too big.'

We talked for a while, but it was hard and difficult. Several people kept trying to close the subject by saying, 'We're being negative', or 'We're being morbid', but instinct told them that we have to persevere, and not just shove our bad feelings into a drawer, because they were too untidy to have on view.

'I realise,' Brother Marcus said gently, 'that this is a very painful area for you all.'

Everyone went on staring at their feet.

'So I'll say goodnight and leave you to continue. But I see that you do know what I've been talking about.'

By Saturday morning spirits had risen and we all worked very hard in our workshops. Here and there, in ones and twos, the debate from the night before continued. Brother Christopher felt that that evening's entertainment should be a little lighter and suggested a party. Grimlington people have the capacity to turn just about any occasion into a knees-up, but given the invitation, the result was bedlam. One by one the Brothers poked their heads around the door to see what the noise was all about. They were either dragged in or disappeared fast. Two people arrived with suitcases for a silent retreat, and I felt sorry for them. It would have been quieter at the Wilton Ballroom. They stared in disbelief as Brother Christopher whizzed round in an Israeli dance at a great speed, faster and faster, habit flying, until the music ended and everyone fell on the floor in an exhausted, hysterical heap.

We tiptoed late to bed and it was a shock to be woken at seven by a Brother with a bell. As he passed down the corridor one or two people managed to stagger to their doors to grin or wave at him, and he responded with a friendly smile. It took us all our time to stop Paula saying, ''Ey up, chuck,' to every Brother she met in the corridors.

The Eucharist was the highlight of the weekend. We had all prepared for it in our workshops and were ready to make it a festive occasion. The Music Group had added to their setting of the Communion service. The Dance workshop had prepared the Gloria and the Lord's Prayer. The Drama Group had interpreted the reading instead of a sermon.

Frank and Marjorie had driven over from Grimlington and were waiting for us in the chapel. Betty was already with us. She could not resist a weekend away and had temporarily joined the Drama Group to justify her coming. As I walked past Frank into the chapel he was grinning from ear to ear and whispered to me loudly, 'Betty doing drama! This I have to see!'

One or two of the Brothers, their visitors and some of the students joined us too. It was an unusual service, to say the least, and we were sad when it came to an end. The Music Group went on playing in an attempt to prolong it a little. Brother Nigel, who had officiated for us and disappeared, suddenly reappeared without his alb and waltzed into the centre of the chapel, hands held high above his head. He danced on his own for some time. Then he held out a hand to Linda, who looked around for advice, and receiving none, shrugged as if to say 'I can't be rude', and got up to join him. One by one everyone got to their feet, including the Brothers and students, and were leaping, jogging and swaying. One of the students did a Cossack dance, or it might have been a 'cassock dance', as, cassock flying, he could have out-danced any Russian. We encouraged him, clapping and cheering. It was a marvellous feeling to let go of every inhibition for once and worship with our bodies as well as our voices. No one was watching. Everyone was too caught up in the joy of the occasion.

'Hey kid,' Betty called out to me as she wafted past, arms outstretched, 'I've always felt I wanted to do this, but never dared.'

I looked round to see Frank's reaction, but he could hardly disapprove, swaying round the altar as he was.

'Do you do this every week?' Brother Nigel asked, when the music finally stopped and we were all lying on the pews panting.

We shrieked with laughter.

'It was you who started it, mate! We'd like to occasionally, but we haven't, not since the Gift Day.'

I suspected the Brothers were not too sad to see us go, though some special friendships were made. Kelly was thrilled with a South African Bishop, who, when she asked him where he had come from, said, 'prison'. He had refused to inform on the flock. Paula could not get over his having a toilet all to himself. 'Reserved for Bishop' said the sign over the door.

'Where do all your wives live?' someone asked at tea one day.

Brother Marcus guffawed, then realised it was a serious question. 'We're celibate,' he said.

'But the children at the services!'

'They belong to the students at the theological college here.'

A whole new world had been opened up to us. We shook hands with the Brothers. Some allowed them-selves to be hugged.

'You must all come again,' they said, smiling and we knew it was more than just a formality.

'We'll come next week,' Linda said, teasing them as she climbed into the back of the car.

They raised their hands in mock despair.

'One of them asked me at tea if we were evan..., evange..., what's the word?' Jan asked as she got in next to Linda.

'Evangelicals?' I suggested.

'That's it. Well are we whatever it is?'

I hesitated, juggling a while with my seatbelt, aware that how I answered could destroy for ever a certain precious innocence.

Linda came to my rescue.

'Does it matter?' she said, waving madly. 'All I know is that I like them such a lot.'

We drove home exhilarated, yet pensive too. In the final session we had discussed how hard it was that a few traditional church members still resented and rejected our creative efforts. The Music Group found it hardest. Most of the hostility to change was directed at them and it could be difficult to sing to such stony faces.

'Then here's your chance to love,' said Brother Marcus. 'Don't patronise them or try to force them to change. The world does that, but it isn't the way of Christ. Look and see what they have to offer and learn to receive from them.'

Once we were home and back into the normal, daily routine, the exhilaration wore off. But Brother Marcus' cutting words, with their challenge to love where we were hurt, lingered and stayed in our minds long after.

Chapter 22

We moved, but it was not without a certain wistfulness and sense of defeat that we left the estate behind for the centre of the town.

'I used to come down back of this street when I were a kid,' Lucy told me, stopping to reminisce as she helped me unpack. 'It were regarded as posh part of town because the 'ouses were so big and pit bankers and the like lived here. We used to come and hunt in dustbins round back because yer could find some real fancy stuff. One day, I must 'ave been about eight, we found a box, lined with white satin, a canteen without the cutlery. We thought it were beautiful, real treasure. We played with it for hours.'

The houses were no longer quite as upmarket. In fact Joel discovered the first day he went out to play that it was a good deal rougher than the estate. Some child grabbed him by the throat and that had never happened before.

Lucy was not the only one who came to help. Church funds were becoming precarious, so what work on the house we could do ourselves, we did. Lots of people joined in, working day after day and night after night, sometimes into the small hours. Lucy and Betty cleared away mounds of rubble and plaster and mopped the floors with such vigour that the water poured down the staircase. Chris cut out hardboard to cover the splintering floorboards, Joe did whatever he was asked, Alicia performed miracles with a screwdriver and Jack used all his creative skills to assemble the kitchen.

'Where is he?' Madge shouted down the phone in the small hours of one morning.

He looked at the clock, then at us, chuckled as he put on his coat and cap and disappeared quickly down the road.

I felt so grateful to the wives who gave up their husbands for all that time. Some came between shifts or just popped home to eat, or they came all day on a day off or if they were on strike. Nothing seemed too much to ask. The house often rang with laughter. It was a good start to a new home.

By the time another autumn crept up on us, we felt more settled than we had felt for a long time. There had been three moves in as many years and it had taken its emotional toll. I longed to put my roots down deep. I began to appreciate why the miners resisted being moved about. To have a mobile workforce might be economically advantageous for a nation, but people's emotional well-being was surely more important. In Yorkshire there was no tradition of mobility. They were not used to the trauma of it, to the effort required in making new relationships. It was a terrifying prospect. They could see that temporary relationships were superficial, compared to those they had now. Their one wish was to live and die where they had been born, where they knew everyone, and parents, brothers, sisters and cousins were just up the road. Was it so much to ask? After all, it meant that the community was almost self-sufficient. It halved the load on the Social Services. People cared for their elderly and infirm and their handicapped children at home, because of the inbuilt support system. But move the men, take the props away, and the community and all it stood for would collapse like a pack of cards.

Nancy was tiny. The bones in her legs were brittle and had to have a series of major operations, which put her in a wheelchair for several weeks at a time. Because her sisters were nearby there was no need for her children to be taken into care.

'We did try going to Selby once, like they said. The pay was much better, but I couldn't stand it. I cried for me mum and me sisters every day. We came back after six months. Just as well. What would I 'ave done up there without me family and friends when I went into 'ospital?'

The Coal Board had been moving men around the pits for some time. It was always a hard uprooting. A year or so later they would close that pit too, and tell the men to move again. It caused a great deal of bitterness. No one trusted the Coal Board's offers of alternative employment with high financial remuneration any more. All the money in the world could not replace a man's roots.

It seemed to me that there was a natural wisdom about living in a close-knit community, sharing one's life and resources. Though the world tries to deny it, a man is his brother's keeper. My Jewish upbringing taught me that. A Jew may not feel love towards his brother, he may not even like him, but he knows his duty. Birth and identity bring responsibility. With the world against us, in joy and in sorrow, we must stick together, they say. Self-preservation requires it.

The miners said the same. And their freedom to choose that way of life was under threat. Men and women who had never experienced communal commitment of that kind could never understand the strike.

'If they don't agree with the strike, let them go back to work,' friends from a distance said to us.

'You don't understand, they can't,' we replied.

'They're just frightened of intimidation.'

Afraid of intimidation, yes, who was not? But more afraid that once the sense of corporate identity began to crumble, there would be no end to it, until nothing was left of an existence that dated back over a hundred and fifty years. Whether they agreed with the strike or not, miners had stuck together in famine and plenty from the beginning of the nineteenth century.

But sadly, few are left in Britain today with any sense

of history or community. The unidentifiable masses live in vast anonymous cities, in ribbon developments, alienated from their neighbours, fiercely self-reliant, enclosed in the nuclear family and trapped within their own privacy. And yet they believe they are more advanced than the Grimlingtons of this world. But how is progress measured? Who knows? In fact such people are blissfully unaware of the poverty of their own lives and do not know that there is a better way to live, for if they did, they would not condemn Grimlington to destruction and its inhabitants to the same lonely, anonymous kind of existence.

The wonders of economics were a mystery to me. I could not understand all the arguments for or against pit closures. But one thing was obvious. With a new industrial estate at the bottom of the town, with our location at the junction of three major motorways and London only two hours away by train, if the pits had to close there was no reason why money should not be invested in many alternative industries in the area. After all, countryside which must have once approached the Dales and the Moors in loveliness was already a treeless wasteland. There was nothing to lose. The train journey to Leeds revealed mile upon mile of bleak, barren landscape, churned and charred, spattered with bricks and rubble, pieces of broken-down fencing and tattered barbed wiring. There was little hope of reafforestation. This was not Sussex or Surrey. No voice of protest would be raised. New industry was therefore sensible and essential. But who cared enough about the North? The 'oppressor', he who would rob us of our jobs and our homes, and leave us with nothing, was seen as a faceless, mindless man from the South, the successor to the landowner, the pit owner, and every other lord and master, who had owned men, patronised them, treated them as cattle and left them to starve in the great depressions.

Temporarily the oppressor acquired a face. Since there was no one else to be the butt of so much anger and bitterness, since he represented Coal Board and Government, was a foreigner who had no understanding of miners and their ways, Mr McGregor would do. The fact that Mr McGregor was also the name of the nasty farmer who chased poor Peter Rabbit for pinching his radishes meant that Joel's familiar bedtime story took on new meaning altogether.

My heart ached for the town as it fought for its life, bruised, battered, weary and confused. McGregor said one thing, Scargill another. They stood in the middle, uncertain whom to believe. There was no trust. The Coal Board had always let them down; managers could be hard, vindictive and impersonal, and had not cared for their workforce. Yet did the Union leaders really care? Would a strike achieve anything? They were helpless, pulled one way by old loyalties and another by hunger. They were pawns on a chess-board in a great political game of power and most of them knew it.

But few families could bear the stigma of 'scab'. Some streets were still known as 'Scab Alley', fifty years after a strike. There was no greater shame to pass on to your children. It was the worst possible betrayal. I suppose it was a bit like the way the Jewish community felt about my becoming a Christian.

Perhaps there was a chance that a strike might work. After all it had always been their only effective weapon against exploitation. If a man had no other control over his destiny, he could at least withhold his labour, and it gave him some sense of his own worth and dignity. This time he was not asking for more money. All he wanted was a job, his home, family, community and future. If there was the slightest chance that a strike could preserve all those, then it was worth any price he might have to pay to achieve it.

Autumn seemed to reflect the mood of the town. It was sad and wistful, with more than its usual hint of farewell to the halcyon days of summer. An insipid, watery sun gave out little warmth and as I walked the children to school through the cemetery, our extremities were frozen before we were half-way there. The bleak and icy prospect of winter was not far away. Families would soon need coal and there was none to be had and no money to afford an alternative. I shivered at the prospect.

The path through the cemetery was the nearest thing in the town to a woodland glade. It was bordered on either side by a few spindly ash and cherry trees. Few people dared walk there alone at night. With its dim yellow lighting and long wispy shadows it looked like a Hollywood set for a Dracula movie and there were rumours of glue-sniffing and other strange goings-on. But by day, if I closed my eyes to the gravestones and piles of litter stacked against the walls, I could almost imagine I was miles from civilisation. The tips of the leaves had turned russet and gold and the effect was quite picturesque.

Then Peter discovered that most of the trees would have to come down. They had Dutch Elm disease. I grieved for my 'woodland glade'. It was hardly beautiful, but I was learning to take beauty where I found it. And there was something infinitely precious about a poor, single tree, which had stood resolute through the years, defying vandalism, pollution, development and industrialisation. Each tree became a kind of symbol to me of the unchanging, undefeated glory of God and all he made, despite man's worst. Autumn always made me a little sad anyway. I hate goodbyes of every kind.

Harvest festival was chaotic. Children juggled their oranges, rolled down the aisle over melons and marrows, munched their way through bananas and got a slap for eating the offering. Despite the strike there was an amazing display of harvest gifts. Why was I surprised? I already knew that people would give away their last potato.

Frank, who had recently become churchwarden, along with Tom, who was doing hours of picket duty, eyed two large boxes of potatoes.

'At least this lot's ready,' he said.

I looked at him quizzically.

'I thought everyone in the town knew. Someone down at the allotments harvested all their potatoes too soon. He left 'em in a mound to rot, but when 'e came back next day, they'd gone. They think some miners must have taken them. They're getting pretty desperate. They've asked around, but no one admits to it. You see, the thing is, if they eat them, they'll poison themselves, poor souls.'

Frank shook his head, then he laughed. 'Eeeh, but I don't know how they got in. So much fruit and veg vanishes that the allotments look like Colditz. I can hardly get in meself and I've got a key!'

'Where there's a will, there's a way,' said our police sergeant with the full weight of experience behind him.

Alicia had the unenviable job of sorting the harvest gifts into parcels and commandeering the workforce who turned up on Monday morning to deliver them. The clergy phones had been ringing all week.

'You will give to the miners, won't you? They're starving and they've always given to the church.'

'You won't give anything to the miners, will you? My business has had to close because of them.'

On the whole community spirit prevailed and the distribution of the parcels was left to Alicia's discretion. She had started a church food cupboard years ago, keeping it well stocked with tins and giving them away when she knew someone was in need. Several church families had had cause to bless her in difficult days. But by the time that harvest came, the shelves were bare. She had been delivering food parcels and seeing to the needs of the various families affected by the strike, especially those connected with the church, for some time.

'I did encourage people to give tins this year,' she said. 'You see we can store tins and give them out as they're needed.'

But there were still relatively few and she rang Mr Mason, the greengrocer, and ordered tins of steak, mince, pease pudding, baked beans and whatever else was cheap and nourishing. I gathered from their discussion that he was quite used to an order of this kind from Alicia.

After much sorting, packing, repacking and debate about what an aubergine was and what you could do with it, and whether green peppers would go down well at the Old Folks' Home, twenty or so volunteers set off on their errands of mercy. Linda arrived back with her parcel half an hour later.

'I knocked and knocked for ages,' she said, 'but no one came to the door. Then a face appeared at the window of the next house. "She's not 'ere, love," the neighbour shouted. "She's in Ossleforth General 'aving 'er legs off."'

Linda laughed nervously, but she was as green as the peppers in her parcel. 'It sounded as easy as 'aving her teeth out,' she said. 'I wonder why it's getting so common to lose bits of yer anatomy these days!' With an uneasy smile, she set off with a new address.

As the helpers came back for more parcels the story was always the same. Many of the regular recipients complained as usual that there was not enough, they didn't eat bananas, they would have rather had something else. But mining families were grateful for the tiniest offering. Everyone who went to a miner's house came back very moved. Lucy went to Ginny's and Ginny almost broke down when she opened the door.

'I can't believe it,' she said, 'it's a gift straight from heaven. Yer timing's incredible. We only 'ad so much money left and it were food or coal. Well the baby 'as bronchitis, so it 'ad to be coal, didn't it? I didn't know what we were going to eat.'

Ginny had been coming to 'Mums and Babes' a few weeks. I noticed her straight away. She always sat with her hands in her pockets, swinging on her chair, with an amused nonchalance which could not hide her interest in every word that was said. She had a ruthless honesty and a determination I admired to settle only for the truth. No platitude was going to satisfy someone with that kind of perception.

'I nearly died of cancer a few years ago,' she told me. 'I was engaged to Doug at the time. You're never the same after that. I don't regret it. It alters the whole way yer see things.'

I told Peter about her. I found her abrasive dismissal of all dishonesty a challenge.

'What did you say her name was? Where does she live?'

'Right opposite the parish hall.'

Peter threw back his head and laughed. I watched him, bewildered.

'Well, well,' he said, 'come to think of it. I thought it was her I saw in church the other day, but I told myself I was seeing things. Don't you know how I know them?'

I shook my head.

'A certain baptismal visit?' he prompted.

Suddenly it clicked into place. Ginny had talked about wanting the children baptised. They were a special gift to her. She was told that with so much of her insides missing she would not have any.

'The most belligerent pair you had ever met?' I asked.

Peter nodded and laughed again.

'Well, I think it's time I visited them again.'

He did, and again, until popping in on Doug and Ginny was such a regular occurrence that I always knew where he was if there was no sign of him at midnight.

Doug hated receiving the parcel from the church. His bulky frame and tough exterior were just a front for the more sensitive character inside.

'We're not reduced to taking charity, y'know, Ginny.'

'I know, love,' she said, 'but yer've got to admit the timing's right. Can't we accept it this time, for the kids?'

'Ay, well, this once,' he said reluctantly, then he

grinned a broader grin than she had seen on his face since the strike began.

'What's up with you?' she asked him, surprised.

'I'm just thinking, it is nice to know that someone cares.'

Chapter 23

'There's smoke coming out of boiler. I don't suppose it's serious, but he ought to know.'

'Thanks for ringing. I'll tell him,' I said wearily.

'Peter!' I called out into the hallway.

He was half-way out of the front door, with a long list of visits he had been intending to do for ages.

'Boiler's on the blink, again! There's smoke coming out of it, this time.'

'There always is these days,' he called back, unimpressed, and sighed.

'Why must things always take up more time than people?'

'Perhaps because you have a way with things you don't have with people!' I said, smiling at him sweetly.

He acknowledged my sarcasm with a snort.

Peter's reputation as a do-it-yourself, mend-anything whizz kid had quickly spread through the parish. One week he walked in from his home Communions with an alarm clock and two vacuum cleaners. All kinds of parish repairs, unmendables, broken appliances and other bric-a-brac began to gravitate in our direction and since I refused to have them anywhere else they ended up in a great heap in the middle of Peter's study. I could always tell when sermon preparation lacked inspiration by the whirring or tinkering sound which escaped from behind the closed study door.

As he visited round the parish, doors which had never shut properly before, shut for the first time. Lights which had not worked for ages lit at his touch. Drains unblocked and boilers staggered into action. There was no way we could gauge his pastoral effectiveness, but as a handyman he was past master. Twice the phone rang calling him out on matters of the greatest urgency. Had a marriage broken down? No, it was the central heating. Still, it was all part of a clergyman's day.

'You know,' I said to him, 'if you had the same effect on people as you had on things you'd be the Archbishop of Canterbury in a year or two.'

'Thanks!' he said. 'I'd better go and have a look at the boiler, I suppose. I might as well go to the parish hall first.' He sighed and the door slammed.

It was as well he did. By the time he arrived, black smoke was pouring out of the building. An excited gang of Scouts were standing outside, laughing and shouting.

'Who's called the Fire Brigade?' Peter shouted. As he approached the doors he saw the flames leaping under the floorboards.

There was no reply. He ran for all he was worth up the vicarage drive past Anna, who had been summoned to the scene, and dialled 999.

Grimlington's part-time fire brigade arrived swiftly, but it look them some time to get the blaze under control.

'Why did no one phone them earlier?' Peter asked. Sparks from the boiler had ignited litter left under the floorboards when the hall was modernised. The fire had been smouldering for some time.

'The boiler's been blowing smoke signals at us for so many months that no one realised what was happening.'

Peter sadly acknowledged the truth of it. He went inside and stood for some time assessing the damage.

'We're insured, aren't we ?' Anna said.

Peter nodded.

'But insurance never covers everything,' he said slowly, looking round at the damp, charred building. 'And the inconvenience! This place will be out of action for ages. No playgroup or toddler club. And we've just had it decorated after dealing with the damp.'

'Buildings!' he muttered to himself through gritted

teeth, 'Buildings and boilers! They're nothing but weight round our necks. A drain of time, manpower and resources. Why don't we just get rid of the lot of them and hire a hall or meet in people's homes?'

He was in no mood for his visits. There was only one place to go. He saw the light in the window of the house opposite and found his feet carrying him across the road.

'By, yer've 'ad some trouble tonight though,' Doug said, as he opened the door and saw the dejected form on his doorstep.

'Come in. Get theesel' warmed up and 'ave a cuppa.'

'It's all that money I mind most,' Peter said, the feeling coming back into his hands as he clasped a mug of tea. 'There are so many other needs at the moment.'

'Ay, well, that's life,' Doug said, settling himself heavily in his favourite armchair. 'I shouldn't worry theesel' too much about money. It comes and it goes.'

Peter smiled.

'You're quite a philosopher in your own way.'

'Well, 'ow I see it is this. I've 'ad weeks when there's been plenty and weeks when there's been nowt. When I've got it, I spend it and when I 'aven't, I do without. Yer 'ave to tek what comes. No use worrying about it.'

'But isn't it hard to be without? I thought miners had quite a good wage.'

'Face-workers do, ay. That's why it's hit 'em hardest now. But not us surface workers. We're lucky to take home ninety pounds a week. But Ginny and I don't complain. We've never starved.'

'We nearly did last week,' Ginny said, with a child under each arm, as she came into the room. 'If God hadn't looked after us and sent us a parcel at right time.'

Doug grinned at her sheepishly.

'She'll not let me forget, will she?'

Peter got up.

'I have to go. The wires under the floor might still be smouldering and the fire brigade says they must be checked every hour through the night.'

'Listen, mate,' Doug said, following him to the door,

'I'm no great sleeper. I'm up with kids every hour or two through the night. I've no work in the morning. So get to bed and I'll keep an eye on parish hall.'

Peter's relief was beyond measure. He could have hugged Doug, but taking another look at his large form, he changed his mind. Doug would think him altogether soft in the head.

It was a Communion service. I looked up during the administration of the bread and wine and realised that at the altar rail, in a row, were miners who were on strike, some who had left the pit in disgust and found other work, Tom, weary with hours of picket duty and Sid, whose fish and chip shop was only just surviving. Such is Yorkshire integrity that I knew that if there had been so much as an ounce of hostility among them, they would not be kneeling there, shoulder to shoulder, waiting to take Communion together.

'Sid, did you realise you were kneeling next to striking miners at the altar rail?' I asked him out of curiosity after the service.

'Was I? It makes no difference to me, not here.'

'There seems no resentment among you.'

'Resentment?' he laughed ruefully. 'This time last year I'd 'ave killed 'em, ruining me business like that. That shows yer 'ow much I've changed. These are me brothers. How can I 'ate them?'

'What are you going to do, Sid? What will you live on?'

'Don't you worry, lass,' he said, patting me on the shoulder. 'Someone's looking after me. I've managed to get a job on a building site for now, so I'll labour by day and fry by night.'

'You'll be shattered.'

'I'm not afraid of hard work. And I'll take Wednesday evenings off so's I can come to the fellowship.'

I marvelled at the spirit of mutual support which seemed to grow daily within the church. Neighbouring towns became frustrated and aggressive, with increasing outbursts of violence. A handful of men from Grimlington went back to work, and the town began to despair. As a Christian community, sharing all we had became a necessity. We learnt to throw nothing away, nor hang on to what was no longer useful. Someone, somewhere, needed it. We sometimes felt we had been given a special chance, which few churches are given, to see how much of our love was real, and how much the sentimental sham Brother Marcus had spoken of.

'Christians should never strike,' a well-meaning woman said to me at a meeting in Sussex.

She had never met a miner, never been to West Yorkshire. Would that life were always that easy, that right and wrong were emblazoned in the sky in illuminated letters. A law for every occasion, so that we would no longer need to think for ourselves. The freedom God gave human beings was a heavy burden to bear. Life would have been easier if we were puppets, so that all the divinity needed to do was pull the strings, but it would never have been so rich and colourful. We would never have wrestled, struggled or prayed.

In the midst of this crisis, one thing was clear. Politics were irrelevant. We could not stand by and watch our brothers starve. As we dashed up to Newcastle on days off and I sat by my father's bed, watching his slow deterioration, I remembered words he had so often spoken when I was a teenager.

'Principles are very important, but people must always come first. When that isn't so, fanatics are born, and fanatics are dangerous. They are without mercy. Politicians and religious people are always the worst offenders.'

Dear Dad, he would never have understood the strike, but I discovered the wisdom of his words over and over again. Perhaps Christ was saying exactly the same thing when they dragged over to him the woman caught in the act of adultery: 'Let him who is without sin cast the first stone.' Principles that never bend for people give a false sense of security and self-righteousness.

We stopped worrying about the church budget, vital repairs, the redecoration of the parish hall and we fed and clothed whoever needed it. And the demand grew with each successive day. Peter encouraged our striking miners who were tempted to go back to work to stay at home. The repercussions for themselves and their families were too enormous. Every day an armoured police van drew up outside the church and under police guard the handful of working miners got out and ran the gauntlet into the cemetery through a jeering crowd. Grimlington had experienced nothing like it.

One Wednesday evening, Barbara broke down in the mid-week meeting and began to sob.

'Let her have a good cry,' Peter said. He could see she was in some distress and three or four pairs of arms were about to smother her. The sobs continued for some time, then gradually subsided.

Eventually she managed to say, 'It's my brother. He went back to work on Monday and yesterday his house and car were smashed to pieces.'

She broke down again and several others began to cry too, either in sympathy or because the strain of the last few months had suddenly become too much to endure alone.

'It's not that property matters,' Barbara said, 'it's that the kids are so frightened. They don't understand what's happening.'

'Neither do I,' Ginny said, 'the world's gone mad.'

Peter made no attempt to call the meeting to order and the crying continued. The wives in particular had had months of hiding their feelings, of coping, of being strong for their husbands and children. Someone had to be brave and keep the home going, find food to put on the table, even though their nerves were taut and their spirits almost broken by the shame of begging and buying rubbish from the butcher's and greengrocer's. Instinctively Ginny, Mavis and Barbara moved together and stood with their arms round each other, swaying slightly and wiping their tears away.

It seemed somehow right and natural and no one interrupted them. The meeting continued. Gradually the tears stopped, they blew their noses, wiped their eyes again and went back to their places, not before Ginny had remembered to go over and give Sid a big hug. It was a kind of apology and he acknowledged it with a wink.

None of the wives had any time for self-pity. It was not in their nature. Once the tears were out of the way, that was that. Life must go on. Support was plentiful, but sympathy was limited and ran out fast. Almost everyone had had some hardship to contend with. That was life. It made them tough and resilient. But the wives at the church not only coped. They began to see the strike in quite a positive way.

Mavis, who came to help Peter with some typing to supplement their income, said, 'If you'd told me this time last year that we'd have gone all these months without a wage coming in, and I'd still cope, I'd have laughed at you.'

She reluctantly accepted the coffee I put into her hands. She was a shy, gentle person and her husband Ron was not really in sympathy with the Union. They lived a quiet life, enjoying evenings in with their records, and I could imagine how much the disruption to their peaceful routine must have upset them.

'The hardest thing I find,' Mavis said, 'is that you feel that everyone else outside the community is against you. I mean, the newspapers and TV make the miners look awful. We're all condemned without a hearing. They don't seem to understand we've no choice. Of course Ron wants to go back. We're ashamed of the pickets. We're ashamed of all the violence. We're a bit ashamed of ourselves for not having the courage, but what would anyone else do? How can we put the children at risk or have them live with their dad being called a scab?'

I nodded and she went on sipping her coffee, thoughtfully. After a while she said, 'Do you know, the

Union rang the other day about some fire-fighting Ron was doing, with their consent, to keep the pit safe. Well, when they said who it was, my legs turned to jelly. Daft, isn't it? But that's my trouble, I'm a born worrier.'

She put the mug down on the table and was about to go back to the typewriter, when she turned suddenly.

'But d'you know, I think these last months are teaching me to stop worrying. Ron and I never realised how much material things had come to matter to us, the house and things like that. You don't, not until you have to do without. I've been thinking about Joe and Linda, watching them give to miners' families. He was unemployed all that time and we did nothing for them. We just didn't understand. We'll never forget though.'

She paused for a moment, then her face suddenly lit up. 'The funny thing is that now we've nothing, we've never been so rich. We get what we need as we need it. I've been down to my last tin and something always turns up. We don't take basics like food for granted any more. So,' she said as she stood smiling in the doorway, 'maybe this strike hasn't been all bad. You always ask yourself whether your faith is real or just a delusion, at least, I do, or I did. You wonder whether it's strong enough to survive a real crisis. Well, I don't regret the chance to find out.'

Nancy's attitude was almost the same. She had had yet another leg operation when I went round to see her and was sitting in her wheelchair, running her home with her leg stretched out in a plaster cast in front of her. She and her three girls were all huddled round a coal fire, the only one in the house.

'These girls,' she said, 'had no coats for the winter, so what was I going to do? I couldn't send them to school with no coats. Someone from church offered to buy 'em one each. That made me feel worse, because she'd no money either. I didn't know what to do, and I thought, "God's supposed to take care of the sparrows, so what about my girls?" The next day there were a knock at the door. It were Dorothy. Now this is honest truth, what do

221

yer think she 'ad in 'er 'ands? Three coats what 'er kids 'ad just grown out of! "Are these any good to yer?" she said. Any good! Each one fitted one of my girls perfectly, as if they were made for 'em. Now yer can't tell me that were coincidence. I wouldn't believe yer anyway. It's been like that all through strike. Our Alf can't get over the way people have given to us without expecting anything back. It's changed 'is whole attitude to church. Maybe we 'ad to 'ave a strike to learn to give and receive.'

It was the week I saw Nancy that the news of the famine in Ethiopia broke. It put Grimlington's plight into a strange new perspective. One after another mining families urged us to bring them no more food parcels, but to send the money to Ethiopia instead.

'At least we've enough for bread and potatoes with the occasional sausage,' Ginny said. 'I can't sit and watch that screen and do nowt. If I could adopt some Ethiopian kids I would. We 'aven't got much in the way of food, but it's more than they 'ave. And yer can starve much quicker without love, than yer can without food. If I've learnt anything these months it's that.'

'And that,' I thought, 'is more than most of us learn in a lifetime!'

Chapter 24

In October my father died. Initially I felt an enormous sense of relief. I could hardly bear to watch his slow disintegration any longer and nor could my mother. Why should such a fine, intelligent man have to spend the end of his days weak, helpless and totally dependent on others? The standard of nursing at the small cottage hospital just outside of Newcastle helped us all to cope. To the end they ensured he was treated with great dignity and respect.

My mother, brother, sister and Peter and I were with him most of the time. I was glad we were able to say goodbye and tell him how much we loved him and what a wonderful father he had been. He need have no cause for regret. Although he was in a coma, his eyelids flickered in response to our voices and we knew he could hear and understand. In a strange way, although one was a sad farewell, and the other a joyful welcome, I felt there were similarities between this moment and Joel's birth. I felt the same awe, the same sense of wonder at being face to face with infinity, the mystery which lies beyond man's limited perception. My father had never feared the moment of death and he went as gently and peacefully as he had lived.

It was later, when the initial relief and numbness wore off a little, that I realised how bereft I was. I had cried so much over the last months and behaved so irrationally at times that I supposed I had done much of my grieving already. But now I became aware of an aching void which no one would ever fill again.

'You know you need never worry about anything,' he

would say to me, despite my not making his ideal marriage, despite everything, 'I'll always be there when you need me.'

But it wasn't true. I still needed him and he was no longer there.

I felt angry he had left me, though it was no fault of his, angry with God for the few paltry years we were allowed, and angry with the ageing process, both my father's and mine! There was no one left to shield me from my own mortality. As the older generation died, and my children grew, I was slowly and inevitably becoming the older generation. I had already lived half a lifetime and accomplished so little. The only comfort was the certainty that my human perspective was inadequate, that probably, once we knew what lay beyond the horizon, we would not say, 'Why did you only give me threescore years and ten?' but, 'why did you leave me down there so long?'

For the seven official days of mourning known as 'Shiva', I stayed with David and Sandy, my brother and sister-in-law. As well as the sadness, there was much laughter in the house too. My father would have enjoyed that. He was not a morbid man. As close family, we were not allowed to cook at a time of bereavement, according to Jewish law, so we waited to see what would arrive at our door and watched in wonder as Sandy's freezer filled from top to bottom. There were chickens, fresh salmon, apple pies and luscious cakes. They so whetted our appetites that David said he had not eaten so well since he got married, and from the look on Sandy's face, I doubted he would eat as well again! We had no heart to shop or cook and were glad it was forbidden anyway. But at the end of a hectic day, with constant visitors and phone calls, it was bliss to sit down and know the food was there and ready. In the Jewish community food is the cure for all that ails you, and in this instance, it certainly helped.

It seemed to me that the way the Jewish community coped with bereavement was wiser and more wholesome than any so-called Christian approach. For one thing it was practical, rather than sentimental. Perhaps the problem was that, apart from sending cards and flowers, Christians have no tradition of how to comfort the bereaved. They feel lost and embarrassed because there are no guidelines, no obvious thing to say or do. It is much easier to visit with a tureen of chicken soup, or a bowl of chopped liver in your hand.

A loss in the Jewish community is not just personal, the whole community feels it. Day after day friends of Sandy's came to take our children out. My mother held court and people came to sit, laugh, cry and remember. They came to join in the prayers every evening, the women in one room, clustered around my mother and me, who sat on low stools, and the men in the next room, reciting 'Kaddish'. The Rabbi was present every evening too. And I thought Peter worked hard! But then my mother could not get over the fact that Peter was not invited to the parties after the weddings and funerals at which he officiated. As an Anglican priest he was a functionary, not a focal point in the community.

We awoke every morning to the sound of the memorial prayers again. An act of worship requires the presence of ten men. The Rabbi would be leading morning prayer at the synagogue. So David had to rely on ten of his friends and relatives coming to pray before they went to work.

Many non-Jewish friends came to the house too. In fact there were so many at the funeral that the Rabbi resorted to reading half the service in English. There were representatives from every organisation my father had served in some way. The St John Ambulance Brigade wanted to lay their cross on his coffin as a sign of respect. We appreciated the thought and Dad would have loved it, but the Rabbi said it was not possible.

There were no flowers at the cemetery. There never are at Jewish funerals, but the house was full of them, sent by non-Jewish friends. Sandy worried about what to do with them at first. The Rabbi said that there was no law, it was simply a tradition, so we relaxed and enjoyed them. We were all quite puzzled about what the laws actually were and what was just tradition. David wanted to be right so he asked the Rabbi endless questions, and in the end was given a booklet so he could look the answers up for himself. Many were sensible and healing, designed to give a mourner space and time, others seemed a bit irrelevant. I was amused. My father had paid scant attention to the written laws himself. His only law had been his conscience, and that he had lived up to it to the best of his ability was evident from the number and variety of people who came to pay their respects.

The Rabbi quite obviously found my presence a bit of an embarrassment. After all he could not be seen to condone what I had done, but nor could he slight the bereaved. He was reserved, yet always gracious. I wondered how Sandy felt too. I knew that 'marrying out' and to a clergyman of all people was an affront to her orthodoxy, but she had never said so and always welcomed me lovingly into her home. We sat up late night after night, enjoying the stillness of the small hours and getting to know each other for the first time. The situation drew us together in a new way. We talked for hours, so much so that when I left to go home, I felt that though I had lost a father, I had found a sister.

Peter had brought me many loving letters and cards from Grimlington, but going back was like coming out of hibernation. With a jolt I was catapulted from my safe, quiet cocoon to a world that was weary and wounded. I went into the kitchen, walked over to the window and looked out at the now familiar sight of the pit head wheels in the distance, unnaturally still and motionless. Something was different.

'Peter,' I called, 'was it my imagination, or did the Council put up a brand new fence around the field at the back a few weeks ago?'

He came up behind me, looked over my shoulder and nodded.

'Thank goodness for that. I thought I must have been hallucinating. Where is it?'

He grinned. 'Every morning when I got up, a little bit more had disappeared. I expect it makes very good firewood!'

I had to laugh.

'Ah well, it was only a fence after all.'

I had managed to push the strike out of my mind for a fortnight, but Grimlington could not forget, not for a moment.

'When it's over . . .' were the opening words of every sentence, as if saying it often enough would convince people that some day life would return to a measure of normality.

But the fact was, it was beginning to seem a never-ending nightmare. Grandparents were sharing their pensions. Retirement savings had long since gone. That little 'nest-egg', a little something put by for the future, had evaporated into the air. No more plans were made, no dreams were dreamed. Life was temporarily suspended and we lived a strange kind of limbo existence.

Jan finally announced that she and her husband were getting divorced. The gulf between them which he said the church created had grown too wide. But there was no chance of a separation until their house sold. And houses were not selling during the strike.

Then, with the worst possible timing, both the DHSS and the binmen went on strike too. According to Linda, the binmen's strike was something to do with a black scab, but whether that was one of the men, or something one of them found crawling out of a dustbin, no one was sure. The dispute started over their refusal to use the black bin liners the Council were now supplying and it continued for weeks. Dustbin bags full of stinking rubbish were thrown into the streets or left in mounds on the street corners. The cats and dogs tore them open and their filth spilt out onto the pavements. Despite the threat of vermin, the Council did nothing. Grimlington once again slipped through the bureaucratic net. A strange stomach virus broke out, and some people, already weakened by a poor diet, were quite badly affected.

The DHSS strike compounded the general hardship and caused chaos. Since I tried to postpone collecting my Child Benefit until I had saved enough to make it feel worthwhile, I was totally oblivious to the problem for some weeks. On a chill November day, when I had just about recovered from the nasty tummy bug, I crawled round to the Post Office, feeling wobbly and washed-out. To my horror the queue went out of the door and half-way up the street. With a sinking heart I joined the weary pensioners and frazzled mums who were trying to keep their bored toddlers off the street and away from the traffic. It began to rain. We huddled against the wall, vainly trying to keep warm and dry.

'They've closed all the blinking sub-Post Offices,' an elderly woman complained. 'I've had to walk nearly a mile from the bottom of the town to get here.'

My turn came at last.

'You'll have to start coming every week for your emergency payments,' the postmistress barked without looking up.

'But I don't need emergency payments,' I said.

'I don't care. I can't be paying out a month's benefit in one go. It mucks up my cash flow. And there are no new allowance books, so I can only give you one week's payment at a time.'

'Have you seen the queue outside?' I persisted, mustering all the strength I had. 'Why should anyone have to wait an hour in the rain for thirteen pounds?'

'If they need it, they'll have to. I can't help that.'

I knew she was under pressure too, but it was hard to sympathise with someone who had simply become a mouthpiece for the system. Why did bureaucracy dehumanise its officials, even in a small town? I walked out and the queue was even longer than before. It reminded me of films of the queues at the soup kitchens in the Depression of the thirties. No pension or no Child Benefit would mean no food. So they waited. There was no choice.

'One of these days there'll be women miners,' I said to Doug. I loved teasing Yorkshiremen about their traditional attitudes to the male and female roles. But with Doug, it rarely worked. He was far too quick for me and Ginny went out to work anyway. He looked at me, his face a mixture of amusement and supreme patience and said, 'Eeeeeh lass, but thar't daft! Where would they pee?'

Now I had not thought of that. Up until that moment it never occurred to me that there were no toilets down the pit. How could there be? I suddenly felt very naive.

'And anyway,' Doug said, grinning, 'no woman would last long down there with all them mice.'

'Mice?' I whispered.

'Ay, if yer don't tie yer snap to yer belt, yer've 'ad it. Mice eat it.'

'Snap?'

'Yer lunch box. Yer can't put it on ground. The mice came down in the 'ay what they used to give pit ponies. By, they must be havin' a lean time of it now,' he chuckled.

I thought for a bit.

'Doug, is it cold down there?'

'No, hot usually, though it should be ventilated properly. It's dark though, and wet.'

'Then why does anyone want to do it?'

He shrugged. 'I suppose because yer dad and grandad did it before yer and there's nowt else.'

'Do you want your lads to be miners?'

The two boys were playing at our feet. Doug looked at them for a while. The little one, angelic with his bright eyes and halo of tight golden curls, gurgled at us, as if expressing his point of view. Doug laughed, then shook his head.

'No, not if I'm honest. No miner does. He always wants his lads to do better. But there's never been owt else, and especially now.'

'If they built the new airport up here, on the M1, instead of at Stanstead, and there'd been the promise of lots of jobs, how would you have felt?'

He threw his head back and laughed.

'But they won't. They've never given the North a chance and they're not going to start now.'

He looked at the children again and a sadness came into his eyes.

'What's for them, that's all I want to know. What kind of future waits for them?'

But on the whole people tried not to think too much about the future. How to survive tomorrow was enough. The thought of Christmas filled most people with gloom. The Union promised every man a turkey, but what of all the other trimmings the adverts said were a necessity? Most people accepted that they would just have to do without that year.

'We're not having tinsel this Christmas,' Mavis said. 'None of the finery, the presents, and all the irrelevant bits. We can't afford them anyway. We'll have a real family Christmas. We'll sing, we'll play games, we'll talk. We might even discover what a real Christmas is.'

No one dared overspend, not even non-mining families. I felt guilty if at the checkout of the supermarket I had chocolate biscuits in my trolley. Members of the Miners' Benevolent Fund sat beside the exit, with a basket at their feet, begging with their eyes for contributions. I suddenly realised how much of my weekly shopping was for luxury, not necessity goods and I became more thoughtful about what I was buying and why. If the strike had not had that effect on the town, I suspected the pictures of Ethiopia would. They took them to heart. Life for all of us that Christmas was altogether simpler and less extravagant.

The church finances were in dire straits. Our determination to keep up the food parcels and the lack of giving took us five thousand pounds into the red almost before we knew it. Everyone was supporting a relative somewhere and no one had money to give to the church. Then came a command from the Town Council to mend the church clock.

'It's a town amenity,' they said.

'Fine,' we said, 'you pay for it then!'

'We've just voted that the church members should.'

'The church members aren't interested.'

'We'll help then . . . but just a bit.'

And so the wrangling continued. Nothing could be done for the time being anyway.

We received our usual mound of Christmas cards and letters from friends and clergy all over the country. Most seemed totally oblivious of what was happening in our part of the world. Some even asked us for money for their ambitious building projects. Their request was like a slap across the face. I smarted. Let them have their plush new buildings. I did not resent them that, but could they not have spared us a thought, a token? Their brothers and sisters were hungry.

One clergyman in the South rang and said his church was concerned. What could they do? Our hearts leaped. Someone did care.

'Send money,' Peter said.

'I meant could we pray? I don't think they'll want to send money.'

'If politics are a problem, don't worry,' Peter said, 'there are plenty of church families in need who have been affected indirectly.'

But we heard nothing and our hearts sank again. It was silly to raise our hopes and we tried not to be disappointed.

'Do they ever think about us?' Linda asked one night at Drama, just before Christmas. We were rehearsing a sketch with a rather cynical feel about it, which seemed to match our mood. She had to stick a picture of a jolly Father Christmas, his sack bulging with presents, over a War On Want poster. She stood for a while comparing the child with its gaunt body and haunted eyes to the rotund, jolly Santa Claus. 'All those Christians in the South, I mean, do they ever think about us or know how we live?'

'I don't think so,' I said. 'How could they?'

'It's just, well, it seems so funny. We're going to be in heaven together, but we don't know anything about each other now.'

She shook her head and smiled wistfully.

'Oh, don't mind me. I'm just sad tonight, that's all.'

It had been a hard week for Linda. She was already upset about Jan's divorce. They were close. Then her brother-in-law, a man in his mid-thirties, collapsed and died while queueing at the pit for his Christmas parcel. There were four children.

'I can't blame the strike,' Linda said, 'his heart would have given way sooner or later. But he was so upset at having to beg like that. He was ashamed. He got into such a state.'

Two days later his near neighbour died too, digging in a local slag heap for bits of coal.

'Better to be cold above ground than beneath it,' most miners said. But his children were cold and he ignored the miners. The coal tip gave way and crushed him. The street was reeling from the shock, while Linda had been comforting Jan and her sister.

Her question stayed with me, perhaps because it was mine too, and I was still thinking about it a few days later when a letter arrived in a strange hand, postmarked Surrey.

'Dear Mrs Guinness, you came and spoke to us a few months ago.'

My initial reaction was relief. Not another invitation to speak. There were so many and it was not something I enjoyed very much. People did not seem to understand how much of a strain it was, though if they were honest, they must, or they would do it themselves and not invite someone else. I read on.

'I sat next to you at the meal and I have not forgotten what you said about the effects of the strike. We have just sold a vase, a family heirloom and it raised more than we expected. Please accept the enclosed as a small gift.'

I looked at the cheque. It was for a thousand pounds.

I threw on my coat, ran through the cemetery and burst into the vestry, where Edward, Alicia and Peter were having morning prayers.

'Look!' I said, waving my letter about.

They looked at me as if I had taken leave of my senses, scanned the letter, and were just as excited themselves. It was not the amount that mattered, although it helped. It was the knowledge that someone had remembered us, and cared. I found Linda and showed her the letter too. She stared at it, then smiled and shook her head.

'Well, you can knock me down. I don't believe it. I just don't believe it.'

It was Lucy and Mary who received the best gifts that Christmas, and from the Council too. Both heard at the same time that they had been given a new house.

'Pinch me, I'm dreaming,' Mary said, wandering round her new house in a daze.

'Look!' she said, pointing at the kitchen counters and throwing open the cupboards.

'And come in 'ere,' she said, dragging me into a large, bright sitting room.

'And what about up 'ere?' she said, rushing upstairs. 'A bedroom each for the kids. And it's warm! No more going to bed in gloves and socks. The radiators run off the fire.'

I followed her round and we ooohed and aaaahed into every nook and cranny.

'I nearly kissed 'em at 'Ousing Department when they told me,' she said. 'I were so happy I didn't know what to do. This is the best Christmas present, it's the best present I ever 'ad. I knew me prayers would be answered one day. I just knew it.'

Looking at the sheer delight on her face, I could not have imagined God holding out on her for very much longer.

Lucy was as thrilled with her new flat. Dad took some persuading that life could be as rich without a coal fire, but once they had moved and he had experienced the joys of warmth at the touch of a button, no more humping, scraping and cleaning, then he wondered why he had made such a fuss. And since the heating was coal-fired, the Coal Board continued to give him the heating allowance they gave to all ex-miners, and he was in his element. In fact he told everyone he had master-minded the whole move. 'Council just 'ad to give in, because wi' me, actions speak worder than louds,' he said defiantly, thumping the arm of his chair to show he meant business.

'Well, Mr Barker, God's good, isn't he?'

A small group had gathered at Lucy's for a guided tour and were now devouring large quantities of her fruit cake, washed down by large mugs of tea. There was silence from the armchair. They tried again.

'God's been good to you, Mr Barker.'

He took his pipe out of his mouth and stared at them suspiciously.

Undaunted, they tried another tack to tempt the old man into discussing his eternal destiny. 'Mr Barker, you're not a drinking man, are you, what do you like doing most?'

'Me?' He stirred at last. A spark came to life in his eyes. 'I like walking, that's what I like.'

'And when you're out there, in the hills, don't you feel as if God is with you?'

There was a moment's reflection. 'No, I'd much rather be on me own.'

And there was no answer to that. Lucy ran out into

234

her new kitchen and clamped a handkerchief over her mouth to stifle the laughter.

Since this was her first real home, Anna organised a shower party for her. There were pots, pans, casseroles and dinner sets. Lucy's eyes filled with tears.

'It's only right,' we said. 'After all, you could put any married woman to shame with your gift of hospitality.'

'Fancy having to wait till yer my age to set up home. Never mind, it's been worth waiting for. I can't thank you all enough so yer must come to my house for yer New Year's dinner.'

I could not think of any way I would have rather started the year.

Chapter 25

Suddenly, after a year, it was all over. There was little elation, no dancing in the streets. In fact there was no reaction at all. Perhaps people were too tired, or hungry. Perhaps they were too numb to absorb the fact. Besides, nothing had changed. They knew it that first day back, when they were given their first pay packet in advance. After deductions on all their debts, fuel, rent, rates, insurance, Union dues, it was almost empty. Oh they had marched in that first morning, heads held high, to the sound of the brass band, and we all turned out to watch our men and cheer them, but they slouched home, shoulders stooping and that empty pay packet scorching their pockets.

Had it really been all for nothing? No Yorkshireman would concede defeat, but it hung over our heads like a giant question mark, which refused to go away. To acknowledge it would be to open a wound too deep to bear. Crushed and scorned by the South he might feel, but a man still has his pride.

The strain of months of interminable waiting, the disappointment, heavy debts, and fear for the future took their toll. Some of the men became ill. They were anxious and nervy. Mick's cousin had alopecia and lost all his hair.

In desperation a number of men felt there was no alternative but to accept work in Selby and commute there every day. The journey took about an hour, not long by London standards, but punitive at four in the morning on hazardous country roads. Then, when they got there, they knew no one. At home, in their own pit, they knew everyone, whatever shift, working alongside fathers, brothers and cousins. That was what made mining bearable. Now there was nothing to relieve the terrible monotony, only the thought that it might keep the town going. The sixteen thousand pounds dislocation allowance seemed like blood money. Small wonder many turned it down, even though it would have paid off their enormous debts overnight.

But slowly, as the daffodils pushed their way through the frozen earth and the milder weather came, spring was again in the air and life began to regain a semblance of normality.

Doug appeared at our house early one morning in an old pair of jeans with his ladders and a huge pot of cement.

'Mornin'. How are we, then?' he shouted cheerily.

It was Saturday and I had just staggered out of bed.

'What's he doing?' I groaned at Peter.

'The pointing,' Peter said with excitement.

'Oh.'

Repairs never filled me with Peter's enthusiasm, but in this case I was relieved. Huge yellowish-grey patches, covered in an interesting kind of mould had been appearing on our newly decorated walls and we hardly dared to mention it to the PCC, given our financial situation. But Peter had been chatting to Doug who, being a man of many parts and desperate to pay off his debts, offered to do it for us at an irresistible price.

'Need any towels or bedding or owt?' he asked me when I took him his first mug of tea. He sat down on our back steps.

'No. Why?'

'I'm setting up a little business. If I can get it going I'll finish with pit. I like the daylight, yer see, and I like being me own boss. I'm not daft, I know where it's all going to end. There'll be no jobs there in a few months and I fancy putting me redundancy money into summat that pays. Anyway, our lass'll help keep me at first. She's decided she likes being out at work.'

'Doug, with your cheek, and sales patter, you should have been one of my race!'

He grinned.

'Only difference is they like saving it and I like spending it. I've told Peter, don't whatever yer do pay me, not till I've finished job or I'll never get rid of me debts.'

From then on Doug might appear at our house at any time of day and at any window. When I walked into a room I might see a pair of shoes, or legs or an arm or two, and then I would hear the unmistakable, 'yoo-hoo!' and like the Cheshire cat in reverse a huge grin would materialise before my very eyes, sometimes sideways or upside down. It was hard painstaking work and sometimes the cold bit through his clothes; at other times the sun brought the sweat out in beads on his brow.

'I've put you a pint in the fridge,' I called to him one day. His face lit up.

'And I've taken it out,' Peter shouted from behind me, 'he's on a diet.'

His face fell, but he worked on.

On the first Saturday warm enough to sit out, Doug stayed at home with the children and Ginny came round with Nancy. We sat drinking tea on what would have been our south-facing patio, had Alicia's architect brother had his way. Peter was trying to create some order out of the overgrown mess of our back garden.

'I like to watch a man work,' Ginny said.

'Hmmmm!' Peter said.

It was the fourth garden we were starting almost from scratch and the novelty was wearing a bit thin. One or two church members walked past down the back alley, stopped, amused to see him naked from the waist up, and leant over the fence to offer advice.

We sat in the sun, lethargic and drowsy, gazing into the distance. Across the fields was row upon row of council housing and beyond and above them the great black mountain which seemed to grow larger by the minute since the strike ended. Towering above that was the huge metal cage with its wheels, familiar symbol of a way of life.

'I remember when that field were all prefabs,' Nancy said, 'and just beyond them were Methodist chapel and none o' them council houses were there.'

Ginny nodded lazily.

'Grimlington's grown right fast.'

'Ay, it's not like it were, it's changed.'

'You sound like a pair of old dears in an old folks' home,' I said.

'I tell yer what though, this strike's aged me years,' Nancy said.

My humour never seemed to reach her.

'Ay, we've changed an' all,' Ginny said. 'I feel like a different person to what I were a year ago, but I wouldn't change that!'

'Wouldn't yer?' Nancy said, with a look of amazement.

'No, I'd do it again, tomorrow if we had to. We showed 'em what we were made of. We showed 'em that Britain doesn't stop at Birmingham. We fought for a man's right to work and we put our stomachs where our mouths were. We've proved that there are more important things than money in this life. We showed 'em all that a man can live on next to nothing, and maybe if we all lived like that all the time there'd be no more Ethiopias.'

Nancy listened to Ginny carefully, but whether she heard was doubtful.

'Well I wouldn't want to go back to living like that,' she said finally, 'it's too much of a strain.'

'Oh, I don't know,' Ginny said, cupping her hands around her mug of tea. 'I'm glad for what I learned. Life was simpler. You found out who yer friends were. I felt much freer in a funny way. I didn't crave for what I couldn't have and I realised that what I couldn't have wasn't worth having anyway.'

Nancy still looked doubtful. Ginny's philosophy was

beyond her. Ginny saw it, thought for a moment, then said, 'Listen, when I were a kid I envied Janice Fairclough because she were nice looking, but most of all because she had a real bath at 'er 'ouse. Now I've a proper bath and I miss old tin one. Yer could sit fer hours in front of fire and when one end got cold, get out, turn cold end to't fire and get back in where it were warm.'

I shivered involuntarily, just thinking about it.

'Well, that's it,' Ginny said, the way she did when she felt something was obvious, 'there's always someone better off. No point wasting yer time worrying or being jealous.'

We were interrupted by the sound of a horn, tooting loudly in the back alley. It was Doug, sitting at the wheel of an old, but immaculate, shining Volvo. He leant out of the window, grinning from ear to ear.

'Like it?' he called to Peter, who went over to look, suitably impressed.

'Ey up, he's 'ere to show off 'is new toy,' Ginny said.

'I thought you were broke,' I said.

'We are. He reckons with all the debts 'e 'as already another'll not be noticed. And 'e's been dyin' for a car. What'll I do with 'im?'

Peter got into the passenger seat and together they stroked the upholstery, twiddled all the knobs, and admired every square inch.

'Your lad's just as bad!' Ginny said to me, lifting her eyes to heaven.

'Just think, Ginny,' I said, watching their glee, 'what a preacher Doug'll make one day. He'll turn Yorkshire upside down and make Billy Graham look like a beginner.'

'That'll be the day,' she snorted. 'Did I not tell you what he did in Filey at the last parish weekend? You know he came into the Communion Service? Well, he saw everyone whispering something to each other when they passed round the bread and the wine, but he didn't know what. So when he got the cup he turned to Ian to give it him and said, "Get this down thee lad, it'll do thee good." Some Billy Graham him!'

'Mmmm,' I said. 'Writing his own liturgy already, is he? You've got to admit, he was right.'

She watched him a while, shaking her head.

'Ah well, the age of miracles isn't over, I suppose,' and the thought of it making her lips curl into an enormous grin.

'Are you coming, woman, or are yer goin' to sit there callin' all day?' he shouted.

The strike also left the church with a new attitude to money, a new sense of proportion. Alterations to the building which would make life a great deal more comfortable no longer seemed so important. Peter longed to move the old oak door out to the entrance to the porch and build new glass doors into the church. The constant to-ing and fro-ing during every service to the toilet down at the parish hall, or out into the fresh air for a coughing fit, bronchitis being rife, meant the constant creaking, groaning and clanking of the latch. Worse, a closed oak door was hardly inviting to a newcomer who arrived late and we gathered that some came and turned away again because they were too frightened to come in.

But there were more urgent needs than new doors. People still needed financial help. Sid's job on the building site had finished, and everyone, especially the miners, felt it only right we should try and help if we could. What were new doors? We could live without them for now. The parish hall was redecorated, thanks to the insurance money, then gallons of water from the boiler condensed in the loft and poured down the new wallpaper. Which all went to prove, everyone said, that buildings were a vicious circle of financial demand and we were right to put people first. The attitude was relaxed without being complacent. Just as at the Gift Day, now past history, we would receive what we really needed, not what we thought we wanted. There were

241

frustrations of course, and Bill, who saw the accounts and knew about the sinking roof, was not always as relaxed as everyone else!

There were other crises too, of equal importance. The manpower, or rather womanpower, we had relied on to run the church had gone to work and had no intention of stopping just because the strike was over. They enjoyed working. They never realised before how hard it was, or how boring it could be, to be tied to the kitchen sink until they were dragged away from it. A long-standing tradition was crumbling, and as it did so, many relationships crumbled too. Change, like a hurricane, leaves all sorts of debris in its wake, and the Marriage Guidance Clinic tried to piece things together. The church found itself lacking leaders for every aspect of daytime activity and the children's work.

Peter understood the struggle many of the men were facing. We had experienced our own crisis of roles too.

'You will stay at home,' he said winsomely the night he proposed, the lovelight shining in his eyes. 'You don't have to go out to work, you know.'

'Oh yes,' I said, swept clean off my feet and in my heart were dreams of baking, cooking, cleaning and a gingerbread cottage with honeysuckle growing up the walls.

We always had the honeysuckle, but the rest of the dream was not quite the same! And then, as work in writing and broadcasting expanded, we seemed to be catapulted into a new kind of existence. Doors opened that I had never forced, never anticipated and we both knew I had to go through.

'Go on,' Peter said and I knew that for him there was a cost involved. 'Take the opportunities and we'll share out the chores.'

If ever I had wanted to be the traditional clergy wife, it was no longer possible. I was working every morning and people found it hard to understand at first that I was there, but not there, because I could not answer the phone or doorbell. But there were no regrets. I had

242

always been determined not to be driven by the need for approval. It could be a terrible tyrant. And fortunately we had found a parish where expectations were not very high, but acceptance was.

So here we were, discovering once again that our struggles were mirrored in the life of the parish. Or was it their struggle reflected in us? Perhaps our lives were now so inextricably bound together that it was all part of the same struggle, the struggle to keep up with a world that was changing so fast that we barely had time to catch our breath, let alone adapt our ways. All was in turmoil, the old values vanishing for ever. Employment could not be taken for granted. There was no longer a set pattern for marriage. Community and culture were under threat. Nothing was safe. Nothing was sure any more.

In the light of all this, for both our family and the church there were two possible courses of action. We could dig in our heels and determine to hang on to the old safe ways and attitudes at any cost, or we could walk out into the uncertainty and despite our insecurity and occasional panic, forge new ways. Peter and I had already made our decision. We felt that the old patterns did not treat the clergy wife as a person in her own right, that children of the vicarage often suffered unnecessarily. Our home, half-Jewish, was unusual anyway. We had to have a little of the spirit of the pioneer to make it stay that way. But pioneering meant adventure and adventure was far more exciting than the safe way.

In reality the church had little choice either. The strike ensured we could not be just as we were before. Change was inevitable. There were no longer glib or easy answers to anything. People needed a Christianity that was true and real, that worked. And once they began to question the old attitudes there was no turning back.

Chapter 26

'It's not going to be one of those success stories, is it?' the Bishop groaned.

We were at a party and he had politely asked me what I was writing now. I looked at him quizzically.

'You know, a *How your church can grow* book?'

'Hardly!' I laughed.

That sounded like a handbook for successful gardeners.

'Knowing Grimlington as you do, you know, it would take more than a little poetic licence to stretch the truth like that.'

'Actually,' Peter assured him, 'this is the antidote to a success story.'

As we drove home the Bishop's words continued to buzz round in my head. Was there ever such a thing as a successful church, in the same way there was a successful firm or business? If there was, was it quantified in terms of money, or building projects, size of congregation, number of meetings, efficient organisation or answers to prayer? The idea was nonsensical, yet some churches, like some firms, enjoyed a reputation. Their system worked. Then why didn't ours? We could try to be professional and jet-set too, but someone always let the side down. If it wasn't an ordinary mortal, it almost seemed to be God himself.

I thought back over the past two years. We had prayed, but the child had died. One month our debts were paid off, the next they were worse than ever. Many found faith, and many seemed to lose it. Change was vital, but costly and painful. Sometimes the church was full. Sometimes it wasn't. There seemed no rhyme or reason for anything. In the same way, some Sunday services took off, while others never left the hangar. Either way no two were ever the same.

'Shall I write a sort of "failure" story then?' I said. Like many couples there were times when we followed each other's innermost thoughts without having to express them verbally. 'Not many people write about coping with frustration and disappointment, do they, and it does seem to play a major part in our lives. Is that what you meant by antidote to success?'

Peter thought for a while as he drove along, then he smiled. 'You wouldn't do justice to the Yorkshire integrity if you were anything less than honest,' he said. 'But what is success anyway? A contemporary western virtue, but certainly not Christian. Our society would hardly call death by crucifixion at the age of thirty-three a roaring success.'

We drove along in silence for a while, Peter concentrating on his driving, as the road to Grimlington was winding and badly lit. I was trying to absorb what he was saying.

'When I think of our church,' he said after a while, 'a picture comes into my mind of a ship in full sail. Some of the passengers keep falling overboard and the rest are so busy pulling them back on, that the ship can't get up any real speed. That tells me we don't fulfil our potential, but I don't think it's the same as failure. The people here are vulnerable. They've experienced great hurt. Perhaps we need to go slowly.'

As he spoke I felt as if a vital piece of jigsaw which would never fit had slotted into place. I had been trying to force it in back to front. A picture was beginning to emerge.

'Are you saying that our human understanding is so warped by the society we live in that our values are upside down? What we call success could really be failure and our apparent failures part of a greater plan?'

Peter nodded.

'So that everything,' I said, 'the heartaches and bewilderment, even Paul's death, had meaning.'

I thought about Mick and Karen and the others who had prayed so much for Paul. They had been hurt, disillusioned, but now they were ready to start praying again for anyone who was ill. At first I marvelled at their courage, their refusal to be defeated and readiness to take a risk. But now I saw that their whole attitude was different. Now there was a deep awareness of our total lack of control over life and death, and that had been the ultimate discovery. We had taken our hands off and having come to the end of ourselves, God was still there, vaster than anything we had ever imagined.

'Perhaps that's why no method or system seems to work for us and we've found no blueprint for success,' I said. 'Self-sufficiency doesn't need God, does it? No struggling or wrestling, but no more adventure either, no mystery to explore.'

'And it does keep us from becoming pompous,' Peter laughed.

'Or cold! No slick and smooth performances!'

'The chance would be a fine thing.'

'But you wouldn't want that, would you?' I said, as the lights of the town came into view just ahead of us.

He shook his head. 'I've learned this much here, that a simple thing like stopping to chat to someone in the street can be more important than running the most efficient church in the country.'

Lucy had done the babysitting for us that night, as she so often did. I had left the children curled up next to her, munching her home-made chocolate crispies while she did her knitting, and I realised how much, as a family with no grandparents or relatives nearby, we needed adopted aunties.

While Peter took her home, I sat in the sitting-room in the dark, watching from the window the town's twinkling lights stretching into the distance. On the horizon the pit-head was flood-lit and, silhouetted against the sky, the slag heap looked dark and menacing, like an angry monster brooding over its prey. I studied it for some time. Every night it was a new shape. Too much slag had accumulated and it was being moved, a little at a time. 'No chance to get tired of the view,' I thought, 'it never stays the same long enough!'

I thought about the strike, now receding fast into the past. It had been a kind of symbolic act, a gesture of defiance and pride to show the country that the cultural identity of industrial Yorkshire was unique and worth preserving. It had seemed to fail, yet the people were as resilient as ever and a flicker of hope still survived. How I prayed that hope would not be disappointed and that someone somewhere would see the potential of the town and pour in resources.

The church was still struggling to reflect that special cultural identity, despite the limitations of any institution, and there were moments of elation when progress seemed almost tangible. Anna often stopped to chat to the assistant in the butcher's in the High Street. She always had an opinion of the church and loved expressing it, though attendance was another matter altogether. One day she handed Anna her chops and said, 'Well I'm glad you've become socialist up there at last.'

Anna blinked and wondered what rumours were rife in the town now.

'I mean,' the assistant said, 'that it's for everyone, not just certain types and classes.'

But, lest we be carried away by the joy of this apparent 'success', we also discovered a strange irony. The more we reflected the life and character of the area, the more that life and character was at risk, because it began to attract professional-class people from miles around. And inevitably they left their own mark, but it was not the mark of the town. Guest services, known locally as 'Parish cabarets', drew some new people in, and Family Services many others who never normally came, but some of our recent growth was by transference from other churches. The two thirds of the town which was council estate was still barely represented in the congregation. When some came, there were so many strangers there that they wondered if it really was their church. Outsiders were hardly aware of the problem, but Linda, Ginny and Ian felt it keenly. Their families lived on the estate and they knew the isolation and rejection people experienced there. The Drama Group planned to take part in the estate's next Gala to say that we did care but it seemed such a small gesture.

'Where do we go from here?' I wondered, as I staggered heavy-eyed up to bed.

But sleep eluded me. I lay awake for ages, trying to answer my own question. Something Linda had said a few days earlier suddenly came back to mind.

'Oh, I used to be all intense once. I tried to look spiritual. I could pray in fancy language, say the right-sounding things, and pretend life was wonderful even when it wasn't. But it got too much. I gave it up and now I'm just me. I know I'm a thorn in the clergy's side, always going on about what this town needs and what the church should do about it, but it is my town and I love it.'

I smiled as I thought about Linda with her uncanny way of expressing thoughts which others buried in the subconscious and hoped would go away. But it was a vital discomfort, like the grit in the oyster which eventually produced the pearl. I knew from that throwaway remark that nothing would make her sacrifice her integrity, submit to the pressures of a middle-class institution and conform to its ways.

It reminded me of my own struggle to come to terms with my identity as a Jew in the Church. It occurred to me that self-acceptance was probably the key to coping with being a clergyman's wife too. I could refuse the role and the pretence that went with it, disappoint people's expectations, because, whether they liked it or not, all I had to offer was myself.

And I began to wonder whether the Church ever really accepted people as they were, or whether we continually forced them to fulfil our expectations. Perhaps that was a signpost to the way forward.

Slowly, as drowsiness came at last, an idea came to mind, an experiment. The Drama Group was always complaining about the church. Supposing they had a free hand. What would they do?

'Imagine,' I said to them the following Tuesday evening, 'that there's no such thing as the church. An itinerant preacher has visited Grimlington and you've all decided Christianity is for you. But there's no building, no clergy, nothing at all except the Bible and you may not be able to read. It's up to you to decide.'

They sat in silence for a while, letting the idea take root.

'I'm in the Grimlington pub,' Ginny said, 'I've a pint here on table.'

'So have I,' Ian said.

Whether it was there nor not, it loosened their tongues and once the conversation got going, there was no stopping them.

'Shhhh!' they all went to Ian, who was holding forth loudly on the effect the preacher had had on him, 'they'll all hear you on next table.'

'Let 'em,' he said. 'They need to hear it,' but he went quiet all the same.

'I think we should meet like this regularly,' Linda said. 'I mean we need to talk together and learn about God. We can use my sitting-room. Joe won't mind.'

And so, for about three quarters of an hour, the newly-formed 'church' met in Linda's sitting-room. Only one of the group decided they would own a Bible and soon the rest deferred to her and treated her as the fount of all wisdom. Until Linda decided she had had enough of listening to someone else. She would get her own, even if it meant learning to read.

Communal prayer caused them some problems. They

were not sure what to do. Linda suggested they all put their fingers in their ears and pray out loud together. They laughed at her, but did it all the same. Ian said he felt stupid, so Jan suggested they wrote some prayers down.

The congregation of imaginary people grew, until, they decided, Linda's sitting-room was too small and they would have to rent a hall. That was the start of a long debate on raising money and the slow realisation that it was becoming increasingly hard to get a consensus of opinion on anything. Eventually Ian had had enough of their 'time-wasting' and walked out in disgust to form his own congregation.

I could not contain my laughter any longer and lay on the floor shaking helplessly while they all looked on in amazement.

'Ignore her,' Ginny said.

Eventually I managed to control myself enough to say to them, 'You realise what you've just done?'

They were puzzled.

'For all your complaints about the church, you've just recreated it exactly as it is, with a building, liturgy, clergy, collections, money hassles and even the denominations.'

They looked surprised at first, then they smiled at each other sheepishly.

'Did it ever occur to you, once you got too big, to form two groups, rather than hire a hall?'

'No,' Ginny said. 'We liked being together. It was cosy. I didn't really want lots of new people coming in to spoil it.'

'Only one of you really cared about sharing the faith he had found and you shut him up effectively.'

'That's right,' Linda said. 'We just assumed no one would be interested.'

'That happens to me all the time,' Ian said, shaking his head. 'Maybe it isn't just...'

He looked round the group. 'What I'm trying to say is that it isn't just the system that keeps people out, is it?'

'The structure doesn't help,' Linda said, 'but it's us, isn't it? It's our attitude that really counts. That's where we need to start.'

About a week later Rick popped in for a chat. He was obviously excited about something.

'I've been thinking about the future of the church and the manpower crisis we're facing at the moment,' he said.

He was right about a crisis. So many Sunday School teachers were wanting to retire that it seemed we might soon have no children's work at all.

'Well, I began to wonder whether we're not rummaging in the wrong place. Maybe we should be concentrating on the things that matter most in the town, like family and community. Why separate the children from the adults? We could have the home groups earlier in the evening and include children. We could have more communal celebrations in the church, when we eat together and let our hair down. New people feel happy at occasions like that. They're a kind of a bridge. A man should feel as at home in church as he does at his Club. It shouldn't be such a psychological leap. Sunday worship should be just as enjoyable, so we're not saying one is religious and the other isn't. The test for whether our services are boring or not is whether the children can sit through them. Mine want to be in church. They love Family Services. That would solve our Sunday School problem. Perhaps we should have them in every week.'

I looked at him a moment, temporarily struck dumb by hearing so many of my ideals on someone else's lips.

He grinned at me.

'I thought it all sounded a bit "Jewish",' he said.

I nodded, my heart sinking at the thought of having the children in the service every week. Joel never could sit still for long. But I knew my motives were selfish. I loved silence as well as exuberance, but I would have to train myself to concentrate despite the distractions.

Besides, it had been an experience to watch little Peta, at eighteen months, stagger out in front of the Music Group whenever they played and dance for all she was worth. Her spontaneity made us feel stiff and reserved. Children have rhythm and movement in their bones. Although there had to be some constraint, too much 'Sssssh', and 'Stand still', drove it out. It made them self-conscious, not God-conscious.

'And is there any chance the children could take Communion one day?' Rick appealed to Peter. 'They are the Church, aren't they? Ours want to so much. How can we deny them?'

'That certainly is Jewish,' Peter said, with a twinkle in his eye. 'In a Jewish home every child shares in Kiddush, the bread and wine, on a Friday evening. That's where the Communion came from. Yes, I think it will come one day, in the Church of England at least, and in other denominations too, I hope. But meanwhile, we do it at home. I think a child understands what it's about as much if not more than an adult. Their perception has not been spoilt.'

'That's what I wanted to ask,' Rick said. 'We want to worship as a family once a week and somehow it seems natural to have bread and wine. Is it all right?'

'You can please yourself in your own home,' Peter laughed, 'but since you ask me, I think it's great.'

'By the way,' I said to Rick, as he got up to go, 'can you do anything with this?'

I took a children's Haggadah down off the bookshelf and handed it to him. 'It's the Passover Service. It's full of psalms and there are dozens of different tunes for them, depending on the family tradition and the country they came from. I see no reason why a church which now has its own setting for the Communion Service shouldn't write a Passover setting too!'

Rick took it, studied it for a while, then smiled.

'Thanks,' he said. 'It's funny, I was going to ask you if you had any records of Jewish music you could lend me.

I have a yen to write some of my own. And perhaps one day we could have a Passover.'

As Rick went out the door I had a strange sensation in the pit of my stomach that a new adventure was about to begin.

Postscript

And so they all lived happily every after. Or did they? So
ends the fairy story, but there is little fairytale about life
in Grimlington. It would have been very convenient for
me if Doug had been gloriously converted and, like
Wesley in the days of old, was saving the country from
certain revolution and bloodshed with his preaching.
But he hasn't – not yet! It would have rounded things off
nicely if Lucy's Old Folk's Home had opened and she
was now caring for the elderly, just as she had always
longed to do. The Home is open, but there was no job
there for Lucy. Her dreams will have to wait for another
day.

As for the future, who can say? One morning about a
third of the men in the church received notice of
redundancy. Within two years all the local pits will
close. What this will mean for the town, no one yet
knows. Of the steadily growing group of young people in
the church, most of the boys are unemployed, with no
prospect of work. When Sarah wrote a song called 'Lord
of my Tomorrows', small wonder that it seemed ours in
a special way. We took it to our hearts and sang it
carefully, counting the cost of every word.

Alicia retired and went back to her native Highlands,
reminding us to love each other. Soon it would be our
turn to leave the parish too.

'We'll give yer a wonderful send-off when the time
comes,' they told us at Alicia's farewell.

My heart sank at the prospect.

One day I biked up to the pit and sat with the wind in
my face, looking down on the town below. It looked like

a miniature village, a cluster of dolls' houses. Perhaps that was all it was to those who held its future in their hands. Most people passing through knew nothing of the life lived behind the drab exterior. I wanted to stretch out my hand, pick up the little community piece by piece and protect it from almost certain disintegration. But I could not save it, any more than I could save myself, from becoming past history. All life slips through our fingers like the sands of time, from and back to him who made it.

I had been so reluctant to come to Grimlington and now I did not want to go. Contrary as ever, just like my ancestors in the wilderness, that was my problem! Mingled in the coaldust, we had found milk and honey. But what lay ahead would be like that too, shrouded in mystery, yet rich in surprises. For the promised land is always now, and not yet.

Child of the Covenant

Michele Guinness

Michele Guinness was brought up to observe all the traditions and ritual of her Jewish culture. When an encounter with a Christian raised questions for her, she turned to the Bible for the answers. In this lively account, she tells how she came face to face with the Messiah and had to make sense of being both Jewish and Christian.

'Her writing, spiced with shrewd observations, sparkles with life and down-to-earth humour and is a delight to read.'
FLOODTIDE

'A vivid portrait ... compelling reading.'
CHRISTIAN ARENA

'The story is told with a style full of zest and sharp but kindly humour. It weeps and laughs in the best Jewish tradition.'
CHRISTIAN RECORD

Hodder & Stoughton
ISBN 0 340 36479 3

A Little Kosher Seasoning

Michele Guinness

'Forget the pressure of work, the need to achieve and the frenetic pace of existence. Just be for a while. And as you read and explore this wonderful new world, let this Mama leave you with the ultimate in Jewish wisdom. "Enjoy, enjoy!"'

Raised in a Jewish family and married to a clergyman, Michele Guinness has long sought to integrate her Jewish roots and Christian beliefs. Here, in a wonderful celebration of the richness of life in all its seasons, she shows how it can be done.

In her customary vivacious style, Michele reveals how life and faith naturally combine: God can be found in the mundane and ordinary as well as in vibrant communal celebration. To help Christians live out their faith the Jewish way, she includes recipes and prayers, meditations and suggestions for services such as a Passover Service. The result is a lively combination of Jewish and Christian spirituality, celebrating the uniqueness and common ground of both.

Hodder & Stoughton
0 340 58600 1

Is God Good for Women?

Michele Guinness

Does God have a down on women? Anyone who judges his personal preferences by the history of religion could be forgiven for thinking that he does.

Traditionally religious institutions do not seem good for women. They have tended to side with a status quo which keeps women in their place, dutiful, domestic and dependent; yet many of the pioneers who have risen to the challenge, who have dared to excel in a male world, have done so because of, not in spite of, their faith.

Michele Guinness has talked to a number of women who have broken new ground in very different ways and this book is a fascinating and inspiring collection. We meet, for example, a rabbi, a police superintendent, an army lieutenant colonel, a chief executive and a gynaecologist. They reflect on similar issues: career and celibacy, marriage and motherhood, ambition and power, loneliness and teamwork, youth and age, yet their stories are very different. Some are well known, others are not. But all have extraordinary insights about what it is to be a woman in relationship with a God who transcends institutions and empowers women to do the same.

Hodder & Stoughton
0 340 67870 4